THE FASCISTS IN BRITAIN

Sir Oswald Mosley inspects his followers on the day of the 'Battle of Cable Street'. Behind him, on the right, is Neil Francis-Hawkins, Director General of the British Union of Fascists and National Socialists

THE
FASCISTS
IN BRITAIN

COLIN CROSS

ST MARTIN'S PRESS
NEW YORK

First published in the United States of America 1963
Copyright © 1961 by Colin Cross
All rights reserved
Library of Congress Catalog Card Number: 63-18765
Published in Great Britain by Barrie and Rockliff, 1961

7- 3 -6 7

CONTENTS

Introduction		7
Chapter 1	Lone Wolf	9
Chapter 2	Furs and Fables	19
Chapter 3	Future Prime Minister?	32
Chapter 4	'For King and Country'	56
Chapter 5	The Instrument of Steel	67
Chapter 6	The Black House	78
Chapter 7	'Hurrah for the Blackshirts!'	94
Chapter 8	Olympia and the Jews	109
Chapter 9	'Mosley Says Peace'	129
Chapter 10	'The Future Is With Us'	137
Chapter 11	The Battle of Cable Street	149
Chapter 12	Decline	169
Chapter 13	Fall	182
Chapter 14	Aftermath	195
Note on Sources		205
Index		207

ILLUSTRATIONS

Sir Oswald Mosley inspects his followers on the day of the 'Battle of Cable Street' *frontispiece*

Sir Oswald and Lady Cynthia Mosley during the Smethwick by-election *facing page* 32

Arnold Spencer Leese, founder of the Imperial Fascist League 32

Miss Rotha Lintorn-Orman, founder of the first Fascist organization in Britain 32

Sir Oswald Mosley with Benito Mussolini in Rome 33

A BUF Mobile Defence Squad parades beside its van at Black House, Chelsea 33

William Joyce 64

John Beckett 64

An anti-Fascist crowd run from a barricade they have erected near Aldgate 65

Police try to force a passage at Royal Mint Street for a British Union car 65

A barricade, surmounted by a red flag, in Long Lane, Bermondsey 144

The head of the South London march 144

Sir Oswald Mosley in 1944, soon after his release from prison 145

Sir Oswald and Lady Mosley in 1960 145

INTRODUCTION

In describing British Fascism I have drawn my terms of reference pretty narrowly, confining it to groups which actually used the word 'Fascist' in their campaigns. Most of the space, naturally, goes to the movement led by Sir Oswald Mosley, whose early career it has seemed necessary to chronicle in some detail. Fascism is a creed requiring vigorous personal leadership, and it would be difficult to describe the British variety without discussing the personality and history of Sir Oswald. The final chapter steps outside the terms of reference to indicate very briefly the way in which the former Fascists have redeveloped their policies since the war; it does not claim to be a full study of post-war developments.

My approach to the subject has been in a spirit of pure inquiry and I have tried to ignore my personal political views, which are anti-Fascist and unsympathetic to anti-Semitism or racialism.

One difficulty has been to avoid any form of McCarthyism. There are a few ex-Fascists who since the war have achieved prominence in politics, the law, medicine and public life generally, and it could be a hardship to them to revive old controversies. I have, therefore, adopted a principle of mentioning nobody simply for the reason that he achieved prominence after leaving Fascism. The names given in the book are of people who played a significant part in the development and organization of Fascism or who were already well known when they joined the Movement.

Unless membership of a Fascist movement is clearly stated, in no case is it intended to be implied that anybody mentioned in this book was a Fascist member or supporter.

I have adopted the convenient habit of dropping all personal titles, save where they are needed for purposes of identification.

The book would have been impossible to prepare without the assistance of a large number of people who have given information and advice and, in some cases, commented on sections of the manuscript. I would like deeply to thank them, at the same time emphasizing that the responsibility for the accuracy or otherwise is entirely my own. They include: The Rt. Hon. Earl Attlee; John Bean, Esq.; J. W. Beckett, Esq.; R. Benewick, Esq.; Fenner Brockway, Esq., MP; A. K. Chesterton, Esq.; Myer Domnitz, Esq.; Geoffrey Dorman, Esq.; E. Evans, Esq.; Dr. Robert Forgan; E. J. Hamm, Esq.; W. Horn, Esq.; W. G. Jackson, Esq.; Colin Jordan, Esq.; W. J. Leaper, Esq.; H. G. McKechnie, Esq.; The Rt. Hon. Harold Macmillan, MP; A. D. Massel, Esq.; Sir Thomas Moore, Bt., MP; Sir Oswald Mosley, Bt.; The Hon. Sir Harold Nicolson; The Viscount Nuffield; W. Risdon, Esq.; Robert Row, Esq.; Ellis Smith, Esq., MP; The Rt. Hon. John Strachey, MP; Hannen Swaffer, Esq.; Arnold Turvey, Esq.; C. F. Wegg-Prosser, Esq.

I am very grateful, too, for the facilities for research afforded by the Union Movement; the Board of Deputies of British Jews; and the libraries of the British Museum, the London School of Economics, the House of Commons, the House of Commons Press Gallery, the Labour Party, the *Daily Express* and the *Daily Herald*.

To the Hon. Mrs. Peter Rodd (Nancy Mitford) I am indebted for her generous permission to quote from *Wigs on the Green*.

COLIN CROSS

1961

Lone Wolf

OSWALD MOSLEY differs from Hitler, who was the son of a minor Customs official, and Mussolini, who was the son of a blacksmith, in that he traces descent from a family established in the landed aristocracy for 400 years. The Mosleys first became prominent in sixteenth-century Lancashire as hatters and clothiers, making shrewd purchases of land in what is now the centre of Manchester. In 1596 a Mosley bought the manorial rights of Manchester for £3,500, including monopoly rights over the markets. The same rights were sold to the town by a later Mosley in 1846 for £200,000. In the late eighteenth century the family moved its main residence from Ancoats, Manchester, to Rolleston Hall, near Burton-on-Trent, where it acquired further landed estates. The line of descent is complicated, the baronetcy having twice been extinguished through lack of heirs and re-created in other branches of the family. The elaborate family tree contains a high proportion of clergy but no serious politicians. Generation after generation of Mosleys lived quietly, piously, caring for their estates and showing little desire to influence the world beyond.

Mosley's father, fifth baronet of the present creation, married in 1894 his second cousin, Maud Edwards-Heathcote of Staffordshire. Mosley, eldest of three sons, was born two years later and given the traditional family names of Oswald Ernald; within his family and among his friends he has always been known as 'Tom'. Mosley's father was an opinionated, fox-hunting squire with a taste for boxing but few intellectual interests. He quarrelled with his wife in 1901 and thereafter lived apart from her. Young 'Tom' was brought up by his mother, who moved to Shropshire, and by his grandfather, the fourth baronet, who lived at Rolleston. The grandfather, a big, red-faced man, was a noted cattle-breeder and a prominent figure at the leading agricultural shows; he was supposed to be the original for the cartoon figure of John Bull. He had a famous collection of stuffed birds. Between Mosley and his grandfather there were close ties of affection; when the grandfather died in 1916 he left his personal estate to Mosley over the fifth baronet's head.

During his schooldays, at West Downs and Winchester, Mosley's tastes ran rather to sport than to academic work. He excelled at the individualist sports of fencing and boxing, becoming at fifteen the youngest boy ever to win the Public Schools Fencing Championship. He was very big, topping six feet at the age of fourteen, and had an aloof attitude to the ordinary schoolboy loyalties and enthusiasms. He left Winchester at sixteen and, after a period of travel, read privately for Sandhurst into which, with a burst of brilliance, he passed top of the cavalry list. His formal education appears to have had little effect on his character or intellect and he is largely a self-educated man. It is possible to draw a parallel between the educational experiences of the young Mosley and the young Winston Churchill, with the difference that Churchill sprang from an intensely political background.

By all accounts Mosley had a zest for the Army but again he asserted himself as an individualist. He was commissioned into his regiment, the 16th Lancers, at the outbreak of the First World War and immediately left it to volunteer for the Royal Flying Corps. He was among the first to fly over the enemy lines as an observer and later trained at Shoreham as a pilot. In 1915, during his training, he crashed and suffered severe injury to his left leg. Before the leg had properly mended he was recalled to his regiment, now serving in the trenches; although he was in great pain he remained in the line during the Battle of Loos and did not report sick until he had physically collapsed. He nearly lost the leg altogether but, after extended hospital treatment, he was invalided from the Army in 1916 with a permanent limp, one leg three inches shorter than the other. For the remainder of the war he worked as a temporary civil servant at the Foreign Office and the Ministry of Munitions.

The more imaginative survivors of the First World War, especially those who entered politics, tended to acquire a sense of mission, a feeling of responsibility to see that their contemporaries had not been slaughtered in vain. Mosley, brooding at Whitehall, certainly acquired a sense of personal destiny which was never to leave him. From the bloodbath of Flanders must come a better world and it was his duty, with his wealth, ability and social privileges, to help to build it. Youth had paid the price and youth must build; youth and age could no longer co-operate. Between them there was an impassable barrier of spent young blood. Mosley read widely about politics, began to formulate his own theories, then sought a seat in Parliament through the Conservative Party, the natural channel for a man of his background. Central Office sent him to the safe seat of Harrow where, a few weeks before the armistice, he was selected as prospective candidate.

Perhaps the knowledge of his money helped the Harrow Conservatives to choose so unfledged a candidate for their safe seat and, certainly, his war injury and commanding appearance were advantages. Above all, however, the Harrow Conservatives seemed quickly to recognize that in Mosley they had a candidate of exceptional power in public speaking. At the selection conference, in his first public speech, the tall dark ex-officer gained a grip on their loyalty which was to stand him in good stead when he later came into conflict with the party machine.

Even in 1918 Mosley rarely, if ever, described himself as a Conservative. He was a Coalition-Unionist, a supporter of the radical Prime Minister Lloyd George, who sounded a high note for his coupon election. 'Let us cleanse this noble land. Let us cleanse it and make it a temple worthy of the sacrifice which has been made for its honour,' said Lloyd George.

The inexperienced Mosley took the cleansing seriously. In his election campaign he propounded a bold programme, including higher wages and shorter hours in industry; public control of electricity and transport; slum-clearance and improved education, child-welfare and health services. He used the curious phrase 'Socialistic Imperialism' – a foretaste of his later National Socialism – and announced that the war had destroyed 'the old parties'.

'Our policy,' he told a meeting, 'is to blot out the manifold disgraces of our national life as far as any government can. We must go forward as a great united people, as the greatest people in the world, with all the force behind us of our greatness, our wealth and our power.'

This mixture of radicalism with patriotism fitted the general mood of the 'brave new world'. Any doubts the Harrow Conservatives may have felt on the score of orthodoxy were dispelled by the oratory of the young war hero. Mosley's only opponent was one A. R. Chamberlayne, a local man, who stood as an Independent Coalitionist. His chief complaint was that the official candidate was 'a bit of a boy'.

Mosley retorted by calling him 'grandfather' and won comfortably by 14,000 votes to 3,000. Thus he was an MP at the age of twenty-three and the first of his generation to reach Parliament. Others of his age group, like Anthony Eden and Harold Macmillan, had passed from the Army to Oxford; Aneurin Bevan was at the Labour College. Mosley, with an active, receptive, self-trained mind, went straight to the strong meat of national politics.

It was the 'hard-faced' Parliament he entered; the Parliament of the men who looked as if they had done well out of the war and who had ridden to Westminster on the Lloyd George coat-tails. Mosley, 'baby' of the House and very impatient, helped to form a 'New Members' Association' to express the views of his generation; the Association was short-lived and Mosley gained a reputation for arrogance. Baldwin, Financial Secretary to the Treasury, semi-anonymously gave twenty per cent of his wealth to the nation, representing the profits his steel mills had made from the war. Mosley suggested that all war profiteers should be forced to do the same, urging a retrospective tax on them back to 1914. Irritated by the patronage of his elders, he toyed with the weapon of sarcasm. In his maiden speech he apologized for his 'crime' of being a young man.

His special Parliamentary interest in his early days was ex-service-men. He peppered the Commons Order Paper with questions on individual cases of injustice over pensions, demobilization and employment. He also pressed for development of aviation. In both fields he found himself crossing swords with Winston Churchill who combined the posts of Secretary for War and Secretary for Air.

Mosley proved one of the rare Parliamentarians capable of standing up to Churchill, and gave as good as he got. The first clash came when Mosley advocated the separation of the War and Air departments, at the same time suggesting the creation of a super-visory Ministry of Defence. The attack reads oddly in view of Mosley's later ambitions.

'I believe we are witnessing a certain disillusionment in the power of one man to do the work of two or three,' said Mosley. 'I believe we are living in a period which is seeing what I may call the "twilight of the gods".'

A bigger clash came when Churchill proposed to put the Guards into red uniforms. Mosley passionately defended khaki which, after the 1914-18 war, should be 'one of our most sacred memories'. The money for the red uniforms could better be spent on fighting the world typhus epidemic. He continued with a sarcastic attack on Churchill:

'The right honourably gentleman has already had full opportunity for the display of his genius in war. . . . May I beg him to turn his attention, flushed as he is with victories won and reverses manfully sustained on far-flung fields – may I beg him to return to the less exciting but none the less exacting pursuits of peace? I am even ready to believe that unless he speedily devotes his great intellect to the furtherance of some great constructive work of peaceful organization – such as, for instance, the League of Nations – he will be in danger of occupying a lesser place in the verdict of posterity than his great predecessor and prototype, the first Napoleon.'

At first Churchill was indulgent, patronizing. He called Mosley his 'young friend' and remarked easily: 'I see a far greater value in continuity, tradition and custom and in the structure of our social and national life than I did when I came here as a young member of twenty-five years of age.'

The antagonism deepened during the later 1920's. Their clashes developed an unusual personal bitterness, with Mosley holding up well against the weight of Churchill's experience. They used a similar technique – an elevated and self-conscious oratory flavoured with sarcasm.

When Mosley was Labour MP for Smethwick, and a newly appointed minister, Churchill, in grandiose style, surveyed the growth of the Labour Movement. In rolling phrases he described how within his own lifetime the Socialists had advanced from insignificance to power:

'They dreamt that they were clearing a pathway along which the toiling millions were to advance towards Utopia, but they wake up to find that all they have been doing is to set up a ladder by which the honourable baronet the member for Smethwick can climb into place and power.'

Retorted Mosley: 'The right honourable gentleman is like a man who, in a spirit of wanton malice, sets light to a house and then throws stones at the fire brigade.'

Later still, Hugh Dalton recalls in his memoirs how Churchill as Prime Minister in 1940 told his first ministerial meeting that if the

Germans won the war they would make Britain a slave state under Mosley 'or some such person'.

Back in the bright dawn of 1919 such a fate for Mosley was never considered – least of all by Mosley himself. He appeared that summer as a champion of the League of Nations and disarmament. Recalling how his friends had been slaughtered in battle, he described the League of Nations as 'the one dominant question in politics, the one thing that really matters'.

On disarmament he struck a note of prophecy. Unless the swollen, conscript armies of the Continent were reduced there would be another war. He urged Lloyd George to use Britain's economic influence to force reductions.

'The League of Nations,' he said, 'has been born amid the tramp of armed men in a world enfeebled by their upkeep. If we allow these miniature Napoleons, who exist in every country, to continue to strut the European stage with these weapons in their hands, there will never be peace . . . and I, for one, am prepared to say that thousands have died in vain and thousands have been cheated of the ideal for which they fought.'

In August 1920 Mosley married Lady Cynthia Curzon, the Foreign Secretary's tall, beautiful daughter, whom he had met when they were both electioneering for Lady Astor at Plymouth. The King and Queen came to the wedding and the Mosleys were much photographed. Many women have found Mosley attractive and Cynthia Mosley was no exception, proving a devoted wife. She was an intelligent girl, bred in an intense political tradition, and was of special service in smoothing her husband's social relationships. Among the guests at the wedding were two who were to become the Mosleys' close friends – Robert Boothby and Harold Nicolson.

Two months later, to the horror of his new father-in-law, Mosley crossed the floor, taking his seat as an Independent on the back row of the Labour benches. He was out of tune with the whole Coalition policy, but the immediate cause of the break was the coercion of Ireland by the Black-and-Tans. Recruited from jobless ex-service-men, the Black-and-Tans were, perhaps, the first organization in Britain of Fascist potential, and Mosley disliked them, criticizing them because they were 'confusing the right of men to defend themselves with the right to wander round the countryside destroying the houses and property of innocent persons'. He complained especially of their lack of discipline, which made them worse than the Germans in Belgium. The Irish reprisals were more like 'the pogrom of the barbarous Slav'. Again he clashed with Churchill.

The Conservatives reacted violently. Against storms of interruptions, Mosley fashioned some effective retorts. He accused the Government of obliterating in Ireland 'the narrow, but very sacred line, which divides justice from indiscriminate revenge'. When interruptions rose to a peak he acidly remarked: 'The purpose of certain honourable members appears to be not to take part in reasoned argument but rather to serve that intolerable organization in this House which howls down any honourable member whose views are not acceptable to the Treasury bench.'

He had his admirers, too. The old Speaker, Lowther, remarked to Edward Wood, later Earl of Halifax, while Mosley was speaking: 'Watch that young man. He will probably be Prime Minister.'* Mosley was, however, roughly treated; and he hated it. His defence was his weapon of sarcasm; he became as dangerous to touch as a porcupine. In his Fascist days he was to take elaborate precautions against being interrupted at all, sometimes pausing for whole minutes in his speeches while Blackshirts removed offending members of the audience.

Another consequence of this rough treatment was to deepen his dislike of the 'old parties', from which, in any case, he felt separated by the barrier of the war. The 'old parties' was a phrase to which he was to return throughout his political life. Another taste of the future came, perhaps, when he violently objected to the use of African troops by the French in the reoccupation of the Ruhr. There was, however, little sign of racialism. Harold Laski, newly arrived at the London School of Economics, wrote cheerfully to his friend Maurice Firuski: 'Oswald Mosley, whom I like more and more, is drifting towards Labour.'† Mosley reciprocated the Jewish professor's friendship.

Mosley was working with Liberals and drifting towards Labour. He was convinced that some new political force was on the point of being born, an apocalyptic vision which has never really left him. In a powerful Commons speech he urged the creation of a third force between Bolshevism and reaction. The Coalition broke up as a result of the Carlton Club meeting of 1922 and Bonar Law, the new Conservative Prime Minister, dissolved Parliament. There was no question of Mosley standing as a Conservative candidate this time. Brushing aside a demand from the Harrow Conservatives that he

---

* *Fulness of Days* by the Earl of Halifax (1957).
† Quoted in *Harold Laski* by Kingsley Martin (1953).

should in future accept the Party whip, he stood as an Independent: a national figure at the age of twenty-six.

'The war has destroyed the old party issues and with them the old parties', wrote Mosley in his election address. 'My intention is not to wear a label which, at present, may be confused with past controversies.'

Cynthia Mosley helped. Her sympathetic manner made her an excellent canvasser and she trained herself as a public speaker. Polling day was her birthday and she artlessly appealed to the electors to choose her husband 'as a birthday present to me'. Mosley argued that the workers should participate in the management of the industries to which they devoted their lives, his first fumbling towards his later advocacy of the corporate state. Gathering Liberal and Labour support, he held his seat by 8,000 against the new Conservative, Major Ward Jackson.

During the short 1922–23 Parliament, in which his father-in-law nearly became Prime Minister, Mosley developed his gifts. With Cynthia Mosley as hostess, their home in Smith Square became a meeting ground for advanced politicians. Although he had little use for small talk Mosley had a gift for fascinating his friends in private conversation. From his lips poured an endless stream of ideas expressed in virile, exciting phrases; most of the ideas were good, but about one in twenty was so absurd as to kill conversation stone dead. In public he could be very rude. He called Garvin, Editor of the *Observer*, 'a musical doormat which plays "See the Conquering Hero Comes" whenever Mr. Lloyd George wipes his boots on it'. Garvin took it well and referred in print to Mosley's 'dazzling prospects'. Massingham, in *The Nation*, wrote: 'If character, a brilliant and searching mind, a sympathetic temperament, and a repugnance from mean and cruel dealing, fit men for the service of the State, Mr. Mosley should rise high in it.' The experienced lobby correspondent of the *Morning Post* observed that 'in many respects Mr. Mosley reminds me of Disraeli before he had taken his bearings'.

Stanley Baldwin, who had succeeded Bonar Law, called a surprise election at the end of 1923, asking for a mandate to introduce tariffs as a remedy for unemployment. Mosley was re-elected for Harrow on substantially his former programme, opposing protection as 'the last gambler's throw of a bankrupt and discredited party'. At about the same time he took lessons in voice production, successfully eliminating a falsetto which had tended to mar his polemics and acquiring a stern, measured rhythm of speech – his calculated changes in pitch sounding like a car changing gear. His majority was just under 5,000 in a straight fight against the Conservative, Hugh Morris. The Conservatives remained the largest party in the Commons, but when Parliament reassembled in January 1924 they were defeated by the combined votes of Labour and Liberals; Ramsay MacDonald, as a result, forming the first Labour Government. During the debate which preceded Baldwin's fall Mosley made a speech which the left-wing ILP-er Fred Jowett said in the *Bradford Pioneer* 'drove the Tories nearly mad'. Jowett added: 'He ought to be in the ILP.'

What still kept Mosley out of the Labour Party was that he was unconvinced that Labour represented the new political alignment he was seeking. For months he hovered on the edge of conversion, his friends likening him to a Victorian Tractarian clergyman trembling on the brink of Rome. But he spoke on Labour platforms and was even taken home by Sidney Webb to meet Beatrice Webb.

'We have made the acquaintance of the most brilliant man in the House of Commons,' wrote Beatrice Webb in her diary.

'Here is the perfect politician who is also a perfect gentleman,' said I to myself as he entered the room. . . . If there were a word for the direct opposite of caricature I should apply it to him. Tall and slim, his features not too strikingly handsome to be strikingly peculiar to himself; modest yet dignified in manner, with a pleasant voice and unegotistical conversation, this young person would make his way in the world without his adventitious advantages which are many – birth, wealth and a beautifully aristocratic wife. He is also an accomplished orator in the old grand style; and an assiduous worker in the modern manner – keeps two secretaries at work supplying him with information but realizes that he himself has to do the thinking!

So much perfection argues rottenness somewhere. . . . Is there in him some weak spot which will be revealed in a time of stress – exactly at the very time when you need support – by letting you or your cause down or sweeping it out of the way?

The question is a pertinent one, as it seems likely that he will either now or in the near future join the Parliamentary Labour Party. J.R.M. [Ramsay MacDonald] is much taken with him and he with J.R.M. Even the Clyde contingent have been fascinated by his personal charm and the wit and wisdom of his speeches. It is, by the way, interesting to note that the

Scottish Covenanters [the Clydeside ILP] are prejudiced in favour of anyone who is particularly hated by the other side. 'There are three men in the House who are detested and reviled by the Tories,' says Johnston, the editor of *Forward*, who is himself in the House – 'Sidney Webb, Patrick Hastings and Mosley . . . because they are traitors to their class.'

One factor which may have held Mosley back was the idea, widely held by people of his background, that only 'gentlemen' were capable of ruling. Meeting the Webbs, Ramsay MacDonald, Laski and others must have helped to convince him of the Labour Party's technical competence. Above all there were the examples of working-class men like Henderson, Clynes, Thomas and Tom Shaw running Government departments as efficiently as their Conservative and Liberal predecessors. Labour had proved fit to rule – a fact which contributed to the virtual annihilation of the Liberals in the next election.

After watching Labour in office for three months, Mosley acted. He joined the ILP, then the normal means of entry for middle- and upper-class recruits, and applied for the Parliamentary Labour Party whip. To MacDonald he wrote in flamboyant terms: 'You stand forth as the leader of the forces of progress in their assault upon the powers of reaction. I ask leave to range myself under your banner.'

The *Manchester Guardian* congratulated MacDonald on 'the fine new recruit he has secured'.

CHAPTER 2

Furs and Fables

OSWALD AND CYNTHIA MOSLEY were a pair of magnificent cuckoos in the Labour Party nest. Or that is how they look in retrospect. At the time of the arrival, however, they had an ecstatic reception. Mosley toured the country and won enthusiastic applause everywhere. Herbert Morrison, Secretary of London Labour Party, arranged a special rally at the New Cross Empire to introduce Mosley to the Movement. There was a particularly warm welcome in Glasgow and the Glaswegian ILP leader Patrick Dollan successfully proposed to the ILP Executive that Mosley should be exempt from the rule that nobody could be an ILP Parliamentary candidate until he had completed a year's membership. There was a welcome, too, from the Parliamentary Labour leaders, especially from MacDonald and Henderson.

One of the best authorities on the Labour Party of the late 1920's was Egon Wertheimer, a shrewd German journalist who was London Correspondent to the Social Democratic paper *Vorwarts*. Constantly amazed at the loose organization and lack of class warfare in the British Labour Party, Wertheimer commented on its affairs from an informed but independent standpoint. He introduced his book, *Portrait of the Labour Party*, with an account of the New Cross Empire meeting:

> . . . A young man, with the face of the ruling class in Great Britain but the gait of a Douglas Fairbanks, thrust himself forward through the throng to the platform, followed by a lady

in heavy, costly furs. 'For he's a jolly good fellow' was sung from
2,000 throats . . . for a man of barely twenty-eight.

Of Mosley's speech Wertheimer wrote: 'It was a hymn, an
emotional appeal directed not to the intellect but to the Socialistic
idea, which was obviously still a subject of wonder for the orator.'
The lady in costly furs was, of course, Cynthia Mosley, and
Wertheimer described how she responded to shouts from the
audience that she should speak:

> . . . The lady in furs got up and said she had never before
> attended a workers' meeting and how deeply the warmth of this
> reception touched her. She said this simply and almost shyly, but
> yet like one who is accustomed to be acclaimed and without
> stage fright to open a bazaar or a meeting for charitable
> purposes.

Later in the book, in a detailed analysis of the personalities of
Labour leaders, Wertheimer wrote of Mosley's skill as a public
speaker and his energy. Young members of the Party were looking
to Mosley as a future leader. In his first edition, published in 1929,
Wertheimer warned Mosley that he was rising too far too quickly
and that impatience might destroy him. In the second edition,
published a year later when Mosley was a minister, Wertheimer
deleted the warning.

During his first four years as a Socialist, Mosley worked mainly
within the ILP which, with its 'living wage' policy, was developing a
new form of left-wing Socialism. Until the mid-1920's it was a
Socialist assumption that capitalism, for all its faults, had solved the
problem of production of wealth. The task of Socialism was to
redistribute the wealth, eliminating injustice. Even the Russian
Communists, in Lenin's time, behaved as if the law of supply and
demand was sufficient to stimulate production, and it was not until
1928, with the first Five Year Plan, that the Russians swung
decisively behind the notion of a planned expansion of wealth. In
the British Labour Movement public ownership was traditionally
regarded as a way of redistributing wealth rather than of facilitating
State planning to produce more wealth. Keir Hardie, for example,
had few ideas for dealing with the unemployed beyond caring for
their physical needs. In the 1920's it was becoming patently obvious
that uncontrolled capitalism was failing even in producing
wealth, and in all three political parties the younger members began

to demand a degree of State planning to overcome the stagnation of the basic industries and to provide work for the unemployed. Mosley helped to pioneer this idea in the ILP, earning a reputation as a rebel among the supporters of Snowden, Chancellor of the Exchequer in the 1924 Labour Government, who believed in the traditional dogmas of free trade, 'orthodox' finance and the Gold Standard. The distinguishing mark of the new rebels was that they no longer gave first place to public ownership – although they assumed without question that over a long period of years successive Labour Governments would nationalize the whole means of production, distribution and exchange – and stressed the importance of the Government stimulating the whole economy to produce more wealth. The obvious weapon was Government control of credit and currency, which Mosley coupled with an immediate nationalization of the banks. The ILP 'living wage' policy was one aspect of this. By forcing industry to pay higher wages, more purchasing power would be injected into the economy and industry would be stimulated into employing more workers. All this was broadly in line with the thought of the Liberal economist, Maynard Keynes, who was just establishing his reputation, and not incompatible with the 'YMCA' Conservatives, led by Harold Macmillan and Oliver Stanley. The common ground was on State planning, not on public ownership, which appeared increasingly irrelevant to the short-term problems.

Between 1925 and 1928 Mosley conducted a vigorous campaign for nationalization of the banks, bringing himself into close alliance with the most militant elements of the extreme left. He won, for example, the friendship and support of A. J. Cook, left-wing Secretary of the Miners' Federation. His friendship with the left produced a reaction in the centre and on the right where there was a tendency to regard him as a playboy; not until about 1929 was it generally recognized that Mosley was a serious politician who worked hard with big ideas – ideas he was desperately eager to see translated into action.

While working with the left, Mosley retained close relations with Ramsay MacDonald and was one of the group of wealthy Socialists who subscribed to the running costs of the Leader's car. He was also on amicable terms with Arthur Henderson, the Party Secretary, who was always anxious to attract middle- and upper-class intellectuals to the Party's service.

With the rank and file of the Party in the country Mosley was very popular. For all their Socialism the Labour Party members of the

1920's tended to retain a respect for the aristocracy. (Wertheimer was bewildered at the attachment of the British working class to royalty and the peerage.) Mosley also had enough money to pay his election expenses. Within six months of his joining the Party he received some fifty inquiries from constituencies looking for Parliamentary candidates; the ILP National Council had a special meeting to consider the flood of applications. Harrow obviously would not stomach a Socialist Mosley and, after long consideration, he decided to fight Neville Chamberlain, former Conservative Chancellor of the Exchequer, at Ladywood, Birmingham – a seat which had been held for fifty years by members of the Chamberlain family. Mosley wanted to win his spurs with a dramatic success. At the back of his mind, apparently, was the additional idea that Birmingham lacked a Labour leader of distinction and that a Mosley tradition might come to replace the Chamberlain tradition.

The fight against Chamberlain was in the general election of October 1924, when Labour gained heavily in votes but the Conservatives, at the expense of the Liberals, gained a majority in Parliamentary seats and the assurance of five years in office. Mosley, with Cynthia at his side, flung himself into a passionate campaign to oust Chamberlain, who had won the previous election with a 3,000 majority.

As a first move, Mosley challenged Chamberlain to a public debate and received the ponderous reply: 'This is a very old trick, which is always played by people who think that they can get a little more limelight at the heels of others who have made a little more noise in the world than themselves.' Retorted Mosley: 'I'm afraid that Mr. Chamberlain is confusing himself with his father.' An irritated Chamberlain referred in his diary to Mosley as 'that viper'.

The result was very close. The first count gave Chamberlain a majority of twenty. A recount reduced it to seven and a third count showed a majority of two in Mosley's favour. New tellers conducted a fourth count which, as dawn broke over the city, returned Chamberlain with a majority of seventy-seven. Had it not been for the Zinoviev letter scare in the last stages of the election it is possible Mosley would have won. Chamberlain, at any rate, regarded it as such a close shave that, to the delight of the Birmingham Socialists, he migrated at the next election to the leafy security of Edgbaston.

With two of the ILP organizers in Birmingham Mosley established close relations. They were Allen Young, a Clydesider and an acute economist, and Bill Risdon, a miner from South Wales whose early political career had been in association with Aneurin Bevan. Young and Risdon were both to follow Mosley out of the Labour Party but meanwhile they buttressed his unofficial primacy in Birmingham and West Midland Labour politics. Under Mosley's vigorous leadership funds were raised, candidates were selected and constituencies were reorganized; so that in the 1929 general election Labour gained fourteen seats, the biggest reverse suffered by the local Conservative caucus in fifty years. G. D. H. Cole commented in his *History of the Labour Party* (1948): 'Mosley, however, did not succeed in establishing any lasting leadership, such as he aimed at, in Joseph Chamberlain's old Radical stronghold. The West Midland members were a mixed bag and by no means all endorsed his leadership.'

One West Midland candidate who did endorse Mosley's leadership was John Strachey, who had appeared as Labour candidate at Aston in 1923 shortly after leaving Oxford, where he had a reputation as a High Tory. Strachey and Mosley became close friends and effective political partners, Strachey's orderly mind proving a useful corrective to Mosley's high enthusiasms. As Editor of *The Miner*, Strachey strengthened Mosley's links with A. J. Cook. The two men had a certain cold-bloodedness in common in their approach to politics. Their relationship was very close; Mosley was definitely the senior partner but Strachey, although half mesmerized by the brilliance of the Mosley personality, retained his capacity for argument. For seven years Mosley and Strachey collaborated as a political team, Allen Young appearing as third man and George Sutton, Mosley's private secretary from 1919 to the late 1940's, acting as research assistant. It is arguable that Mosley's political effectiveness was permanently weakened when Strachey and Young left him in 1931.

Mosley and Strachey collaborated during 1925 in drawing up detailed schemes for Government control of credit. Their ideas, first entitled the 'Birmingham Proposals', received the endorsement of the ILP annual conference and of Birmingham Labour Party, and were outlined by Mosley in a pamphlet called *Revolution by Reason*. Strachey later amplified the proposals in a book under the same title as the pamphlet, in which he first revealed his skill as a popularizer and expounder of political and economic theory. Mosley and Strachey worked together on the book during a summer holiday at Venice, and a close friend of them both, Robert Boothby, aged twenty-five and just elected as a Conservative MP, was there to watch them. He recorded the scene in his autobiography *I Fight to Live*.

The first time I went there [Venice] I was guest of the Mosleys; and I shall never forget my first sight of the Piazza. They took me there after dinner with a handkerchief across my eyes, and when it was removed I found myself in the middle of a scene which must have been without parallel even in the pre-war world. The blazing lights, the band playing *Lohengrin*, the throngs of interested and interesting people strolling up and down, and St. Mark's in the background.... Every morning Tom Mosley and John Strachey, who was also a guest, discussed *Revolution by Reason*, a book which they were writing together and which I then thought the height of political audacity, although it seems very reasonable stuff today [1947]. This was the period when Mosley saw himself as Byron rather than Mussolini; and to me it was infinitely preferable. He was certainly a powerful swimmer and used to disappear at intervals into the lagoon to commune with himself. . . .

Strachey dedicated his book 'To O.M., who may some day do the things of which we dream'. The underlying argument was that there should be enough purchasing power within the economy to keep the machines busy and the workers at work. 'Poverty, when joined to our modern capacity to produce, is a twice-cursed evil. It curses the humble because they cannot buy. It curses the great and rich because they cannot sell.... Today its continuance is unforgivable, since for the first time in history it is unnecessary.' Socialists had tended to blame maldistribution of ownership as the principal evil but equally important – and Strachey quoted Keynes – was lack of money within the economy. 'We do not in this free and happy country of ours pay the very slightest attention to the price level when we are issuing money.' Two brief Acts, which could pass quickly on to the Statute Book, would provide a public banking system and an Economic Council for the control of productive capacity.

There were a variety of methods by which extra money could be injected into the economy – minimum-wage legislation, family allowances, and generous credit from the banks to enable industry to produce before a market was immediately available. The corollary, of course, was detailed State control to prevent the extra money causing a runaway inflation. The issue of extra money should be matched, step by step, with the production of more goods. In a foreshadowing of Mosley's later 'corporate state', Strachey said that the Government should have power to compel employers and workers in the basic industries to come together to form what he called 'national corporations'. A second corollary was that Britain would have to abandon much of her international trade, prices fetched by exports being outside Government control. 'We should be content to regard the object of British industry as the humble and straightforward one of satisfying the needs of British men and women.'

Revolution by Reason gave basically the economic policy which Mosley was to advocate as a Fascist; although on becoming a Fascist he abandoned the idea that it should be accompanied by a parallel programme of taking industries gradually into public ownership, and added to it the distinctively Fascist principles of authoritarian government and the corporate state.

In retrospect, as Boothby remarked, the *Revolution by Reason* policy seems commonplace, so complete has been the Keynsian revolution. But in the mid-1920's it was regarded even on the left as novel, dangerous and revolutionary. It cut sharply across the objective of the orthodox politicians and economists to reduce prices even at the cost of creating unemployment and to reduce wages even at the cost of the most bitter industrial strife. The orthodox policy reached its climax in the 1925 Budget when Winston Churchill, as Chancellor of the Exchequer, restored the pound to the Gold Standard. Snowden approved, and the only influential voices raised against it were those of Beaverbrook, Keynes and Vincent Vickers, a director of the Bank of England who resigned in protest. The consequent rise in British export prices led directly to the lock-out of the miners in April 1926, and thence to the so-called General Strike. Mosley, working with the left wing of the ILP, bitterly attacked the Gold Standard decision. The campaign was, however, ill co-ordinated. Among the trade-union leaders Ernest Bevin was the most powerful opponent of the Gold Standard, but he regarded Mosley as the kind of unreliable intellectual who might at any moment stab him in the back. Mosley, in his turn, seemed unable to appreciate the abilities of working-class leaders, who distrusted him. Unlike, for example, Hugh Dalton he made little attempt to penetrate and to understand the ethos of the working class. The friendship he developed with Beatrice Webb may have tended to confirm his attitude.

Only with the miners did Mosley establish close relations. In their long, miserable fight against wage reductions Mosley championed

their cause, winning the high regard of A. J. Cook, who was to
prove himself not ungrateful. Cook, a former Communist, had a
revivalist fervour and, with splendid disregard for tactics, led the
miners through severe privations under the slogan 'Not a penny off
the pay, not a minute on the day'. Mosley had tumultuous receptions
at miners' rallies, especially the Durham miners' galas where both
he and Cynthia Mosley were among the most popular speakers. As
he watched the Durham miners marching with bands and banners
through the narrow streets of their cathedral city, Mosley gained,
he said later, the inspiration for his Fascist marches of the 1930's.
Mosley's advocacy of the miners' cause did not aid his popularity
in more orthodox trade-union circles, where Cook was regarded as
an embarrassment. At the 1926 Labour Party Conference the
National Executive, accepting the TUC line, proposed a resolution
which offered sympathy to the miners but little practical help,
although Ramsay MacDonald handed to the miners' funds a gift of
£60 he had received from the delegates as a sixtieth-birthday present.
Mosley, on behalf of the ILP, moved the reference back of the
resolution and called on the Labour Movement to use 'its whole
strength, political and industrial' on the miners' behalf. The reference
back was supported by such variegated speakers as Harry Pollitt,
David Kirkwood and W. J. Brown, but the Executive won by
2,159,000 votes to 1,368,000.

At the following year's Labour Party Conference Mosley himself
reached the National Executive, a rare achievement for a man who
had been a member of the Party for only three years. He was elected
to the constituency section of the Executive with the solid support
of the miners. The voting figures for the successful candidates
were:

George Lansbury	2,183,000
Charles Treveleyan	1,675,000
J. H. Hayes	1,644,000
Oswald Mosley	1,613,000
Herbert Morrison	1,562,000

(At that time the whole conference, not merely the constituency
delegates, voted in the constituency-section election.)

Meanwhile Mosley had returned to Parliament. In December 1926
J. E. Davison, a railwayman, resigned unexpectedly through ill
health from his seat at Smethwick, and Mosley, supported by the
whole weight of the Midland Labour Movement, took his place.
The by-election attracted a good deal of publicity, with Conservative

newspapers concentrating on the human story of the rich Socialist soliciting working-class votes. Cynthia Mosley, it was confidently reported, was telling the Smethwick housewives that if they voted for Mosley they would all get furs like hers. The Conservative Leader, Stanley Baldwin, ridiculed 'the spectacle of wealth posturing as the sympathizer of poverty'. Cynthia tartly replied: 'It is no doubt sound Conservative doctrine that those who are not themselves in miserable conditions should do nothing to help those who are living in miserable conditions.' There were long descriptions of the Mosleys' hotel accommodation, and of Cynthia's jewels and furs. There were pictures of the Mosleys sunning themselves at Biarritz and Venice. Most startling of all, there was an attack on Mosley from his own father:

'I could never understand the line my son has taken,' Oswald Mosley senior grumbled to the *Daily Express*.

He was born with a gold spoon in his mouth – it cost a hundred pounds in doctors' fees to bring him into the world. He lived on the fat of the land and never did a day's work in his life. . . . He has a big income from his own family and from the other side. . . . If the working class, for whom I have always stuck up, are going to be taken in by such nonsense, I am sorry for them. How does my son know anything about them?

In the *Daily Herald* Mosley issued a reply: 'My father knows nothing of my life and has very seldom seen me. He contributed nothing to my education or upbringing, except in the form of alimony which he was compelled to contribute in a court of law.'

The attacks in the newspapers and from his own family appeared to strengthen Mosley's sense of isolation – and of personal mission. He hit back warmly at the 'furs and fables', at 'the dope poured out by scores of newspapers in the hands of two or three millionaires', and, possibly, made a mental note that one day the Press should be dealt with. His consolation came from the applause of the Labour audiences. Arms loose at his sides, Mosley would lift his chin as the cheers echoed round him. He could move himself to tears with his own speeches, the tears repeated with an actor's skill when he repeated the same speeches to different audiences. Some doubted whether the tears were genuine, but the fairest judgment may be that Mosley's technique was as unconscious as that of a revivalist preacher – or of an actor – who with perfect sincerity can repeat the same forensic tricks night after night. The content of Mosley's speeches was too closely argued for him to be accounted a mere demagogue. He had, too, much more than a demagogue's skill at answering questions from a public platform. He disliked interruptions but always allowed time for questions when he had finished his speech – a habit he continued in his Fascist days. The brilliance of his technique as, with arms akimbo, he used an opponent's question as a means of hammering home his own case made him a most difficult man to challenge. He did, however, display some of the demagogue's appetite for power over an audience and obviously enjoyed being cheered.

Even better than the applause was the Smethwick result. Mosley won with a majority of 6,500 – five times that of his predecessor.

Back in the Commons, Mosley was surprisingly quiet. Some thought he looked uncomfortable in his new surroundings and noted how he seemed to vary his way of life; appearing at one moment as the austere, plain-living Socialist and at the next as the young aristocrat, fond of fast cars, good clothes and fine food. In the House the Conservatives thought it good sport to try to cut him back to size and punctuated his speeches with ribald interruptions. For them Mosley showed biting contempt, calling their interventions 'strange noises representing the dumb, instinctive yearning to achieve the heights of human speech'. He clashed again with Churchill and with members of his own front bench, notably Snowden. The Government produced a scheme for evacuating unemployed workers from the distressed areas to the more prosperous Midlands and south – importing unemployment, therefore, into Mosley's own area. In the debate on the King's Speech in 1928, Mosley attacked the scheme in words which provide a good illustration of his sardonic, argumentative, Parliamentary style:

'We now have the extraordinary theory that if you take a man who is unemployed in Durham and put him down in Birmingham, where there is considerable unemployment, you are assisting the aggregate of employment. . . . Until you can expand your market, until you can increase your demand for goods, and thus increase the demand for labour, you have not begun to deal with the problem. . . . In recent years we have exported enough to pile up in 1927 the favourable trade balance of £97,000,000 which was largely spent on creating industries abroad and which might better have been used to create them in the suffering districts of our own land.'

In 1928 Mosley secured re-election to the National Executive. He was aged thirty-two, being eight years younger than Morrison and nine years younger than Dalton. The voting figures were:

George Lansbury	3,071,000
Herbert Morrison	2,823,000
Oswald Mosley	2,153,000
Charles Treveleyan	1,882,000
Hugh Dalton	1,774,000

The same year his father died aged fifty-four. Mosley attended the funeral and afterwards found that he had been excluded from the personal Will although, as the last heir to the entail, he received the family landed estates worth just under £250,000. He did not inherit Rolleston Hall, which had been demolished in 1923 to make way for a housing estate. There was some speculation about whether he would use his new title, Lady Cynthia having earlier announced her wish to be known in the Labour Movement as plain 'Cynthia Mosley'. Mosley's publicly declared view was that the baronetcy was 'not worth renouncing'.

After the miners' defeat, Mosley turned his main attention away from domestic economic affairs towards foreign and imperial issues, working closely with MacDonald on the International Sub-Committee of the National Executive. He was in indifferent health, his wartime leg injuries still troubling him, and he devoted a great deal of time to travel. He toured India where, as son-in-law of Curzon, he received a respectful welcome but broke convention by shooting a tiger that had been reserved for the Commander-in-Chief. He returned with the conventional left-wing view that India should proceed quickly towards self-government. During a visit to the United States he went on a fishing trip with Franklin Roosevelt. Cynthia Mosley travelled with an ILP delegation to the Soviet Union and expressed the customary approbation of the Communist experiment. In the summer of 1928 MacDonald was Mosley's guest on a tour of European capitals. Fenner Brockway, Secretary of the ILP, afterwards recorded the whisperings which went round the Labour Movement about this trip – how Cynthia Mosley fussed over MacDonald, 'flattered him with attentions on train journeys and in hotels and saw that his every need was met'.* MacDonald and the Mosleys were certainly on terms of mutual admiration and, according to Hugh Dalton in *Call Back Yesterday*

* *Inside the Left* by Fenner Brockway (1942).

(1953), at about this time MacDonald sounded the TUC General Secretary, Walter Citrine, to see whether Mosley would be acceptable as the next party leader. Citrine opposed the idea.

MacDonald and Mosley found themselves on opposite sides in a sub-committee of the National Executive appointed to draw up a programme for the 1929 general election. MacDonald, supported by Snowden, wanted a general statement of Socialist aims and principles, from which the next Labour Government could, according to circumstances, select which measures it thought most practicable at the moment. The left suspected that this was an evasive manœuvre, designed to enable the next Labour Government to retreat from Socialism altogether. Mosley, who because of his bad leg had to be carried into the meetings, worked with Treveleyan to advocate what he afterwards described as 'a crisp, practical programme of measures which Labour could carry in the lifetime of one Parliament'. The fifth member of the sub-committee, Arthur Henderson, acted as mediator and at his suggestion the task of writing the manifesto was delegated to R. H. Tawney. The result was the 42,000-word *Labour and the Nation*, which MacDonald revised and diluted during a week-end at Lossiemouth. In its final form it was a Utopian document which bound a Labour Government to no timetable.

Even in phraseology Mosley's view was strikingly close to that of Ernest Bevin, who told the 1927 Labour Party Conference: 'When some of our friends draw up programmes, they are something like manifestos. . . . I would rather see a short programme of immediate objectives that Labour can really hope to accomplish and then we can go back and say: "At least we have done what we said we would; we have delivered the goods." ' From an electoral point of view MacDonald's judgment was vindicated. The Liberals went into the 1929 election with their detailed *Yellow Book* proposals for massive State intervention to cure unemployment but, in spite of an expensive campaign, gained only twenty seats. Labour gained 130 seats and for the first time became the largest party in the Commons, although still dependent on Liberal support for an absolute majority.

Mosley added a further 1,000 votes to his majority at Smethwick. Cynthia Mosley became MP for Stoke, ousting the sitting Liberal by a majority of nearly 8,000. She had nursed the constituency for three years but by the time of the campaign was in poor health and suffered a miscarriage shortly after the poll. Mosley gave her a diamond brooch in the shape of the Palace of Westminster, the figures of her majority running across it in red rubies. John Strachey fought again at Aston, this time winning by 1,500. Other Mosley group gains included Oliver Baldwin, the Conservative Leader's son, at Dudley; W. J. Brown at Wolverhampton West; J. F. Horrabin at Peterborough and James Simmons at Birmingham Erdington.

'At last England has arisen and the day is here – the new day when the people of Britain shall come into their own,' wrote George Lansbury in the *New Leader*.

Never were so many high political hopes to be more cruelly disappointed.

CHAPTER 3

Future Prime Minister?

THERE is evidence to suggest that on the formation of the 1929 Labour Government Oswald Mosley nearly became Foreign Secretary. It rests on a letter, dated 15th June 1929, written by Harold Laski and summarized by Kingsley Martin in his *Harold Laski* (1953):

> MacDonald had sent for Laski and talked about the Government. He had agreed that Sankey should be Lord Chancellor: they had argued about the Foreign Office, which MacDonald first thought of giving to J. H. Thomas, and then would have given to Sir Oswald Mosley had not Arthur Henderson 'stood out to bursting point'.

Laski's fondness for colouring his anecdotes with imagined detail made him not the most reliable of witnesses, but Mosley himself declares (1961) that at the time he had an inkling that he was being considered for the Foreign Office. The notion ties in with MacDonald's known views. MacDonald's chief interest was foreign affairs and in 1924 he had been both Prime Minister and Foreign Secretary. The Party would not have tolerated his taking both posts in 1929 and it was, therefore, natural that he should toy with the idea of appointing a young, inexperienced Foreign Secretary who would work under Downing Street tutelage. For three years MacDonald and Mosley had been working harmoniously together on the National Executive foreign-affairs sub-committee. Could not the

Sir Oswald and Lady Cynthia Mosley during the Smethwick by-election, 1926

Arnold Spencer Leese, founder of the
Imperial Fascist League

Miss Rotha Lintorn-Orman, founder of
the first Fascist organization in Britain

(*Keys*

(*above*) Sir Oswald Mosley with Benito Mussolini in Rome, April 1933

(*below*) A BUF Mobile Defence Squad parades beside its van at Black House, Chelsea, *circa* 1934

(*Daily Herald*)

partnership be continued in government? It is questionable whether Mosley would have long been content to be Foreign Secretary on leading strings, but if he had been given the appointment there is at least a chance that he would have either remained in the Labour Party during the 1930–31 crisis, and survived as the senior ex-minister, or have followed MacDonald and made a new career in the 1931 National Government.

In the event, the Foreign Office went to Arthur Henderson, with Hugh Dalton as Under-Secretary, MacDonald retaining the conduct of Anglo-American relations in his own hands. Mosley was considered for the post of First Lord of the Admiralty† but was eventually appointed the sinecure of Chancellor of the Duchy of Lancaster, ranking above the under-secretaries as a senior minister outside the Cabinet. Morrison became Minister of Transport, also outside the Cabinet. Attlee, busy as a member of the Simon Commission on India, was not in the Government at all.

Mosley had no reason for complaint and made none. Chancellor of the Duchy was a brilliant appointment for a man aged thirty-two who had never previously held office. It was the more brilliant because his special brief was to assist J. H. Thomas, Lord Privy Seal, in solving the unemployment problem. Unemployment was the big issue of the day and the one on which Labour had won the election. MacDonald attached so much importance to the unemployment problem that he handed responsibility for it to a committee of four ministers: Thomas as chairman and chief spokesman; Mosley as Thomas's understudy with special oversight of local-authority works schemes; George Lansbury, First Commissioner for Works; and Tom Johnston, Scottish Under-Secretary.

'A more ill-assorted team could scarcely be imagined,' Johnston recalled in his autobiography.* According to Lansbury* the committee

> met many times in a sort of semi-dungeon high up in the Treasury offices. We were surrounded by the reputed élite of the Civil Service. . . . There was, however, always present one faithful watchdog who represented the Treasury. . . . The Treasury could always be counted upon to find good and excellent reasons why nothing should be done.

Backing the Treasury watchdog was the brilliant, bitter Philip

*These quotations are from *Memories* by Tom Johnston (1952) and *My England* by George Lansbury (1934).
† *An Autobiography* by Philip, Viscount Snowden (1934).

Snowden, who as Chancellor of the Exchequer inflexibly upheld the canons of traditional finance. To Snowden the principal meaning of Socialism was the nationalization of industries. Since Labour had no Parliamentary majority nationalization was impossible, and therefore Socialism was impossible. While awaiting a majority, Labour should prove its respectability by balancing the Budget, upholding the Gold Standard and maintaining free trade. For the Unemployment Committee's works schemes Snowden laid down the strict rule that they should be financially self-supporting. He dominated the Cabinet and had no difficulty in getting his views accepted. Certainly J. H. Thomas could not stand up to him. A genial and successful railwaymen's leader, Thomas's skill lay in negotiating and in public relations; for the detailed work of tackling unemployment and fighting the Treasury he was entirely unsuited. A flamboyant visit to Canada as a super-salesman of British goods seemed to exhaust his ideas.

Beatrice Webb recorded in her diary on 2nd December 1929 that she had been talking to Henderson who had told her of

> the collapse of Thomas who is completely rattled and in such a state of panic that he is bordering on lunacy. Henderson reported that the Prime Minister feared suicidal mania. Meanwhile Thomas . . . regards all suggestions as accusations of failure. Henderson is now suggesting to the PM that he himself must take the subject in hand, that there must be a committee of Home Defence against poverty, that Cole must be engaged if possible, and a proper department started – and that Jimmy [Thomas] must be sent away for a rest and Oswald Mosley installed, under the committee, to carry out agreed plans.

Thomas had reason for panic. During the last six months of 1929 unemployment remained rock steady at 1,300,000, representing over one in ten of the insured population. His committee was making not the slightest impact. The Conservatives were mocking him and the Labour Party was becoming restive.

The first puff of discontent came at the Labour Party Conference in September 1929, just three months after the Government had taken office. There was no disposition to attack the leaders – the rank and file still idolized MacDonald. The resentment took the form of a vague feeling that aristocrats and intellectuals were gaining too much influence. The conference rejected a proposal from the Executive to create a category of 'national associate members' which would have enabled middle-class people to join the Party without identifying themselves with local branches. 'We do not want the formation of any rich caucus inside our movement,' declared a delegate of the Transport and General Workers' Union. A more concrete blow at the aristocracy was the dismissal of the two Labour baronets, Mosley and Treveleyan, from the National Executive. It was an unfair penalty, for both were among the most industrious members of the Government. The voting figures for the successful candidates in the constituency section were:

George Lansbury	2,016,000
Herbert Morrison	1,693,000
Hugh Dalton	1,575,000
Morgan Jones	1,121,000
George Dallas	935,000

Mosley, as Strachey recorded, had a 'genuine, unsophisticated desire to do something'.* He moved into Treasury Chambers, Whitehall, and brought in Allen Young, the Birmingham ILP organizer, as private secretary. Strachey became his Parliamentary Private Secretary. At first his main work outside Parliament, beyond attending the fruitless meetings of the Unemployment Committee, was to persuade local authorities to run works schemes to help their unemployed. Local-authority deputations found Mosley blazing with enthusiasm and returned to their towns with a high opinion of the young minister. Mosley was less satisfied. He was irritated that he, a minister of the central government, had to persuade rather than order the local authorities to carry out national plans. In his later, Fascist, policy Mosley insisted that the central government should have complete power of command over local authorities. The existing system, he said, was as unworkable as a business organization would be if it allowed local branches to disobey head office.

By the autumn it was clear – if it had not been so before – that local-authority works would provide, at best, a marginal impact on unemployment. If any remedy were possible, it would have to be a fundamental remedy reorientating the whole national economy. Thomas had no idea of producing such a remedy and Mosley decided to take the initiative. With eager industry he and his assistants, with

* *The Menace of Fascism* by John Strachey (1933).

the collaboration of Lansbury and advice from Keynes, produced a comprehensive set of proposals which they boiled down to twenty-five pages of typed foolscap and submitted to the Cabinet in January 1930. This was the document which was to become known as the *Mosley Memorandum*.

The *Mosley Memorandum* postulated a form of siege economy not dissimilar to that used by the Churchill Coalition during the Second World War and by the 1945 Labour Government. It would probably have worked, although at the high cost of State intervention into private industry, the dismantling of foreign trade and mass migrations of workers from one industry to another. The unemployed, who at the peak of the crisis numbered three million, might have thought the price worth paying. Of the *Memorandum* G. D. H. Cole, in his *A History of the Labour Party* (1948), wrote: 'I feel sure it was largely right.'

The ideas in the *Mosley Memorandum* were obviously drawn from a variety of sources. From his own *Revolution by Reason* policy Mosley drew proposals for expanding purchasing power, and for a liberal credit policy by Government-controlled banks. From the tariff reformers he drew the idea of excluding foreign goods from the British market; he refined the cruder ideas of the Protectionists by saying that goods should be excluded, by tariff or direct control, only on condition that the equivalent British home industries were efficient and paid fair wages. His aim, as he put it, was to 'insulate' the British economy to make efficiency and full employment possible. To reduce the cost of food imports, Mosley proposed a big, protected development of home agriculture. For the nation's remaining food and raw-material requirements he proposed bulk-purchase agreements, preferably with the Dominions. To make immediate inroads into the unemployment figures, Mosley advocated the raising of the school-leaving age from fourteen to fifteen and giving insured workers an option of a pension at sixty; these points were not dissimilar to a scheme propounded by Bevin a year earlier. Similar to the Liberal *Yellow Book* policy were proposals for public-works schemes, notably for roads and slum-clearance, and for a Government board to supervise investment and the rationalization of industry.

The whole was not very different from the ILP 'Socialism Now' policy, but in essence it had little to do with Socialism. It was capable of being implemented in almost any but a purely free-enterprise framework. Vigorous Government leadership might have carried it even through the 1929 Parliament, rather as Roosevelt carried through his New Deal three years later.

In preparing so far-reaching a scheme Mosley acted beyond his ministerial brief. It was not for the Chancellor of the Duchy to reorganize the nation's economy. There was irritation within the Cabinet, Clynes, the Home Secretary, finding the *Memorandum* 'something approaching insanity'.* Support within the Cabinet came from Lansbury and a certain amount of sympathy from MacDonald, who insisted that the *Memorandum* should at least be examined. Snowden's Treasury officials carried out the examination and their verdict could never be in doubt. They riddled the whole document with detailed objections, but the unyielding adherence of Snowden to free trade and a balanced Budget was the decisive obstacle.

News that Mosley had submitted a memorandum leaked quickly to the Press, appearing first in the London Letter of the *Manchester Guardian*. There followed weeks of newspaper speculation and by the time the Cabinet finally rejected it, in March 1930, Mosley's public reputation was at stake. The subject was the more newsworthy because of the staggering rises in unemployment which followed the American slump at the end of 1929. By the end of January 1930 British unemployment passed the 1,500,000 mark and by April it reached 1,700,000. By July it was to pass 2,000,000.

On the rejection of his proposals, Mosley addressed a series of sharp letters to MacDonald arguing against the Cabinet decision. Argument failing, Mosley decided to carry his case to the House of Commons and on the 20th May sent a letter of resignation to a puzzled Prime Minister. He had been a minister for eleven and a half months.

MacDonald was sufficiently shocked by the resignation – which he had not expected – to make changes in the allocation of responsibility in the Cabinet. He took charge of unemployment himself, moved Thomas to the Dominions Office, and promoted Attlee from the back benches to be Chancellor of the Duchy and Thomas's assistant in preparing for the forthcoming Imperial Conference. Attlee later became Postmaster General. Lansbury considered resigning on the same grounds as Mosley but, remembering an incident earlier in his career when precipitate resignation had proved a mistake, held his hand.† Mosley had no hesitation at all. 'I was in

* *Memoirs* by J. R. Clynes (1937).
† *The Life of George Lansbury* by Raymond Postgate (1951).

his room at the House of Commons the night he resigned and well remember his relief and satisfaction, his determination to go forward and "bring these grave matters to the test",' wrote Robert Boothby.*

The first test was a special meeting of the Parliamentary Labour Party on the 22nd May. Mosley moved a resolution calling for a new policy on unemployment 'in accordance with the programme and pledges of the Party at the last election'. His speech was powerful, detailed and persuasive and, by all accounts, he won the sympathy of most of the meeting. The difficulty was that if the resolution had been carried it would have entailed the destruction of the MacDonald administration, which for the overwhelming majority of the MPs was unthinkable. Henderson, in a friendly speech, urged Mosley, having made his point, to withdraw the resolution. Mosley insisted on a vote and was beaten by 210 to twenty-nine, the ILP voting with him.

Mosley's insistence on a clear-cut decision was the first step towards his breach with the Labour Party. The time for compromise, he believed, had passed; the Party must either accept Mosley's ideas or lose Mosley.

I recollect the spectacle of Mosley sitting silent and alone, brooding with an indescribable bitterness, as the elderly, portly trade union officials and nervous pacifist intellectuals filed out of a party meeting at which they had demonstrated their continued confidence in Mr. Ramsay MacDonald [wrote Strachey]. A stab of premonition flashed through my mind. How had the Italian Social Democrats looked at the Congress of the Italian Socialist Party which expelled the Editor of *Avanti*? Had they not been sure that they had finished with that tiresome fellow Mussolini? I do not know if Mosley's premonitions were of a more detailed character.†

Mosley's premonitions at this stage appeared to be more concerned with an all-party movement against the 'old men' by the politicians of his own, post-war generation. On 28th May he carried his campaign to the floor of the House of Commons in the most outstanding speech of his Parliamentary career. He was on his feet for an hour and ten minutes; slowly, dramatically, he analysed the country's economic plight. Stabbing the air with his favourite

* *I Fight to Live* by Robert Boothby (1947).
† *The Menace of Fascism* by John Strachey (1933).

gesture of a man throwing a dart, he pleaded passionately for a programme of action:

'I begged the Government to make up its mind how much it was prepared to spend on unemployment, how much money it could find, and then to allocate the money available according to the best objects we could discover. As it is, no such system has ever been adopted. Departments have come crowding along, jostling each other with their schemes, and, like bookmakers on the race course, the man who can push the hardest, make most noise, and get through the turnstile first, gets away with the money. . . . To grapple with this problem it is essential to have a revolution in the machinery of government.

'Why is it right and proper and desirable that capital should go overseas to equip factories to compete against us, to build roads and railways in the Argentine or in Timbuctoo, to provide employment for people in those countries; while it is supposed to shake the whole basis of our financial strength if anyone dares to suggest the raising of money by the Government of this country to provide employment for the people of this country? . . . Let us run up the white flag of surrender if we cannot have the money to pay for unemployment.

'You have in this country resources, skilled craftsmen among the workers, design and technique among the technicians, unknown and unequalled in any other country in the world. What a fantastic assumption it is that a nation, which within the lifetime of everyone has put forth efforts of energy and vigour unequalled in the history of the world, should succumb before an economic situation such as the present.

'If the situation is to be overcome, if the great powers of this country are to be mobilized and rallied for a great national effort, then Government and Parliament must give a lead.

'I beg the Government tonight to give the vital forces of this country the chance that they await. I beg Parliament to give that lead.'

The speech had an unusual reception. The cheering was as loud on the Conservative and Liberal benches as among the Labour MPs, most of the enthusiasm coming from the younger members. For a brief moment Mosley was the leader of his generation – an experience he was never to forget.

Lloyd George and Churchill, the speakers who followed, both praised the speech, albeit with reservations. Lloyd George called it 'a mixture of Karl Marx and Lord Rothermere'. Churchill observed that Mosley's ideas would work 'if you had an archangel to manage these things – a perfectly trustworthy archangel'.

The Conservative Party at this time was in hardly a happier state than the Labour Party. On the right, Lord Beaverbrook and Lord Rothermere had just launched their United Empire Party. On the left, the forceful young men of the Macmillan–Boothby–Stanley group were calling for the Party to modernize its ideas. In their book *Industry and the State* (1928) they had joined forces to advocate Government control of credit, the creation of an 'Economic General Staff' and compulsory rationalization of backward industries under State control. Using experience gained in the war, the Government could effectively master economic slumps. The whole was a mild prevision of Mosley's later corporate state, although it was less systematized and proposed no change in political institutions.

In the face of the mounting crisis in economic affairs it seemed possible that Conservatives of this stamp might work together with Mosley. During the summer and autumn of 1930 the newspapers were intrigued by what they called the 'Mosley conversations', in which Walter Elliot, Boothby, Stanley and other Conservative MPs called at Mosley's home to discuss future policy. Macmillan, temporarily out of Parliament, also took part.

At the same time Mosley continued to try to convert the Labour Party. In preparation for the Annual Conference at Llandudno he travelled the country on speaking tours, shining to many as a beacon of hope. The climax came when from the conference platform on 7th October 1930, in a twenty-minute speech, he told the delegates that the crisis was Socialism's greatest opportunity: 'When, within the memory of any man or woman in this hall, has the nation demanded action as it is demanding it now? With courage, vigour, decision and a policy we can use the situation to remodel the whole structure of the country. Let us not shrink before a great opportunity; let us not shrink in fear before it, let us seize it and use it to give the country a lead.'

This was the peak of Mosley's Socialist career. The cheering delegates hailed him as their Messiah. Hardly a man in the hall doubted that he was Labour's next Prime Minister. 'The delegates rose *en masse*, cheering for minutes on end. I have never seen or heard such an ovation at a Labour Party Conference,' wrote Brockway.*

Lansbury, replying for the National Executive, was openly sympathetic. He told Mosley to continue to educate public opinion on the rights of the unemployed. 'Educate, agitate, organize,' he urged.

The National Executive escaped defeat by only 1,251,000 votes to 1,046,000 on a pro-Mosley resolution from Doncaster. Because of a breakdown in a taxi, A. J. Cook arrived at the conference too late to take part in the vote. Had he arrived in time, it was rumoured, he would have been able to persuade the miners to vote with Mosley, thus ensuring the defeat of the Executive.

In the National Executive election J. H. Thomas lost the seat he had held for many years in the trade-union section and Mosley was elected to the constituency section. The figures in the constituency section were:

George Lansbury	1,916,000
Herbert Morrison	1,730,000
Hugh Dalton	1,431,000
Oswald Mosley	1,362,000
George Dallas	1,209,000

Most politicians in Mosley's position would have regarded the Llandudno Conference votes as a good base for future campaigning within the Party. Mosley did not take that view. He regarded his defeat as the Labour Party's last word, and straightway began to organize a new and independent movement. The old political leaders, he believed, were failing the nation and the only hope was for the post-war generation, under Mosley's inspiration, to sweep away the old politics in favour of something new. The Conservatives had failed, the Liberals had failed and the Labour Party had failed. Like a black plague the depression was spreading over the entire country, closing down great industries and adding tens of thousands every week to the unemployed. A new force was needed to which the people, in their extremity, could turn.

To bring Conservatives into the new movement proved unexpectedly difficult. Able young men were willing to admire Mosley and to sympathize with his policy, or at least some of it. But to leave the Conservative Party and to follow this strange man into the unknown was something quite different; there was nothing wrong with the Conservative Party which could not be put right from inside.

* *Inside the Left* by Fenner Brockway (1942).

To his disappointment, Mosley found only one Conservative MP with the right cast of mind for the new venture. This was W. E. D. Allen, first elected to Parliament a year earlier as an Ulster Unionist. Allen was a widely travelled man with a somewhat romantic political outlook and a taste for political philosophy. He shared Mosley's belief in the need for a government of action and decided that Mosley was the man to provide it and became his personal and influential friend.

Prospects in the Parliamentary Labour Party were, for a while, more encouraging. Disappointment with the Government's record had brought the Party to a highly fissile state. The seventeen members of the Parliamentary group of the ILP were already in a state of semi-independence, with James Maxton as their leader and John Beckett, MP for Peckham, as their whip. Another group, less closely organized, was the 'intelligentzia', consisting of MPs who would not go to the left-wing extremes of the ILP but who criticized the lethargy of the Government and of the solid mass of trade-union MPs who supported it so unquestioningly. After Mosley's resignation the intelligentzia coalesced into a 'Mosley Group', holding regular meetings and frowned on by the whips. An ILP member, W. J. Brown, acted as secretary and tried to create a definite alliance between the Mosley Group and the ILP. Brown succeeded in establishing co-operation on day-to-day issues and the ILP-ers attended the Mosley Group meetings, but there remained a well-founded suspicion that Mosley's proposals were an alternative to Socialism rather than a means towards it. At its peak, in the autumn of 1930, the Mosley Group numbered about fifty Labour MPs including the ILP Group and including some who attended meetings mainly from curiosity.

The inner core of the Mosley Group was Mosley, Cynthia Mosley, Strachey, Brown and Aneurin Bevan. At that time Bevan was vocally on the extreme left but, in the new Parliamentary world he had reached only in 1929, was cautious in action. The ILP nicknamed him the 'armchair revolutionary'. With Mosley he was to be very cautious. He admired Mosley's political ability and found the fare and company at the Mosleys' Smith Square house to his liking. His active young mind was receptive to Mosley's bright new ideas. On psychological grounds alone, however, it would have been difficult for him to leave the miners of Ebbw Vale to follow the leadership of an ex-Tory baronet. Jennie Lee* gives an account of the

* *Tomorrow is a New Day* by Jennie Lee (1941).

trend at this time of Bevan's conversation: 'I tell you it's the Labour Party or nothing. I know all its faults, all its dangers. But it is the Party we have taught millions of working people to look to and regard as their own. We can't undo what we have done.'

On the project for a new movement, Bevan, according to Miss Lee, was yet more explicit. 'Where is the money coming from? Who is going to pay? Who is going to call the tune? I tell you now where you will end up. You will end up as a Fascist party. . . .'

But Mosley pressed ahead. Strachey rewrote the *Mosley Memorandum* proposals into the form of a political manifesto – the *Mosley Manifesto*. The aim was to persuade the whole of the Mosley Group and the ILP Group to sign it, the list being skilfully circulated so as not to reach the weaker Mosley adherents until it had already obtained a substantial number of signatures. The results were disappointing. All but three of the ILP Group refused to participate. The seventeen Labour MPs who did sign represented a broad cross-section of the Party from left to right. Two of the signatories, J. Lovat-Fraser and Frank Markham, were to follow Ramsay MacDonald into the National Labour Party. Three others, Oliver Baldwin, Brown and Strachey, were to become Independents. One, John McGovern, was to remain with the ILP when it parted company with the Labour Party. Three – Cynthia Mosley, Oswald Mosley and Robert Forgan – were to go into Fascism. The remaining eight, who all remained within the Labour Party, were J. Batey, Aneurin Bevan, W. G. Cove, J. F. Horrabin, J. J. McShane, H. T. Muggeridge, Phillips Price and James Simmons. The miners' leader A. J. Cook, not a Member of Parliament, also added his name. In a Press statement the signatories declared: 'We surrender nothing of our Socialism.'

The main difference between the *Memorandum* and the *Manifesto* was that the latter went into more detail on the machinery of the Government. The *Manifesto* called for a Cabinet of five non-departmental ministers – 'the five dictators', the newspapers called them – with sweeping powers to legislate by Order, subject to the veto of the House of Commons. This would by-pass the muddles of the 1929 Parliament where, because the Government had no majority and no power to enforce the closure, its Bills were piling into a log jam. (After the fall of the Government the Labour Party itself was to adopt somewhat similar proposals for defeating Parliamentary obstruction.)

The *Manifesto*, published in the Sunday newspapers of 6th

December 1930, had a good reception. Garvin in the *Observer* wrote that anybody who rejected the Mosley thesis had a duty to produce an alternative. L. S. Amery, in a speech denouncing the 'three old gangs', declared that he had read it with 'interest and sympathy'. Moore-Brabazon wrote: 'Along the lines of the *Mosley Memorandum* lies the escape for the moment from make-believe into reality.' Walter Elliot wrote to *The Times* to praise it. Opponents tended to ignore rather than to attack it.

From outside politics came a statement on 18th December by Sir William Morris (later Lord Nuffield), chairman of the National Council of Industry and Commerce, in which he called Mosley 'a courageous young man'. Morris said his mind was 'harassed day and night by the plight into which this England of ours is rapidly falling'. There was 'one bright spot – the forceful gesture of a young and virile section of the Labour Party . . . providing concrete evidence of the possibility of the foundation of a vigorous Industrial Party'.

'Show me,' said Morris, 'a successful business, anywhere in the world, that is operating on the principles utilized a century ago. You cannot. Then what hope is there of a Parliamentary system that has remained unchanged so long?'

Mosley himself was calling for a 'new psychology' and repeatedly declared that Parliamentary democracy was 'on trial' – a phrase he meant more literally than most of those who use it. To a luncheon of printing-machinery manufacturers he said the proper relationship of Government to Parliament was that of company directors to shareholders – the shareholders should decide broad policy then give the directors complete freedom to carry it out, not harassing them with day-by-day questioning and obstruction. We could not go on 'shouting the meaningless slogans of a century-old contraption which has no more in common with the modern age than crinolines and whiskers'.

If at this stage Mosley had paused to allow opinion to consolidate, and had insisted less on his personal mission, he might still have kept within the orthodox political framework. But despite the protests of most of the Parliamentary Mosley Group he pressed ahead with organizing and raising funds for his new political party. By January 1930 he had rented an office at 1 Great George Street, Westminster. The same month the proposals of the *Memorandum* and *Manifesto* appeared in a sixty-one-page pamphlet entitled *A National Policy*, published by Macmillan's with Bevan, Brown, Strachey and Young given as the authors. The pamphlet was an appeal to Conservatives and Socialists to work together to meet the national crisis, leaving the question of whether industry should ultimately be publicly or privately owned on one side. Parliament should be re-formed to give the Government power to act swiftly and with precision, 'the only way the reality of democracy can be saved'. There should be 'a programme of disciplined national effort' under Government direction to take the unemployed off the dole and direct them to useful work. The aim should be to produce a planned, high-wage economy insulated from the world depression.

Unemployment continued to soar dizzily upwards. The Government was taking no action at all. The chief preoccupation of the Cabinet was the rising cost of unemployment benefit, which was endangering the stability of Snowden's beloved Gold Standard. Beatrice Webb, whose husband was in the Cabinet, noted in her diary on 24th February: 'It is an absurdity that the Labour Party, as at present constituted, should be in power. The Labour Movement had better be referred to its studies. In home affairs it has no policy – it has completely lost its bearings.' In March she recorded a shrewd criticism of Mosley's proposals:

> The *Mosley Manifesto* is an able document – its argument in favour of a general plan, and there is much reason for it, is well done. But its proposals are as grandiose as they are vague. From the standpoint of propaganda it is a failure; it falls dead in the No Man's Land between those who wish to keep and those who wish to change the existing order. . . .

She compared Mosley with Hitler, not yet in power, and observed that the British electorate would not stand a Hitler. 'Mosley has bad health, a slight intelligence and an unstable character – I doubt whether he has the tenacity of a Hitler. He also lacks a genuine fanaticism. Deep down in his heart he is a cynic. He will be beaten and retire.'

Beatrice Webb's reference to Hitler was apposite. Few even of Mosley's closest associates realized how seriously he was taking the concept of a 'modern movement' in Britain, running parallel with the 'modern movements' in Germany and Italy. He received the sympathy shown from many quarters with undue optimism, and tended to regard it as the pre-natal stirrings of a British 'modern movement'. He was aggrieved and disappointed when, in March 1930, the New Party formally came into existence but with only a handful of members. Of the seventeen signatories of the *Mosley Manifesto* only six joined the New Party – the two Mosleys, Oliver Baldwin, Brown, Forgan and Strachey. Baldwin and Brown remained members for only one day, resigning when they read a statement by Mosley to the *Observer* in which he likened the New Party to the Continental modern movements. Oliver Baldwin sat in Parliament for a while as an Independent but returned to the Labour Party in time for the general election six months later. Brown became a permanent Independent, convinced that the old parties had outlived their usefulness but not convinced that Mosley's version of the modern movement was the right answer. From the Conservatives the New Party recruited W. E. D. Allen, who crossed the floor of the Commons to sit with his new colleagues on the Labour back benches below the gangway.

Allen Young took charge of the New Party organization, working from the Great George Street office. In the Commons Robert Forgan became the New Party whip. Son of a Church of Scotland minister in Aberdeen, Forgan was a medical man who had become a Socialist as a result of his experiences in the public health services of Glasgow and Lanarkshire. He had a sincere, somewhat naïve enthusiasm for slum-clearance, better nutrition and preventive medicine generally. His allegiance had been to the Clydeside ILP-ers and he had joined quietly in their rebellions against the Government, being regarded as a sincere, hard-working but inexperienced politician. Soon after his arrival at Westminster in 1929 he decided that the stagnant Thames air, piped through the ventilating system, caused an enervating atmosphere in Parliament. He attracted a little publicity by urging Lansbury, First Commissioner of Works, to install air-purifying equipment which would make MPs attend to their duties with more vigour. Later he appeared to decide that something more fundamental was wrong with Parliament and that a more authoritarian system of government was necessary to secure the health and housing reforms he wanted.

From the start, misfortune dogged the New Party's footsteps. The early confusions about who was and who was not a member were followed immediately by Mosley catching influenza which turned first to pneumonia and then to pleurisy, putting him out of action for the first six weeks. The work of launching the Party fell on Forgan, Cynthia Mosley and Strachey, who travelled the country to carry out a speaking programme which had been planned for double their number. The Labour National Executive immediately expelled them all – a redundant step since all had resigned – and declared the New Party a proscribed organization. Henderson, the Party Secretary, regretted the loss of Mosley, to whom in biblical terms he was wont to refer as 'the rich young man', but he would not tolerate any attempt to split the Labour Movement. Under Henderson's guidance Transport House prepared plans to crush the New Party at birth. Everywhere the New Party speakers met violent opposition, being treated as upper-class traitors to the workers' movement. Cynthia Mosley wept on the platform when her consti-tuents booed her at Stoke. At Dundee an angry audience drowned Strachey's voice by singing 'The Red Flag'. The Labour Movement was now in a rough, angry mood; attacking the New Party not only for its actions but also as a target against which to work off the frustration engendered by the shortcomings of the MacDonald Government.

Mosley, convalescing at Monaco, was at first remote from the fight. Brooding on his own, he decided to hit back at the Labour Party in the place where it would hurt most. Through the death of the sitting Labour member, a by-election occurred in the marginal seat of Ashton-under-Lyme, held by Labour in 1929 by a majority of only 3,407. Mosley decided to fight the election even at the risk of splitting the left-wing vote and handing the seat to the Conservatives. The Manchester committee of the New Party resigned in protest, but Mosley, insisting that the modern movement would appeal to right as well as left, pressed ahead and chose Young as the New Party candidate. With Risdon, late of the Birmingham ILP, as agent, Mosley and Strachey moved into Ashton to conduct a vigorous campaign. Conservatives and Labour retaliated by con-centrating their Lancashire resources on Ashton.

The outcome was a Conservative win with a majority of 1,415. Young polled 4,472, just saving his deposit. During the count a crowd of angry Labour supporters filled the market square outside the town hall. When they heard the voting figures their mood turned ugly and they roared with rage. The police warned the little group of New Party leaders that they were in danger of physical assault and offered to smuggle them quietly away through the town hall back door. According to Strachey,* Mosley looked down from the town hall steps at the sea of angry faces and remarked: 'That is the crowd that has prevented anyone doing anything in England since the war.' In that moment, Strachey believed, Mosley finally became a Fascist.

* *The Menace of Fascism* by John Strachey (1933).

Risdon's recollection (1961) is that Mosley said: 'We saw worse than this in the war, Bill.' At any rate, Mosley refused the offered police protection, and with shoulders squared and chin held high led his followers through the crowd to their cars.

In June the New Party MPs crossed the floor of the Commons as a protest against a Government Bill to reduce the cost of unemployment benefit by abolishing 'anomalies', the last time they worked in association with the ILP Group. Forgan negotiated for a place on the Conservative benches, displacing Brendan Bracken from his accustomed seat. For Allen it was the second time he had crossed the floor in three months.

Three weeks later Strachey and Young resigned from the New Party. The occasion for the break was Mosley's refusal to accept a policy drafted by Strachey in favour of trade with Russia. It was, in fact, the culmination of a series of disputes which had split the New Party Council ever since Mosley returned from Monaco. Strachey and Young were Mosley's oldest political friends and, possibly because of this, had been slow to understand the direction in which his mind was moving. They saw the New Party as a kind of Keynsian ginger group – 'a Utopian appeal for social compromise' as Strachey put it.* For the much more fundamental programme Mosley was planning they had little taste. Strachey rebounded to the extreme left, worked closely with the Communists for six years, and with his book *The Coming Struggle for Power* became the leading Marxist popularizer for the generation of the Left Book Club. Young became political secretary to Harold Macmillan and later a Board of Trade civil servant.

Young's successors at the head of the New Party organization were F. M. Box, a former Conservative Party agent, and Leslie Cumings, an electrical worker who had been prominent in the London ILP.

One of the principal causes of the split was a proposal by Mosley to create a New Party youth movement, in which Strachey and Young detected a Fascist potential. The aim, apparently, was to create a network of youth clubs which would combine physical with political training and make the New Party distinctive in its methods. There was a fund for the clubs to which, among others, William Morris, the motor manufacturer, contributed generously enough to affect the New Party's whole financial standing.† The nation-wide

* *The Menace of Fascism* by John Strachey (1933).
† In a personal communication to the author (1961), Viscount Nuffield said the extent of his financial support to Mosley was a gift of a substantial sum for the clubs.

network of clubs was never developed but the New Party did run an active club in King's Road, Chelsea, which included boxing, fencing and physical training in its activities, together with political debates and discussions. There were also a few clubs in the provinces, notably at Stoke and Birmingham. Another cause for disagreement was Mosley's decision to organize what he called 'a body of young men to give physical support to our programme'. They were based partly on the youth clubs, where they were members and instructors. Their function was primarily to keep order at meetings and to enable New Party speakers to win a hearing, but they were also to be available to protect law and order in the event of a Communist uprising – a possibility much in Mosley's mind as the economic crisis deepened towards the disasters of the autumn of 1931. 'We shall use no sticks, no knives and no bombs,' Mosley told the *Daily Express*, 'we shall rely on the good old English fist.' Strachey and Young saw this force as Mosley's equivalent of the Nazi storm-troopers. The Press nicknamed them the 'biff boys' and it was as the 'biff boys' that they first went into action in the summer of 1931, trained by the Jewish boxing champion 'Kid' Lewis, a man of lively social conscience and simple outlook who had volunteered to act as Mosley's personal bodyguard.

The 'biff boys' were about a hundred strong and were predominantly of the 'hearty' undergraduate type. They had plenty of work, the Ashton episode having deepened the Labour Party's fury against the New Party. The Communists, eager to hasten the arrival of a revolutionary situation, also joined the fight. At Glasgow a crowd of 3,000 tried to rush St. Andrew's Hall where Mosley was to speak. 'Biff boys' and police fought to eject them, but enough remained in the hall to render Mosley inaudible, somebody having cut the wires of his microphone. Escorted by Lewis and the 'biff boys' Mosley left the hall and, with courage that won respect, addressed the crowd in the street.

An even bigger battle was fought in Birmingham Rag Market, where a meeting of 15,000 developed into a free fight, Mosley descending from the platform to help his stewards. Chairs were smashed and combatants were carried from the hall streaming with blood. His opponents took out a summons against Mosley, alleging assault, but the magistrate dismissed the case without hearing evidence for the defence. At Manchester, in contrast, the 'biff boys' had a quiet time. A meeting at the Free Trade Hall heard Mosley with close attention and, at the end, gave him a standing ovation. 'His ideas,' reported the *Manchester Guardian*, 'swept a great audience off its feet and the scene at the end was a matter for thought to any "elder statesman".'

But in addition to the 'biff boys' the New Party had its intellectuals. Harold Nicolson who had just left the diplomatic service and was an old friend of the Mosleys came in to edit *Action*, the Party's weekly paper. C. E. M. Joad hurried in and hurried out again when he detected 'the cloven hoof of Fascism'. Osbert Sitwell spoke on its platform. *Action* had thirty-two pages for twopence and Nicolson made it a political and literary review intended at once to appeal to the general reader and to give editorial support for the New Party. His model was *John o' London's Weekly* and there was a distinguished set of contributors, including E. Arnot Robertson, Cecil Melville, Raymond Mortimer, Peter Quennell, Eric Partridge and L. A. G. Strong. In an editorial Nicolson said *Action* would be 'contemplative, ruminative, mild'. Mosley would have preferred something more in the nature of a fighting propaganda sheet, but made no attempt to interfere. *Action* was a paper of contradictions, Mosley's polemics running in an adjoining column to Victoria Sackville-West's gardening notes.

> We must create [wrote Mosley in the first issue] a movement which aims not merely at the capture of political power; we must create a movement which grips and transforms every phase and aspect of national life to post-war purposes; a movement of order, of discipline, of loyalty but also of dynamic progress; a movement of iron decision, resolution and reality; a movement which cuts like a sword through the knot of the past to the winning of the modern State.

The orthodox politicians, meanwhile, were busy withdrawing purchasing power from an already anaemic economy. The extraordinary May Committee reported by a majority in favour of a £120,000,000 reduction in Government expenditure, including a twenty per cent cut in unemployment benefit. On the industrial front the National Confederation of Employers pressed ahead with a campaign for further reductions in wages.

It would be difficult to dissent from the view that the whole course of events since 1931 has proved that Mosley and the New Party were, in essentials, right; and that the established political, financial and industrial interests were following a mistaken policy. There was, however, an element of tragedy in the self-confident way Mosley broke free to form an independent movement over which he could have complete control. Mosley was not the only man who was right. Although slow to say so publicly, for fear of splitting the Labour Movement, the Trade Union Congress under the intelligent leadership of Citrine and Bevin was strongly opposed to Snowden's deflationary policy. Bevin, the most powerful member of the TUC General Council, agreed with the *Mosley Memorandum* although he distrusted Mosley's personality.* Had he been more at home in the inner life of the Labour Movement, Mosley, after his resignation, might have drifted towards an understanding with the TUC instead of engaging in his unrewarding work of seeking support from miscellaneous elements outside the Labour Party. If Mosley was precipitate, the TUC was, possibly, too slow, delaying its showdown with the Government until August 1931, when it was too late. A combination of Mosley's energy with the TUC's authority might have changed the course of history, at least to the extent of giving the Conservative Party the duty of carrying through an essentially Conservative policy. The notion of such a combination seems to have occurred to neither side.

Through August 1930 the Cabinet bickered over cuts in expenditure. Snowden insisted that the only way the confidence of foreign bankers could be retained was by following the May Committee's recommendation to cut unemployment benefit. Eight – or possibly nine – Cabinet ministers stuck in their heels firmly on the principle that the crisis should not be solved at the expense of the unemployed; the Government reached deadlock and resolved to resign. To the surprise of the Labour Party, MacDonald returned from Buckingham Palace to form a 'National' Government in alliance with the Conservatives and Liberals.

The new Government carried out the May Committee's cuts – with no discernible influence on the confidence of foreign bankers. Unemployment continued to rise sharply and in October 1931 MacDonald, breaking a previous pledge to the contrary, dissolved Parliament and appealed to the country for a 'doctor's mandate'. The election took place in a fervour of patriotism and the voters, seeing the leaders they knew concentrated in only one place, returned the Government to power with a Commons majority of 498.

Mosley saw it as a patriotic duty to give qualified support to the

* *The Life and Times of Ernest Bevin, Volume One* by Alan Bullock (1960).

National Government's immediate programme. On his instructions, Forgan secured an interview with Neville Chamberlain, Conservative Party Chairman, to see whether New Party candidates could be allocated a few Labour-held constituencies in which they could fight without National competition. Chamberlain curtly refused.

Just before the dissolution, Mosley made his last Parliamentary speech:

'It seems to me,' he said, 'that Britain in her crisis is being asked to turn her face to the wall and to give up like an old woman who knows that she has to die. I want to see this country at least make an effort. I do not believe, and never have believed, in the cure of fasting but in the cure of effort. I believe that the way out is not the way of the monk but the way of the athlete. . . . I venture to suggest that the simple question before the House in this debate is whether Great Britain is to meet its crisis lying down or standing up.'

The timing of the general election was, for the New Party, the final stroke of misfortune. Mosley had expected at least two years in which to build up an organization for an electoral contest. Even without the wave of patriotic fervour which rallied to support the National Government, the New Party would have been doomed to defeat. Before polling day Nicolson warned *Action* readers to expect no dramatic New Party successes. 'Our day will come in 1933,' he explained. But the results were far, far worse than the New Party's worst fears. There were twenty-four candidates, nearly all in Labour-held seats. Of these all but two lost their deposits, all but four polled under 1,000 votes. Even the Communists did better.

Cynthia Mosley was expecting a baby and Mosley moved to her constituency at Stoke, polling 10,534 votes and coming bottom of the poll. Forgan was ejected from West Renfrew with a vote of only 1,304 – he had polled over 14,000 there as Labour candidate in 1929. Major Randolph Dudgeon, Liberal MP for Galloway, joined the New Party at the last moment and polled only 986 in the constituency he had represented through three Parliaments. Sir John Pratt, a former Liberal minister of Coalition vintage, polled 1,565 as New Party candidate at Hulme, Manchester. Nicolson had 461 votes from the Combined English Universities, but even this was better than the lowest vote of all: 'Kid' Lewis's 154 in his native Whitechapel. W. E. D. Allen did not stand.

Obviously the New Party was not to be the vehicle for the British 'modern movement', and Mosley decided that he would have to look more closely at the experience of the Continental leaders.

Nicolson wrote in *Action*: 'We consider that the petty bullying and intimidation of the Fascist regime is as unintelligent as it is inhumane'; but Mosley, a couple of issues later, was remarking: 'In every country the founders of the Modern Movement have had far worse experiences than any we have yet endured.' The crime-novelist Peter Cheyney wrote a series of *Action* articles calling for a 'Nupa-Shock Movement', a disciplined force to be directly responsible to the Leader at National Headquarters. By the end of the year Mosley had finally come down in favour of a corporate state – 'a society working with the precision and harmony of a human body. Every interest and every individual is subordinate to the overriding purpose of the nation.' In his *Action* article a week later he was explaining that 'personal liberty is not expressed in the right to vote for one or two dummies once in four years'. He called for disorder in India to be 'sternly repressed' and said that the Indian people should have vigorous government with rising standards of living instead of 'the illusion of political freedom'.

The final issue of *Action*, published on 31st December 1931, announced that Mosley and Nicolson were to visit Italy and Germany to study the modern movement. 'We go to collect information from all sources, to compile and to collate information so that if and when the time of this country comes to pass through great events, a few of us may be prepared.' Nicolson, in his last article, said that *Action* had a sale of between 15,000 and 20,000 and had been losing £340 a week. Soon afterwards he published a futuristic novel in which he envisaged a 'Churchill-Mosley' coalition government in power by 1936.*

Mosley was in heroic mood. He had just rejected a tentative overture from MacDonald to become a supporter of the National Government, and in the last issue of *Action* he wrote:

> Better the great adventure, better the great attempt for England's sake, better defeat, disaster, better by far the end of that trivial thing called a political career than stifling in the uniform of blue and gold, strutting and posturing on the stage of Little England, amid the scenery of decadence. . . .
> We shall win; or at least we shall return upon our shields.

In retrospect it is clear that, by cutting himself adrift from the main political parties, Mosley forfeited a brilliant political future.

* *Public Faces* by Harold Nicolson (1932).

He could certainly have become a Cabinet minister and, possibly, he could have risen to be Prime Minister. The careers of Churchill, Cripps and Macmillan have shown during the past generation that a man may quarrel with his party and yet rise to a high place within it.

The game of historical 'ifs' is a fascinating one and Mosley provides a superb subject.

Suppose, first, that he had remained within the Labour Party.

The 1931 election might have cost him his seat at Smethwick, but he would have found little difficulty in returning to Parliament at an early by-election. During the period 1931–35 the Labour Party was lacking experienced leadership in the Commons. The three predominant figures were George Lansbury, Clement Attlee and Stafford Cripps; of whom Lansbury was elderly and in poor health, Attlee was unknown and Cripps was a Parliamentary novice. Mosley could have established himself as the leading figure on the Opposition front bench and the Party might well have preferred him to Attlee as Deputy Leader. In 1935, after Lansbury's resignation, Mosley might have become Leader instead of Attlee. He would have achieved high office in the wartime coalition when his gifts of leadership and oratory would have made him predominant among Churchill's henchmen. In 1945 he would have become Prime Minister and, with verve, leadership and imagination, would have presided over the post-war social revolution. It is arguable whether or not a leader of his type would have been successful in holding the Labour Party together from 1950 onwards. He is now (1961) aged only sixty-five. His Parliamentary experience would stretch back longer than that of any other active politician and, either in office or opposition, his status would be comparable only to that once held by W. E. Gladstone and Churchill at the peaks of their careers. If he had not become Leader in 1935 he would have had a second opportunity on Attlee's resignation in 1955, when he was aged fifty-nine.

Alternatively, he might have chosen to throw in his lot with Ramsay MacDonald in the National Government in 1931. By degrees he would have moved back into the Conservative Party and become a candidate for the leadership. The critical point might have been the resignation of Anthony Eden in January 1957, when Mosley was sixty.

Where Mosley differed from most other political rebels is that he attached permanent importance to what should have been a temporary quarrel. Some observers, for example Hannen Swaffer, say this was because as a rich man he was accustomed to getting what he wanted. A poorer man would have accepted temporary defeat within the Labour Party and remained within the Party to fight another day. A deeper explanation is the extraordinary sense of personal destiny which has haunted Mosley's political career. He seems seriously to have believed that he had been born to be the saviour of the nation and appears to have had difficulty in accepting that his opponents could have been acting in good faith. In cutting adrift from the main political parties he was aiming for something much more than an ordinary Prime Ministership. He believed that his destiny was to change history, that he was another Cromwell, Napoleon – or Adolf Hitler.

CHAPTER 4

'For King and Country'

NICOLSON accompanied Mosley on his tour of the modern movements in the belief that first-hand observation would cure Mosley of his pro-Fascist tendencies. The cure started when their train reached Milan, by Nicolson purchasing on the station platform a copy of a State-controlled newspaper devoted almost entirely to the doings of Mussolini. He handed it to Mosley as an example of what newspapers were like under a Fascist regime. To Nicolson's surprise, Mosley grinned with delight, slapped his leg and joked: 'I'd like to make Max [Beaverbrook] produce a paper like that.' In Rome Mosley arranged an interview with Mussolini. Nicolson did not go and waited in the hotel. Mosley returned ablaze with enthusiasm and said that Mussolini had invited them both to stand with him on the saluting base during a Fascist parade. Nicolson flatly refused to appear in public with the murderer of Matteotti, quarrelled with Mosley, packed his bags and left Rome and the New Party.*

Mosley, without Nicolson, travelled on to Munich where he studied the Nazi organization and met Nazi leaders, but not Hitler. At this stage Mussolini was the decisive influence. At their first meeting the two men had acquired a mutual and lasting regard for each other. Mussolini at this time – possibly through Mosley's influence – was wondering whether the pragmatic measures he had taken in Italy could be turned into a coherent political doctrine of

* Verbal account by Sir Harold Nicolson to the author in December 1960.

universal validity. Later the same year Mussolini declared 'the twentieth century will be the century of Fascism' – a reversal of his earlier line that Fascism was suitable only for Italy. He certainly seems to have inspired Mosley with the idea that what could be achieved in Italy could also be achieved in Britain. Mosley's remaining doubts vanished.

Soon after his return to London, Mosley described the Fascism he had seen in an enthusiastic article in Lady Houston's *Saturday Review*:

> It is [he said] as remote from stand-pat Conservatism as it is from the woolly-headed Socialism or the destructive Communism which it overthrew. It brings to post-war politics a new creed and a new philosophy which cannot be tucked away in any of the old pigeon-holes of thought.... This Fascism challenges alike the 'Right' and the 'Left' of old world politics. It has produced not only a new system of government, but also a new type of man, who differs from politicians of the old world as men from another planet.

Straightaway Mosley contacted the existing Fascist organizations in Britain, which were indeed as different from his previous Socialist connections as if they were on another planet. It is necessary here to break the chronological account of Mosley's career and go back to the political underworld of the early 1920's in which British Fascism first developed.

The oldest and biggest organization was the British Fascists, organized conventionally enough as a limited company and, by 1932, practically moribund. The leader and founder was a Field Marshal's grand-daughter, Miss Rotha Lintorn-Orman, a forthright spinster of thirty-seven with a taste for mannish clothes. At private Fascist rallies, it was rumoured, she wore a sword.

The story ran that the idea of Fascism came to Miss Lintorn-Orman one day in 1923 while she was weeding the kitchen garden of her dairy farm at Langford, Somerset. She was gravely alarmed at the rise of Socialism and Communism and decided to insert a series of six advertisements in the Duke of Northumberland's paper *The Patriot*. The advertisements asked for recruits for a 'British Fascisti' to act as an organized force to combat Red Revolution.

It was psychologically a good moment. The arrival of the Labour

Party in office in January 1924 seemed in thousands of secluded middle- and upper-class homes the prelude to a Red Terror in which property would cease to exist and no woman's virtue would be safe. Sophisticated Conservatives at Westminster who, like Stanley Baldwin, believed it was desirable for Labour leaders to gain experience in office, were slow to convince their more elderly supporters in the country that there were important differences between Ramsay MacDonald and Lenin. The British Fascisti became a rallying point for the sections of society which had never adjusted themselves to the death of Queen Victoria. Within weeks of her advertisements Miss Lintorn-Orman had enough support to take offices in London. In the early part of 1924 recruits were pouring in at a rate of 'hundreds a week'.

There was no uniform, but Miss Lintorn-Orman bade her members carry black handkerchiefs and wear a badge on which the words 'For King and Country' encircled the inch-deep initials 'B.F.'. Under later military influence the badge was changed to a simple 'F'. There was also a salute.

'The Fascisti salute,' wrote Miss Lintorn-Orman in her *Bulletin*, 'is made by bringing the right hand across the chest and touching the badge. Fascisti will stand at the salute during the playing of the National Anthem. All members will salute each other on meeting.'

There was no attempt at a Fascist policy. Indeed it would have been difficult to formulate one. Mussolini came to office in 1921 virtually without a programme. He built Fascist Italy on the basis of his experience in power; not until the end of the decade was it possible reliably to adduce Fascist principles. Mussolini's own attitude was that 'Fascism is not for export' and he was at first surprised when he found movements in other countries looking to him for inspiration.

The British Fascisti stood simply on the basis of defending King and Parliament against the forces of Communism, Socialism, Anarchism, free love, atheism and trade unions, which the members tended to lump into a mysterious single entity. They were not particularly anti-Semitic, although they had dark suspicions that 'aliens' were at the root of the Red disorder. So far were they from having a policy that they constantly proclaimed themselves 'non-political'. In practice this meant that they supported the Conservative Party. Proudly they quoted letters of thanks from Conservative MPs for the services of British Fascisti stewards at public meetings – including one from the Jewish Conservative Sir Philip Sassoon. One

Conservative MP, Colonel Sir Charles Burn, became a member of their Grand Council.

Under the Grand Council was a hierarchy of units, troops and companies under quasi-military leadership. As membership swelled the aim was to give every locality a British Fascisti unit. By August 1924 the Movement was claiming 100,000 members, organized to maintain essential services during strikes and to aid the civil power in the event of revolution. There was special stress on the organization of 'flying squads' of cars, motor-cycles and pedal-cycles. Miss Lintorn-Orman had been an ambulance driver in Serbia during the war; women Fascisti complained that she made them learn to change tyres.

Stewarding Conservative meetings brought some excitement. There was a special citation for one William Joyce who was 'attacked in a most dastardly manner while acting as a steward on the night of 22nd October (1924) at the meeting of the North Lambeth Conservative candidate at Lambeth Baths'. Joyce, then a student at Birkbeck College, was slashed across the right cheek with a razor. He bore the scar until as 'Lord Haw-Haw' he died on the gallows of Wandsworth Prison on a dark January morning twenty-two years later. It appears that Joyce found the British Fascisti unsatisfactory; at any rate he left soon afterwards and became an active Conservative.

Meanwhile Miss Lintorn-Orman had been dropping into the background. In most parts of the country landed proprietors, minor industrialists, retired officers and a sprinkling of Anglican clergy were taking over the leadership. In London the presidency passed to Brigadier-General R. G. D. Blakeney, late Royal Engineers, who until 1922 had managed the Egyptian State Railways. Blakeney, a vigorous, well-connected man aged fifty-one, determined to build a disciplined organization of the highest respectability, dedicated to the maintenance of law and order. He was greatly angered when Sir Henry Slessor, the Labour Solicitor General, referred to the British Fascisti as 'this dangerous and seditious organization'.

Blakeney organized the Movement into a private company, limited by guarantee with a capital of 100 £1 shares. At the same time he anglicized the name to the British Fascists. There followed a controversy in *British Lion*, the Movement's paper, about the correct pronunciation of 'Fascist'; some favouring 'fassist', others 'fashist'. This was a perennial problem in Fascist circles right through to Mosley's day. The tendency was for the inner circles of Fascist

leaders to use 'fassist', which became, so to speak, the 'U' pronunciation. Opponents preferred 'fashist', possibly because it has a harsher
and more foreign-sounding note.

A fair idea of the nature of the British Fascists in 1924 can be
given by citing some of their officials, selected at random. In London
Major-General T. D. Pilcher was lecturing the members on 'the
correct tactics for handling a Communist mob'. General Carruthers
was Company Officer at Camberley. Blakeney's deputy was Rear-
Admiral A. E. Armstrong. The Rev. J. L. Kempthorne was in
command at Falmouth. Bournemouth had a particularly strong
branch with Sir Michael Bruce in command and General Geoghegan
and General Tyndell-Biscoe as area commanders. The O.C. London
was General Sir Ormonde Winter, who tried to get the members
enrolled *en bloc* in the Special Constabulary. Captain the Earl of
Glasgow ran the Scottish area. Admiral Tupper commanded at Liss.
Colonel Dan Burges, v.c., Governor of the Tower of London, who
was criticized for wearing the Fascist badge, replied: 'British Fascism
has nothing to do with politics at all.' All over Britain retired war-
horses were scenting battle and emerging from retirement, just
as they did sixteen years later on the formation of the Home
Guard.

The constructive ideas of the Movement were elementary. An
article in *The British Fascist Bulletin* dealing with unemployment,
then running at about a million, came ponderously to the conclusion
that income tax should be lower, thus enabling gentlefolk to reduce
unemployment by engaging more servants. There was strong
support for private enterprise. If capitalism were abolished, *The
Bulletin* explained, there would be no capital and industry would
die.

Blakeney himself developed a more distinctively Fascist approach.
'A gang of internationalists seek to control the world,' he said in a
speech at Portsmouth in 1925. Communism was run by 'international
Jews'. Admiral Armstrong, his deputy, went to Italy to study
Fascism. In 1926 the British Fascists sent a deputation to Mussolini
to congratulate him on his escape from an attempted assassination.
The Movement's Propaganda Officer, E. G. Mandeville Roe, a
twenty-three-year-old schoolmaster in South London, wrote a book
describing Mussolini's system and advocating the principle of strong
political leadership.

The British Fascists were highly fissile. Extremist little groups,
dissatisfied with the Movement's staid activities, were continually

breaking away to set up on their own. There were the British Empire Fascists, the Fascist League and the Fascist Movement, pocket parties enjoying brief lives under pocket Mussolinis.

A more serious split came in October 1925 when a dissident group set up as the National Fascisti and adopted a black-shirt uniform. The advent of the National Fascisti lost the British Fascists about a hundred of their most active members. *The Bulletin* was worried but eventually decided that the universal troublemakers, the Communists, were to blame.

'Fascists take care!' it proclaimed. 'Remember your oath! This agitation is being so carefully propagated that there is a very real danger in the near future. Rally round General Blakeney! Do not betray *him* who gives his whole life to the Movement. *He* will not let you down. No discussion, only obedience!'

The National Fascisti themselves split after a few weeks' existence, their most active members re-forming themselves as the British National Fascists under the slogan 'Hats off to the past, coats off to the future!' The British National Fascists ran for three or four years as a mixture of Ku-Klux-Klan and undergraduate rag, breaking up Labour Party meetings, defacing left-wing posters, kidnapping *Daily Herald* vans and making threatening telephone calls to Labour leaders. They broke into a meeting addressed by Mosley at Cambridge in 1927. Even smaller groups included the United Empire Fascists under the leadership of Serocold Skeels, the British Empire Fascists and the Fascist League.

For the main British Fascists the big event was the 1926 General Strike. One member wrote to *The Bulletin* suggesting that members of the TUC General Council should be shot out of hand. Others prepared to help the Government in the maintenance of essential services. Members had already succeeded in keeping the Cambridge gasworks in operation during a strike arising from a demand for a closed shop, and were ready for bigger game.

The Government, too, with its Organization for the Maintenance of Supplies, was preparing for the General Strike. The British Fascist Grand Council, claiming an absurdly inflated membership figure of one million, approached the Home Secretary, William Joynson-Hicks, with an offer to help. The answer was disappointing. Joynson-Hicks, his Permanent Under-Secretary John Anderson at his elbow, said he would accept the Movement's help only if it dropped the name 'Fascist' and abandoned its paramilitary organization. Blakeney and Armstrong favoured acceptance, were defeated in the Grand Council by Miss Lintorn-Orman, and quit the Movement. Thereafter Miss Lintorn-Orman reassumed active command.

The British Fascists did, in fact, help during the General Strike, although rarely in organized units. They even acquired a martyr, Kenneth Reavell. While acting as a locomotive fireman, Fascist Reavell put his head too far out of the cab, struck a bridge and died.

After Blakeney's departure the British Fascists rapidly declined. Most of the colonels and admirals resigned and the remnants of the Movement assumed an urban, back-street character, their main activity being to try to break up Communist street-corner meetings. Their last big public appearance was when they provided 600 stewards for a Conservative patriotic rally at the Albert Hall addressed by Sir Henry Page-Croft, MP, in the autumn of 1926. The Fascist stewards paraded through the hall carrying their silver and black flag with the fasces emblem, to the strains of 'Land of Hope and Glory'.

Miss Lintorn-Orman vainly threatened in her new paper, *British Lion*, that the Conservatives would go to the wall if they did not stand by their principles. 'Fascism will replace milk-and-water Conservatism,' she proclaimed. There were demands for the 'purification of the British race' and for special taxes on aliens. In the Lewisham 'Parliament' Mandeville Roe led a Fascist opposition. To try to revive her members' enthusiasm Miss Lintorn-Orman created a Fascist Order of Merit, with silver and bronze fasces badges for diligent service. She put her men into black shirts and her women into black blazers. Her only success was with the women, who patrolled the London streets in uniform on a mixed mission of rescuing prostitutes and heckling Communists. The women also held mock political meetings which ended in rough-houses as they practised their technique for ejecting hecklers.

The final blow came with the formation of Mosley's British Union of Fascists in the autumn of 1932. Almost the entire active membership melted away, although Miss Lintorn-Orman continued her activities until her death in March 1935. The limited company was wound up shortly after the founder's death with assets of £20 and debts of £1,706. Figures published during the winding-up proceedings show that the subscription income had been £6,848 in 1925, £604 in 1928 and thereafter less than £400 a year. Copyright of *British Lion* passed to the Unity Band, an eccentric, semi-Fascist group which had the proclaimed intention of restoring all things to the state they were in before the 1914–18 war.

A second mainstream of Fascism owed its inspiration to Arnold

Spencer Leese, a retired veterinary surgeon. Although Leese's movement never obtained a membership of more than 200, it had a coherent doctrine and both obstinacy and courage in spreading its views. In racialism Leese came nearer to the German National Socialists than any other British political leader.

Born in 1877, nephew of a baronet, Leese showed no interest in politics until he was nearly fifty. He worked for twenty years as a vet in India and Africa, becoming a specialist in the diseases of camels. He wrote a standard textbook on camels, of which he sent a copy to King George V. The 1914–18 war brought him back to Europe and, after service in France with the Royal Army Veterinary Corps, he settled in private practice at Stamford. He was a non-smoker and teetotaller and had individualistic ideas on diet. He was fond of producing medical and pseudo-medical arguments to justify his tastes. He loved animals and it is possible that his violent anti-Semitism resulted from his distaste for the Kosher method of slaughtering animals. At any rate he always devoted great energy to attacking Jewish butchers. He disliked Christianity, which he believed was part of a Jewish plot to undermine the virility of the Nordic races. In his personal life he appears to have been a straightforward man, honest in his dealings and unafraid of the consequences of his actions. He stood over six feet tall, was powerfully built and sported a blond, Hitler-shape moustache. As a public speaker he was indifferent; he liked best a lecture-room atmosphere in which he could discourse quietly on his principles.

Leese joined the British Fascists in 1924 and organized the Stamford branch, which he ran on individualistic lines. Before long he parted company with the leaders in London and ran the Stamford Fascists as an independent group. They were, Leese later claimed, the first in Britain to wear the black shirt. They advocated a system by which people would have to pay to vote in Parliamentary elections; this, Leese argued, would incline the electors to use their votes with greater care. Above all, the Stamford Fascists broke a cardinal rule of the British Fascists by actually intervening in an election. In 1924, when two Labour candidates looked like being returned unopposed in a Stamford municipal election, Leese and a fellow Fascist, Henry Simpson, successfully stood against them. Simpson was re-elected in 1927, this time against both Conservative and Labour opposition. These appear to be the only occasions on which candidates labelled as Fascists ever won contested British elections.

Stamford was a poor base from which to run a national revolution.

In 1927 Leese sold his practice and transferred his activities to London, purchasing a home at The White House, Pewley Hill, Guildford. He was not rich but husbanded his resources with sufficient care to be able to devote his whole time to politics for the rest of his life. By 1929 Leese had attracted enough supporters—about a dozen—to form a new organization, 'The Imperial Fascist League', with himself as Director General and Leslie H. Sherrard as 'Commandant General of the Fascist Legions'.

From the start the Imperial Fascists wore black shirts and black breeches. At first they used the fasces as their emblem but in 1933 they changed to the swastika, which they superimposed on the Union Jack for their banners and armbands.

The parade strength of Sherrard's 'Fascist Legions' was always small. At a major meeting in 1933 they could assemble only sixteen members in uniform. Earlier they seem to have been a little stronger and to have attracted a steady trickle of converts from the British Fascists. The foundation of the Mosley Fascists in 1932 stopped the supply. Leese admitted in his monthly paper *The Fascist* that nine out of ten recruits lapsed soon after joining. He was not worried. His aim, he said, was quality rather than quantity.

The most notable recruit was Brigadier-General Blakeney, the former British Fascist leader. Blakeney held no office in the Imperial Fascists but between 1930 and 1933 was a regular speaker at their meetings. He appears to have shared Leese's extreme anti-Semitism.

In their early days the Imperial Fascists made a sketchy attempt to advocate a comprehensive political programme. In 1929 they propounded a three-point policy: (1) Recognition of the failure of political democracy. (2) Formation of a new 'governing caste'. (3) Organization of trade and industry into a 'Corporative State', members of the legislature to be elected by industry instead of by regional constituencies. Their slogan was 'Boycott the ballot box!' and their members heckled the meetings of all the political parties. Leese admitted that there might eventually be 'a loathsome need' for the Imperial Fascists to take part in elections but they would only do so with the aim of destroying the democratic system. After the first few months the Imperial Fascists concentrated almost entirely on the Jews, their anti-Semitic theories growing ever more elaborate. By 1930 they were attacking freemasonry as an instrument of the Jews. In 1931 Leese announced 'with deep regret' that Mussolini had fallen under Jewish influence.

Leese's paper *The Fascist* was based on the model of the Nazi *Der*

William Joyce
(*Planet News*)

John Beckett
(*Radio Times Hulton Picture Library*)

(*Radio Times Hulton Picture Library*)

5th October 1936

(*above*) An anti-Fascist crowd, some of them carrying missiles, run from a barricade they have erected near Aldgate. The police are charging on the far side of the barricade, which has been reinforced with paving stones

(*below*) Police, some with drawn batons, try to force a passage at Royal Mint Street for a British Union car, escorted by Blackshirt motor-cyclists. Neil Francis-Hawkins is in the rear seat of the car

(*Associated Press*)

Stuermer, edited by the violently anti-Semitic Julius Streicher. Leese admired *Der Stuermer* and frequently quoted from it. Like Streicher he enjoyed publishing cartoons which showed the physical characteristics of Jews as offensive or sinister. In the pages of *The Fascist* the stock caricatures of Jews were shown cracking whips over the backs of British workmen, threatening in lisping English the editors of Fleet Street newspapers, presiding over the League of Nations, with blood dripping from their hands.

In February 1932, acting on Mosley's instructions, Robert Forgan approached the British Fascists with the proposal that they should accept Mosley's leadership and merge with the New Party. There was also an approach to the Imperial Fascist League. The terms were stiff. Mosley was to be Leader in the full Fascist sense, with complete control over organization and policy. The aim of the new organization would be to win political power as quickly as possible, and to build a corporate state on the lines of *The Greater Britain*, the Fascist handbook which Mosley was then preparing for publication.

Arnold Leese turned down the offer outright. With the British Fascists the results were, for a while, more fruitful. Neil Francis-Hawkins, a member of the British Fascist Grand Council, was already an admirer of Mosley and agreed to negotiate. Francis-Hawkins was a short, tubby man in his early thirties, a salesman of surgical instruments. His political imagination was limited but he had a clear idea that the country needed tidy, orderly administration to replace what he considered the confusions of democracy. Forgan introduced Francis-Hawkins to Mosley and agreement for a merger was quickly reached. In May Francis-Hawkins took the proposal to his Grand Council where it ran into violent opposition from an enraged Miss Lintorn-Orman, who still regarded Mosley as a near-Communist. On a vote the Grand Council rejected the merger by a majority of one. Francis-Hawkins thereupon resigned from the British Fascists and joined the New Party. With him went Mandeville Roe and several other officials, taking with them copies of the British Fascist membership and subscription lists.

Through the summer of 1932 there was bickering in the New Party about the wearing of uniforms and the use of the term 'Fascist' but, at the cost of further resignations, Mosley won his way. He prepared a circular letter to his members and to the people on the Fascist membership lists provided by Francis-Hawkins. It announced the formation of a new political movement, the British Union of Fascists:

Dear Sir,

You have, no doubt, read in the papers of the recent formation of the British Union of Fascists and I am enclosing herewith a short manifesto and membership form in the belief that they will be of interest to you.

A fuller statement of policy explaining the need for such an organization will be found in my new book, *The Greater Britain*, which can be obtained either from your local bookseller or direct from these Headquarters.

The Movement is indeed a 'Union of Fascists' and many members and officials drawn from all existing Fascists' organizations are now in the ranks of the British Union of Fascists.

Recent events more than confirm the necessity for Fascist organization. Our object is no less than the winning of power for Fascism, which we believe is the only salvation for our country. We appeal for the co-operation of those who have long believed in Fascism, but have been disappointed with the lack of progress and want of constructive policy in former Fascist organizations. We are now organizing active measures to advance the Fascist cause, including constant propaganda meetings and route marches through our great cities. We need your help. Will you give it?

Yours faithfully,
Oswald Mosley

CHAPTER 5

The Instrument of Steel

MOSLEY formally launched the British Union of Fascists on 1st October 1932, which was also the publication day of his book *The Greater Britain*. There were thirty-two founder members, most of whom attended, in black shirts, a solemn inaugural ceremony at the former New Party office in Great George Street. Mosley unlocked the door, pausing for photographs, and with a broad grin unfurled a black banner emblazoned with the fasces emblem in silver. In later years the ceremony was to be held in mystic remembrance, the gathering of the founders 'in an upper room' being recalled on every anniversary. Quietly Mosley spoke of the need for utter dedication to the Fascist cause. 'We ask those who join us,' he said, 'to march with us in a great and hazardous adventure. We ask them to be prepared to sacrifice all, but to do so for no small and unworthy ends. We ask them to dedicate their lives to building in this country a movement of the modern age. . . . Those who march with us will certainly face abuse, misunderstanding, bitter animosity and possibly the ferocity of struggle and danger. In return we can only offer to them the deep belief that they are fighting that a great land may live. . . .'

From the start it was a movement of youth. Mosley himself was thirty-five and most of his associates were younger. They saw themselves as the post-war generation come to sweep away the corruption of the past and often referred to themselves as 'a movement of ex-servicemen'. The foundation members were predominantly the remnants of Mosley's Labour Party and ILP following. Forgan was the

Movement's first Director of Organization. Risdon was the first Director of Propaganda. Cumings was sent to organize the Movement in South Wales, but does not appear to have remained with the BUF for very long. Of the early rank and file many came from the ILP which, recently disaffiliated from the Labour Party, was shedding members in every conceivable direction. Mosley appeared most interested in recruits from the Conservatives, the old British Fascists and from outside politics. He may have taken the loyalty of the ex-Socialists rather for granted and believed that he should concentrate on cementing the loyalty of those who distrusted his left-wing past. Or, more simply, he may just have felt at home with people who shared or admired his social background.

By proposing himself as Leader of a Fascist Britain, Mosley stirred up such a tumult of opposition that, in comparison, the New Party fights looked like a tea party. His first priority, carefully planned in advance, was to build up the uniformed Fascist Defence Force to protect his meetings and to ensure that he and his speakers would be able to present the Fascist case without interruption. The essence of Fascism was authority and the first proof of the BUF's authority was to be its ability to silence hecklers. Mosley justified this as his right to free speech, but it was a novel idea that a political leader should systematically organize a uniformed force to enable him to say whatever he liked in public. Without the Fascist Defence Force, Mosley claimed, he would have totally failed to win a hearing – an assertion which was probably true.

It was part of the left-wing dogma at the time that declining capitalism would seek survival in Fascism and Mosley arrived just in time to prove the dogma right. A blow at Mosley was a blow at capitalism and he was a much easier target to reach than the anonymous capitalists in City boardrooms. The Communists saw the British Union of Fascists as the herald of the revolutionary situation, an idea with which Mosley tended to agree. In the early days of the BUF he half expected that the Fascists would reach power in conditions of civil war, as Mussolini had reached power in Italy eleven years previously.

> We seek our ends by legal and constitutional means. . . . We desire to avert the collapse which has led to bloodshed and violence on the Continent [Mosley wrote early in 1933]. On the other hand, we recognize that things may be allowed to drift

too far and that other methods may thus become necessary. . . .
We must be prepared to save Britain by force from those who
would seek to destroy her by force.

The first commander of the Fascist Defence Force was Eric
Hamilton Piercy, an insurance agent who had worked with the New
Party 'biff boys'. Aged thirty-three, Piercy was a big, bluff man who
held the rank of inspector in the Special Constabulary. He had great
faith in athletic exercise and worked hard to bring his Blackshirt
stewards to a high standard of fitness. He also trained them in drill.
Somewhat disingenuously the BUF used to claim that their drill
was not military; the Army marched in fours whereas the Fascists
marched in threes. Neil Francis-Hawkins was the Defence Force
adjutant.

A pattern of violence and counter-violence quickly developed. The
Blackshirt stewards travelled to meetings in black vans, protected
from brickbats by thin armour plating and wire mesh over the
windows. Opponents called the vans 'armoured cars' or even 'tanks'.
At open-air meetings the Blackshirts ranged themselves below the
speaker's platform, eyeing the audience. At the first interruption the
speaker would give a warning that Fascists did not tolerate hecklers.
A shiver of anticipation would run through the audience, some
passers-by joining the meeting less to hear the speaker than to see
what would happen next. At the next interruption the chief steward
would bark a sharp order; two or three Blackshirts in a disciplined
manœuvre would remove the culprit from earshot, perhaps smashing
their fists in his face. As often as not the initiative for fighting would
come from the opposition. Whether the Fascists or anti-Fascists
started the fight, the result was usually a general *mêlée* with the
Blackshirts trying to win before the police arrived to close the
meeting. Trained, disciplined and vigorous, the Blackshirts generally
had the advantage. At indoor meetings the Fascist advantage was
even greater. Stewards would line the walls of the hall ready to
pounce on opponents; there was generally a quiet foyer where
'punishment' could be administered. Police and Blackshirt stewards
outside the hall could prevent anti-Fascists breaking in to rescue
their outnumbered comrades. Manchester set a useful precedent to
local authorities by insisting that the Fascists could have municipally
owned halls only if the police were allowed to do the stewarding.
The BUF complained that the police allowed too many interruptions.

The extent of Blackshirt violence varied very greatly. There was a minority of thugs and sadists who joined the Movement simply because it offered opportunities for copying the worst activities of Hitler's storm troopers, as described in the left-wing papers. Within the BUF dark stories circulated of needles being driven into hecklers' testicles, of castor oil being forcibly administered. Such men did not make the most efficient Blackshirts and they rarely lasted long in the Movement. The larger Blackshirt element had a simple hatred for 'Reds', were not averse to a scrap and often got as good as they gave. Mosley advocated the use of bare fists and, on at least one occasion, ordered his stewards to be searched for knuckledusters. In the early days the favourite Blackshirt weapons were lengths of rubber hosepipe loaded with shot, but these, too, were discountenanced by Mosley. Left-wing accounts often refer to the hosepipes and Mosley admitted in the witness-box at the High Court that they were used at the Free Trade Hall, Manchester, in March 1933. He added that he had given instructions for them to be banned.

A common cause for hurling an anti-Fascist into the street was his refusal to stand up for the National Anthem which closed every Fascist meeting. This was excused by the BUF on grounds of patriotism rather than that the meeting was being disturbed. Insults to stewards were another reason for ejection. The BUF paper *Blackshirt* reported how one man had been ejected because he called a Fascist 'a lousy bastard' – 'the filthiest observation one man can address to another' *Blackshirt* commented.

The typical long-service Blackshirt was a man of the lower middle class, not particularly clever but capable of loyalty and sacrifice. Fascism had an appeal because it attacked both the capitalism he resented and the Socialism he feared. Without sacrificing his social rank, which was a grade above the manual worker, he could take part in a revolutionary movement. For his work he received little reward. He bought his shirt for five shillings and paid a subscription of one shilling a month if in work or fourpence a month if unemployed – the same rates as those in the Communist Party. If he travelled a long distance to a meeting he would have free transport in van or hired bus and, perhaps, a free meal. Devoted Blackshirts would stand night after night on street corners in the lonely task of selling the Fascist publications. The party meetings had a semi-religious air, with salutes for the pictures of Mosley which hung in every headquarters.

Mosley reciprocated the Blackshirts' devotion. It became hard to convince him that a Blackshirt was ever at fault. At the end of a big public rally it was his custom to gather the Blackshirts privately round the platform, thank them for their services and ask for still further sacrifices in the future. On one occasion, deeply moved, he stretched his arms towards them and cried: 'You are blood of my blood, spirit of my spirit!'

'Crikey, has the old man gone off his head?' whispered E. D. Randall, nineteen-year-old author of the Movement's marching song, who was in the audience. Randall was a representative of a much smaller element, the intellectual Blackshirts, who tended to see the pageantry, emotionalism and authoritarianism as means to an end. The Movement was unsuccessful with intellectuals, few of them remaining members for very long. With his charm and ability Mosley had little difficulty in attracting the interest of some of the best minds of his generation, but he lacked the capacity to turn interest into allegiance. The intellectuals who did stay within the Movement over a long period were not particularly bright and suffered catastrophically from lack of a sense of humour.

Mosley was self-confident in his abilities both as Leader of the Movement and potential Leader of the nation, a characteristic which opponents and some friends tended to dismiss as vanity. Granted the basic Fascist assumptions, however, there is no reason to suppose that anybody could have done the job better and few could have done it so well. Mosley had personal magnetism, a capacity for very hard work, an inventive, original mind and outstanding gifts of persuasion. Had it been possible for him to use a nation-wide television network in 1933 the BUF might have become a much more formidable force. On the debit side he had poor tactical judgment, a crippling inability to judge people's characters and, ultimately, a ruinous unwillingness to acknowledge the existence of unpalatable truths. His methods of organization tended to encourage bureaucracy within the Movement.

While Mosley had some characteristics in common with both Hitler and Mussolini he was, fundamentally, a different type of man from either. Above all else Mosley was an intellectual, applying theoretical arguments to the solution of practical problems. Mussolini, in contrast, made up his theories as he went along, declaring a few weeks before winning power: 'Our programme is simple: we wish to govern Italy. It is not programmes that are wanting for the salvation of Italy but men and will-power.' Hitler was a mystical believer in the destiny of the Germanic race, and in *Mein Kampf* committed himself to very little beyond a campaign against the Jews and a plan for extending German boundaries. Mosley set out in advance his detailed, practical proposals for a British revolution. In his speeches and in his books *The Greater Britain* (1932), *One Hundred Questions* (1936) and *Tomorrow We Live* (1938) he covered every aspect of political, economic, industrial and social organization. His aide, A. Raven Thomson, even designed routes for the motorways the BUF promised to build on achieving power.

The top priority of Fascist policy was to rewrite the British Constitution, Mosley asserting that effective government was impossible within the existing framework. There would be only one political party, the British Union of Fascists, and the only allowable criticism of the Government would be 'the constructive criticism of technicians'. The Fascist Government would be answerable not to Parliament but directly to the people in plebiscites every five years. If the Prime Minister died, retired or suffered defeat it would be the King's duty to choose a successor, the King's choice to be ratified by plebiscite. To advise the King on such an occasion there would be a Grand Council of Fascist veterans. The Privy Council would be abolished. There would be a House of Commons elected on a basis of occupational franchise, miners voting for miners, doctors for doctors, housewives for housewives and so on. The MPs would not be politicians and would have no duty to survey the Government's work as a whole; there would be short Parliamentary sessions in which, from an expert point of view, MPs would examine the legislation submitted to them by the Government (ministers would not be MPs). The House of Lords would be abolished and replaced by an Upper House of notable citizens; the Upper House would rarely meet as a whole but would provide panels of experts which the Government could consult on specialized matters. Existing local government would be abolished in favour of local leaders appointed by the central government and advised by local councils elected on the occupational franchise.

The Press would remain free – provided editors and proprietors printed the 'truth'. It would be a criminal offence for them to publish untrue news 'and the penalty will be particularly severe if it can be shown that such publication was deliberately and maliciously conceived in support of a private interest, to the detriment of the national interest'. For the private individual the corporate state was designed to provide a mechanism by which he could make his views known in the highest quarters. 'Contact between Government and people must ever be so close that the flame of our own revolutionary passion may pass continually from the souls of the pioneers to fire and maintain the spirit of the people at a white heat of ardour.'

Like Hitler and Mussolini, Mosley disliked the word 'dictatorship', because it carried the implication of a ruler existing independently of the will of the people. He preferred the term 'leadership' – the Fascist Leader being the embodiment of the people's will. Since the people's will should be all-powerful, nothing should be allowed to obstruct the Leader's work.

At first Mosley tended to shy away from the notion that the ex-Chancellor of the Duchy should become the nation's sole political leader. In the first, 1932, edition of *The Greater Britain* he wrote: '. . . Leadership may be an individual, or preferably, in the case of the British character, a team with clearly allocated functions and responsibility. In either case, the only effective instrument of revolutionary change is absolute authority.' In the revised, 1934, edition the same passage reads: 'Leadership in Fascism may be an individual or a team, but undoubtedly single leadership in practice proves the more effective instrument. The Leader must be prepared to shoulder absolute responsibility.'

The political proposals were to be carried out very quickly. The first election in which the Fascists secured a majority would be the last under the old system. Fascist MPs (forbidden even to speak to MPs of other parties) would, on obtaining a majority, pass a General Powers Act giving the Government wide authority to legislate by Order. Parliament would then adjourn, the Fascist MPs acting as executive officers of the Government in the country and the Opposition MPs having no role at all. By the time the next election came round the new political system of the occupational franchise would be working, and a start would have been made on the main objective – the construction of the corporate state.

Based mainly on the Italian model, Mosley's corporate state was to organize the whole industrial and commercial life of the country into a network of twenty-four 'corporations', each to include representatives of employers, workers and the Government. Corporation decisions on wages, working conditions, output and modernization would have the force of law on ratification by the coordinating body, the National Council of Corporations. The aim was to combine the vigour of private enterprise with a Socialist regard for the interests of the workers and the consumer. Capitalists would be allowed to compete with each other within the corporate framework, but it would be a criminal offence for them to disobey corporate regulations. Trade unions would be reorganized to provide the workers' side of the corporations; the 'power action' of the workers representatives within the corporations would make strikes 'unnecessary'. Housewives were to have their own corporation which would have special responsibility for women's interests, child welfare and food standards. Married women were to be encouraged to stay at home to look after their families but if they did go out to work they would be entitled to equal pay with men. 'We want women who are women and men who are men,' declared Mosley. The Medical Corporation would have the duty of providing a National Health Service which would not, however, be free.

The whole would exist within a self-contained Empire economy 'insulated' from the shocks of world conditions. Wages would be progressively raised to enable the people to buy the expanding output of British industry. To solve short-term unemployment there would be a big programme of public works, including a labour corps to construct new roads and to rebuild slum areas. The Government would closely control the banks, making it a criminal offence to lend money abroad when it could be invested in Britain. The banks would not be nationalized but the bankers would be gaoled if they disobeyed the Government.

Mosley's mixture of Conservatism and Socialism reached its subtlest point in his proposals for dealing with class distinctions. Men, he said, were born fundamentally unequal, some being fitted to follow and others to lead. His system would concentrate authority on those fitted to lead. On the other hand, he rejected the existing class structure as being out of date. All schools would be State-controlled, parents retaining only the right to choose the religious atmosphere in which they wanted their children educated. The school-leaving age would be eighteen, but from fifteen upwards there would be a sharp differentiation between the potential leaders and the others. Within the hierarchy of the Fascist State every man would rise on merit, being entitled to earn big monetary rewards and to bequeath them to his children. The State through 'equity tribunals of people's justice' would confiscate the estate on the first heir's death if he had not performed public services equivalent to its value —an adaptation of the 'Rignano Principle' on inheritance which was much in vogue among Socialist economists in the 1920's.

The policy, as a whole, reads more like a blueprint for an imaginary and authoritarian Utopia than like a practical political programme. Few leaders can have announced their intentions in so much detail as did Mosley. His proposals were to build 'a civilization that shall be the sum and the glory of the travail of the ages'. The British Union of Fascists was to be the 'instrument of steel' which alone could turn his ideas into reality.

Many recruits found the measure of faith required of them to be too great and they left the Movement. Others left because of the internal dissensions which racked it from the beginning to the end of its history. The BUF was a Fascist state in miniature with all authority concentrated in the Leader. There were no party conferences to decide policy, no elections to choose officers. On important matters Mosley was in the habit of consulting a vague group called the Policy Directorate of six to eight senior members, but decisions were his alone. He would hear the officials' views and then announce his verdict. Lower down the hierarchy the same principle held good. The District Leader and, below him, the Blackshirt Unit Leader were miniature Mosleys, with their own sphere of absolute authority. Some of the junior leaders even aped Mosley's personal mannerisms. The penalty for disobedience and often for criticism was expulsion. On occasion Mosley expelled whole branches for disobeying a local leader appointed by National Headquarters. In some respects the autocracy was successful. While Communists and Socialists were indoors, quarrelling about abstruse points of discipline or policy, the Fascists were in the streets selling pamphlets and canvassing voters. A District Leader of the quality of W. E. A. Chambers-Hunter (Aberdeen) or Vice-Admiral G. B. Powell (Portsmouth) could build up a serviceable team spirit. In other, more important, respects the autocracy was disastrous. It encouraged toadying and petty bullying. Some District Leaders seemed to delight in being unpopular. In the higher reaches of the Movement there was an atmosphere of intrigue, with officials competing against each other for access to Mosley's ear. Within four years of the Movement's foundation control had passed into the hands of a set of bureaucrats who tended to see the organization as an end in itself rather than as a means of winning political power.

The inner life of the Movement was important. The BUF ran its own holiday camps, produced its own brand of cigarettes, and had its own ceremonial for Fascist weddings and funerals, all of which were intended to build up a corporate loyalty. Most important of all were the insignia and uniforms, symbols of the Movement held in semi-religious awe. First came the black shirt itself, which was not really a shirt but a tunic modelled on the garment Mosley wore for his favourite sport of fencing. It had a high, polo neck and fastened with buttons over the left shoulder. Mosley and officials who could afford them had tailor-made shirts in black silk. There was also an 'undress' black shirt which could be worn under an ordinary suit with collar and tie. For wear with the full black shirt the regulations originally stipulated grey trousers but most members preferred to wear black. Members giving more than three nights' service a week were allowed black riding breeches with jackboots. Headgear proved troublesome. Most Fascists followed Mosley's example in preferring to go bare-headed, but there were experiments with caps, berets and forage caps, the latter winning official approval in 1935. A year later Mosley introduced a totally new 'Action' uniform similar to the dress of the Nazi S.S. but this was not much seen outside the East End of London.

Mosley's original plans provided for a big force of Brownshirts, industrial workers enrolled in the Fascist organization without political duties, but this idea was stillborn. There were also to be Greyshirts, probationary members training for Blackshirt status, but by 1935 the grey shirt was being used for the youth movement, consisting of young men and girls aged under eighteen.

Women members, first recruited in March 1933 under the leadership of Mosley's mother (who was very active in the Movement), wore black blouses with matching skirts and berets.

In the early days the badge was the fasces, the Roman emblem of authority which had been revived by Mussolini. The Fascists wore it on their uniform shirts and as a buttonhole badge with plain clothes. It appeared also on the Movement's flags, posters and printed literature. The fasces was an axe with a handle of rods bound by a triple cord. Around it developed an elaborate symbolism: the axe representing the power of Fascist government cutting through all obstacles, the rods the varying interests within the nation and the cords the unifying power of Fascist discipline. The fasces was never formally abolished but after 1935 it tended to give way to a new insignia – a flash of lightning within a circle which, from a distance, looked like a Nazi swastika. The lightning represented the Fascist power of action and the circle represented the unified Fascist state. Opponents called it 'the flash in the pan'.

From the start the BUF adopted the Roman salute with out-stretched arm.

Thus did Mosley construct the mould in which he hoped to shape his instrument of steel. The circumstances at the beginning were hopeful. Three months after the foundation ceremony at Great George Street, Adolf Hitler became Chancellor of Germany. In the same month Britain's unemployment figures soared to the all-time record of 2·95 million. The MacDonald-Baldwin National Government appeared incapable of providing a solution and the Parliamentary alternative, the Labour Party, was pitiably weak with only fifty MPs. It was a time to ask if Britain under the leadership of the 'modern movement' should seek to copy Germany and set up an entirely new form of state. In the early months of 1933 the beginnings of a mass membership began to pour into the mould Mosley had prepared.

CHAPTER 6

The Black House

'WE SHALL advance to power quicker than the Germans,' announced Mosley two months after Hitler had achieved power. He had reason for optimism. Within weeks of its foundation the BUF was a nationally known movement and was fighting its first battles in the streets. Hitler's success had great publicity value. Newspapers were eager to speculate whether Mosley would be the British Hitler. In the general view, Mosley was the abler man. There was steady recruiting, mainly in London but also in Birmingham, Manchester, Tyneside, South Wales and Bristol. In Scotland the advance was slow; Motherwell branch's claim of 200 members in the spring of 1933 was, if true, a flash in the pan.

With eight pages for a penny, the Movement's first regular paper *Blackshirt* started publication in February 1933, under the editorship of Cecil Courtney Lewis, a solicitor who had served in the Indian Army and as a political officer in Iraq. Lewis pioneered a Fascist literary style of violent invective: all opponents became 'scum' or 'sub-human'. Although Lewis's importance dwindled as new and more notable recruits came into the Movement, he continued in the vital role of legal adviser (the BUF had civil and criminal cases frequently before the courts).

The recruits of the first half of 1933 were of decisive influence; second only to Mosley they were to shape the techniques of the BUF and its pattern of development. They were especially influential in developing the anti-Semitic tendency which in 1934 turned into an official campaign against the Jews.

On the organizational side the most important acquisition was Ian Hope Dundas who, at the age of twenty-four, became Mosley's Chief of Staff. Dundas, who had recently resigned a commission in the Royal Navy, had an impeccable social background, his father having been twenty-eighth Chief of Dundas and an admiral. His duties were to act as a kind of personnel officer and he carried them out in a semimilitary manner, with a bugler to accompany him on his daily 'rounds' of National Headquarters. In December 1933 he married Pamela Dorman in the first 'Fascist wedding', complete with Blackshirt escort and Mosley as best man. Dundas wore his Chief of Staff's uniform with crossed fasces on his chest and the bride wore a gold fasces badge on her white dress. (Mosley's previous experience as best man had been at John Strachey's wedding in 1929.) The Fascist marriage was a failure, ending in divorce after five years. In so far as he reduced to order the chaotic affairs of a rapidly growing movement, Dundas was a success, but his methods created a faintly Ruritanian atmosphere.

At about the same time Mosley recruited Alexander Raven Thomson who was to rank as the BUF's leading intellectual. He was aged thirty-four and the possessor of a sufficient private income to have enabled him to devote several years to a variegated study of politics. He had read economics at German and American universities and had for a brief period been a member of the Communist Party. For four years before joining the BUF he had devoted his time to writing an involved book called *Civilization as Divine Superman*, a neo-Fascist work intended as a reply to Spengler's *Decline of the West*. Briefly, Thomson's thesis was that civilization could avoid decay if it adopted as close a communal spirit as the 'insect communities'. Civilization was the master, not the servant, of man, granting him 'the immense advantages of co-operation and specialism only as a reward for surrendering his freedom to the higher aims of the communal spirit'. In the BUF Thomson was very loyal to Mosley and busied himself with expanding and elaborating the Leader's ideas. Some members regarded him as a 'yes man'. He was rotund, dark and jovial; Arnold Leese of the Imperial Fascists used to claim that he looked Jewish.

A recruit of more independent character was Arthur Kenneth Chesterton, second cousin of G. K. Chesterton. A fervent patriot, with a schoolboyish enthusiasm for the British Empire, for a while A. K. Chesterton saw Mosley as the man who would remove the stains of industrialism from England's green and pleasant land.

Chesterton is a polemical writer of the top rank and as such was of great service to the BUF. He is a man of contradictions. Emotionally he is probably a nonconformist, a rebel against established conventions. Intellectually, he has supported ideals of authority and order. The contradictions may have produced the inner strain which seems to have prevented him from fully developing his literary talent. In 1933, when he joined the BUF, he was working as public relations officer at the Shakespeare Memorial Theatre, Stratford-upon-Avon. He was a newcomer to politics; a likeable, opinionated man of thirty-four; tall, lean, a pair of piercing eyes lighting his narrow face. His high enthusiasms were tempered by a charming sense of humour. He won the M.C. in the First World War and saw active service again in the Second.

William Joyce, who joined at about the same time as Chesterton, was a patriot of quite another stamp. A short man with a hard, intelligent face, Joyce was aged twenty-nine. He had taken a first-class-honours degree in English at London University and was a very successful tutor at a correspondence school. In the BUF he quickly developed a brilliant talent as a public speaker, within months ranking second only to Mosley in popularity. His style was somewhat similar to that of Hitler's Propaganda Minister, Josef Goebbels. Against Risdon's advice, he abandoned his teaching career to take a salaried BUF post, first as Area Administrative Officer for West London and later as Propaganda Officer at National Head-quarters, where his classes for speakers were a big attraction. He seems to have been a shy man who cloaked an inferiority complex behind an arrogant manner. He could be amusing but his wit turned too often to sarcasm for him to be a comfortable companion. His friends remember him in affectionate bewilderment.

The mainspring of Joyce's life was a grotesquely inflated patriotism. He was not, in fact, even a British subject. Son of a naturalized American, he was born in New York and brought up in Ireland, where his family sided with the British during the troubles. To Joyce, the Flag, the Crown and the National Anthem were symbols deserving profound respect. 'A pacifist, being unwilling to risk danger in defence of his land, is lower than the lowest kind of protoplasmic life known to science,' he declared.

His other governing emotion was a bitter hatred of Jews.

Although he was a successful speaker and organizer, Joyce had little contact with reality. Inside his mind there may have existed a rich, colourful dream-world where he was the universal teacher, the model patriot and the scourge of the Jews. Even in the hothouse atmosphere of the BUF he could sometimes appear ridiculous, and stories about Joyce became part of the Movement's folklore. A typical anecdote is how Joyce, accompanied by the usual busload of Blackshirts, went to address a meeting of market gardeners at Evesham. The market gardeners had suffered a bad season and were in a receptive mood to hear the BUF proposals for a protected market for British agriculture. Joyce made a speech lasting four hours in which he analysed the world situation, arguing brilliantly in favour of friendship between Britain and the Fascist countries. It did not appear to enter Joyce's head even to mention market gardening. When the dazed audience went home, at about midnight, somebody told Joyce that there was a group of Italian immigrants living in the town. The tireless Joyce was delighted and on the spot decided to hold a Fascist parade. He marshalled the Blackshirts and, to the strains of the Italian Fascist song *Giovinezza*, led them through the town towards the Italian quarter. Bewildered Evesham people woke from their sleep to hear Blackshirts tramping past their homes in full song. The episode ended with the arrival of a police inspector who said curtly to Joyce: 'Go home, little man!' White with humiliation, Joyce called off the march and, with the Black-shirts, returned to London.

The story illustrates not only Joyce's detachment from reality but also his command over the rank-and-file Blackshirts. He was an effective disciplinarian and physically brave; in spite of – or possibly because of – his small stature, he would wade into the thickest part of a fight.

The early BUF battles were on two fronts, against the minority Fascist groups on one side and against the militant anti-Fascists on the other. The dissident Fascists received much attention, their existence being regarded as a slight on the authority of Mosley's leadership. Arnold Leese's Imperial Fascists were the most danger-ous; they wore uniforms similar to those of the BUF and the public found it hard to distinguish the one organization from the other. The Mosley Fascists tended to get the blame for Leese's violent outbursts and for the anti-Jewish slogans and swastikas which Leese's men painted on synagogues. The *Jewish Chronicle* was at some pains to distinguish between Mosley and Leese, declaring in March 1933: 'The Mosley Fascists themselves are our best supporters in the fight against the Imperial Fascist League.' Leese caused intense irritation among the Mosley Fascists by calling them the 'Kosher Fascists' and by hammering away at the allegation that Cynthia Mosley, through her grandfather Levi Leiter of Chicago, was half Jewish. *Blackshirt* retaliated by calling Leese a 'little tyke'. The feud reached its climax when fifty Mosley Fascists in plain dress smashed up an Imperial Fascist public meeting at Trinity Hall, Great Portland Street. Leese's 'Imperial Fascist Guard', only sixteen strong, was heavily outnumbered and unable to prevent the invaders tearing to shreds the IFL banner – the Union Jack with a swastika in the centre. Leese himself was debagged but, with his economical turn of mind, appeared to bear less resentment against this indignity than against the fact that he had to pay for several chairs smashed in the *mêlée*. Another participant in the fight was Brigadier-General Blake-ney, late of the British Fascists, who had joined forces with Leese; the Imperial Fascists afterwards claimed that Blakeney had lost the sight of one eye through being struck by a chair leg. If Blakeney did in fact suffer so severely he must have been a man of forgiving dis-position; four years later he was writing for Mosley's weekly paper. The BUF denied that the attack on Leese's meeting was officially organized but did not contest that their members were involved.

At about the same time a BUF unofficial striking force smashed up the office in Kensington of a mushroom group, the British United Fascists. Two of the raiders, members of the BUF, were arrested and bound over at London Sessions to keep the peace.

By the end of 1933 the BUF decided that the most effective way of dealing with the dissident Fascists was to ignore them. The BUF was overwhelmingly the strongest Fascist organization and had attracted to its ranks almost the entire active membership of the British Fascists, the Imperial Fascist League and the mushroom groups. The British Fascists went bankrupt in 1935 but Leese fought on until 1940, alleging that the BUF was an ingenious weapon devised by the Jews to keep public attention away from Leese's true anti-Semitism.

Against the anti-Fascists the fighting was to be much more severe and more prolonged. From the start the BUF principle was to invade the enemy's territory, to carry out intensive campaigns in working-class districts. Had the Conservatives done this they would, in the conditions of 1933, have encountered violent opposition. A Conservative speaker appearing night after night on a slum street corner would have been lucky to escape abuse and probably brick-bats. The Fascists not only spoke in the 'Red' districts but guarded themselves with a uniformed defence force and appeared positively to look forward to a fight. To the Socialists and Communists, the Blackshirts stalking through the streets looked like so many agents of Adolf Hitler and were hated accordingly.

When the BUF opened its first office at Walworth in March 1933 the anti-Fascists picketed the premises for a fortnight. Ultimately an angry crowd of 300 tried to force their way inside and were dispersed by the mounted police – a foretaste of the mounted-police charges which became a regular accompaniment of Fascist activity in the East End three years later.

On Mosley's first appearance at Kentish Town there was a pitched battle, with Piercy, Richard Plathen (National Political Officer) and other Blackshirts removed to hospital with superficial head wounds; anti-Fascists also suffered casualties. Soon afterwards Piercy was required to resign his inspectorship in the Special Constabulary, his political activities having been declared incompatible with police work.

In the provinces, where BUF branches were small and widely dispersed, the organizers developed an efficient technique of concentrating their forces from a wide area in one particular spot. A good example of the technique was an incident in September 1933, at Stockton-on-Tees, where a Fascist speaker had been heckled. Blackshirts were transported by bus and lorry from as far away as Manchester and Newcastle to take part in a counter-attack on a Sunday afternoon.

> They then marched in their well-known column of threes into Stockton where they found some sort of meeting going on in the Market Square [*Blackshirt* reported]. Amid an appalling din of catcalls and howls several of our speakers attempted to give the policy, but it was obvious that the Reds were going to prevent any resemblance to free speech. . . . The crisis was reached when one of our members was attacked by a man thrusting his forefingers into his eyes. The man was knocked down immediately and the Blackshirt stewards moved forward like a machine against the Communist section of the crowd. Fighting desperately, the Reds were swept back forty yards right across the Market Square, and the platform was left isolated in the centre, surrounded by a small Fascist guard. It was indeed a beautiful sight.

So the pattern of violence and counter-violence developed nearly everywhere the Fascists showed their faces. Sir John Gilmour, Home Secretary, reported to the House of Commons that there had been a sharp increase in convictions for disorder at political meetings since the BUF had introduced uniforms, but at this period, and for four years afterwards, the overwhelming majority of convictions were of anti-Fascists. Not until 1937 did it become Blackshirt practice to interfere with anti-Fascist meetings.

In the spring of 1933 Mosley, Cynthia Mosley and twelve senior BUF officials had a respite in the calmer atmosphere of Rome. The occasion was Mussolini's International Fascist Exhibition, which attracted representatives from all the European 'modern movements', including a German group led by Hermann Goering. The BUF group had a warm welcome and received from Starace, Secretary of the Italian Fascist Party, the gift of a black banner bearing a small Union Jack and the inscription 'For King-Empire and International Justice'. The BUF carried it publicly in Rome but, probably because of the quaint wording, they rarely or never used it in England.

Mussolini awarded the Mosleys the special honour of sharing his saluting platform at a march-past on 21st April of Fascist contingents from all over Italy. The other members of the BUF were allotted a place immediately under the platform, where they were to parade with their new banner and the Union Jack. At the last moment Mussolini failed to appear; it was raining and he decided to take the salute on a covered balcony a quarter of a mile away. The Mosleys were alone on the official platform and for two hours they, and the British Blackshirts below, stood in the streaming rain to acknowledge the salutes of the entire parade.

'In a stand behind her husband stood Lady Cynthia Mosley in a light mackintosh, brown felt hat and – to mark the occasion – black gloves, which are the correct wear when giving the Fascist salute. This she did repeatedly as unit after unit obeyed the order "Eyes left!" ,' the *Daily Telegraph* reported.

This was the only occasion on which Cynthia Mosley showed sympathy with Fascism at a major public event. It was her last public appearance. A month later she died in the London Clinic from peritonitis, having been in poor health since the birth of her youngest child in April 1932. At the time of her death she was aged only thirty-three and considered to be one of the most beautiful women in London. Her Labour Party friends found difficulty in believing that she had turned Fascist, but her guiding principle appears to have been absolute loyalty to her husband – a principle she maintained under every stress.

For Mosley her death marked the end of a public as well as a personal epoch. In the 1920's it had been 'Tom and Cimmie', the rich, talented couple who mixed widely in political and intellectual society. Cynthia Mosley had a good brain and a gift for friendship and human sympathy which complemented her husband's virile qualities. Robert Boothby* remembered her as 'a perfect hostess, a wonderful companion and a friend beyond price. I think of her now as a lighthouse standing like a rock in the stormy sea, whose steady beam brought comfort to all in difficulty or in trouble.' After Cynthia's death Mosley became totally immersed in the affairs of the BUF and for the remainder of the decade cut himself off from wider social contacts. 'This is now my only home,' he told his staff at BUF headquarters when they gave him a clock for his next birthday.

The King and Queen and the Prince of Wales sent their sympathy and there was a well-attended memorial service at St. Margaret's, Westminster. Churchill, Lloyd George, Lansbury and MacDonald issued a public appeal for a memorial fund which, with the aid of London County Council and Lambeth Borough Council, resulted in the erection of a Cynthia Mosley Day Nursery at Kennington. Winston Churchill was seen to weep at the opening ceremony which was conducted by the Archbishop of Canterbury. For a year after her death Cynthia Mosley's body lay in a private chapel at Cliveden, home of Lord and Lady Astor. An elaborate tomb was constructed to the design of Edwin Lutyens on the banks of the River Colne in the grounds of the then Mosley home, Savehay Farm, Denham. It consisted of a circular, sunken garden, a hundred feet in diameter, descending by terraces to a sarcophagus in golden Travertine stone. Mosley, the bearers and two workmen were the only people there when the coffin was finally laid to rest.

Responding to the sympathy he received from his fellow Fascists, Mosley issued a brief statement: 'Thank you, my friends. Now onward!' He plunged himself into a welter of work, becoming the busiest opposition politician in the land. He addressed two or three major public meetings a week, visited new BUF branches which were springing up like mushrooms and supervised a torrent of printed propaganda. Half fashionable London turned out to hear him debate with Maxton at the Friends' Meeting House, Euston Road, with

* *I Fight to Live* by Robert Boothby (1947).

Lloyd George in the chair; ILP members in red shirts co-operated with Blackshirts in stewarding the audience. Bernard Shaw, who two years earlier had advised Mosley to stay in the Labour Party, shocked the Fabian Society with a lecture in which he said Mosley was 'one of the few people who were writing and thinking about real things and not about figments and phrases'. In June 1933 Mosley led the first of the marches which were to become an essential part of BUF technique; with their Leader in front, and accompanied by bands and banners, about 900 male and 100 female Blackshirts marched three miles through the West End of London. This first march was quieter than most of its successors, arousing little interest from the general public and largely ignored by the anti-Fascists.

The strength of the march – about 1,000 – probably represented the greater part of the active membership in London. But to attract even 1,000 members was not bad progress for so young a movement. By October, the first anniversary of the foundation ceremony, the BUF was a long way from winning political power but it had established at least the skeleton of a national organization and was recruiting more members every week. Never before in modern British history had the spontaneous idea of one man flowered so quickly into a national movement. The success, as W. E. D. Allen, Mosley's Ulster friend, wrote in the *Quarterly Review* of October 1933, marked 'a revolt against the whole theory and system of Democracy in Britain'.

The BUF quickly acquired the resources to move from its small quarters in Great George Street and early in 1933 rented a suite of offices at 12 Lower Grosvenor Place. Mosley wanted something still bigger and rumours appeared in the newspapers that he was negotiating to buy Wellington Barracks from the War Office. He settled eventually on Whitelands Teachers' Training College, Chelsea, of which the BUF Trust, Ltd. (holder of the Movement's funds) bought the lease in the autumn of 1933. It was a substantial building complete with lecture rooms, dormitories, a gymnasium and a parade ground. In an emergency, the BUF declared, 5,000 Black-shirts could live there as a self-contained unit. Mosley renamed the building 'Black House' but opponents preferred to call it the 'Fascist Fort' or the 'Fascist Barracks'.

The Black House [Chesterton* wrote] served Fascism well for many months. It was the centre of its gay, bustling, and in a

* *Oswald Mosley, Portrait of a Leader* (1936).

sense turbulent life – the intellectual and social as well as the organizational centre. Its offices were occupied by men working fourteen and fifteen hours a day; its lecture halls were the scene of Joyce's brilliant policy lessons, filled with students eager to learn everything about this new, exciting crusade; its club-rooms rang with the laughter and song of men who felt that the advent of Fascism had made life again worth living.

A less cheerful side of Black House could be found in the cellars, where the Blackshirts made ready for the day when they could seize political opponents and bring them in for punishment, as the storm troopers had done in Hitler's Brown Houses. One cellar had a skull and crossbones on the door and was nicknamed the 'death cell'! It was said at the time by opponents that the cellars were used for disciplinary purposes within the Movement. The residents of Black House were a miscellaneous collection and there were fights, disobedience of orders and petty thefts. Rather than call in the police the resident Blackshirts may have on occasion maintained their own discipline with the aid of castor oil, truncheons and locked cellars. It is difficult to define the extent to which 'Blackshirt Justice' of this kind was used, since the whole thing was unofficial and included a generous measure of play-acting.

There were, broadly speaking, three categories of Fascists in the Black House.

In the top category came the Movement's senior officials, headed by Forgan as Director of Organization, and including Dundas, Joyce, Box and Francis-Hawkins. They numbered between twenty and thirty, including the Movement's two leading journalists, Rex Tremlett and W. J. Leaper.* The officials treated Black House as an office and slept there only if they were kept late at work.

The second category was a much larger one, numbering at various times anything between fifty and 200. They were the resident Blackshirts who received free accommodation and one or two pounds a week pocket money and did duty as guards, messengers, drivers and paper-sellers. They lived a semi-military life with meal-times, parades and 'lights out' regulated by bugle calls. At a time of high unemployment it was easy to attract young men to this kind of existence and there does not appear to have been much discrimination about the type selected. The inner core of the group were the

* Tremlett left during 1934. Leaper, a former I L P man and a New Party Parliamentary candidate in 1931, left at the beginning of 1936.

'I' Squad which regarded itself as an élite and wore jackboots. The 'I' Squad acted as a special escort for Mosley and as a mobile guard which could be rushed to the East End to rescue a Fascist speaker in trouble. At Black House the members guarded doors and patrolled the corridors, keeping a sharp eye open for intruders and helping to maintain a general Fascist atmosphere. Yet another group, nicknamed the 'Pansies', wore plain clothes and had a special reputation for brutality. About twenty strong, the 'Pansies' were paid thugs plain and simple with no political interests. Most of them had criminal records for violent crime.

The third category consisted of the hundreds of unpaid Blackshirts who used Black House as a social centre and operational head-quarters. If kept late on duty they could stay the night and, if they lost their jobs, they could easily become full-time Blackshirts.

Whether the maintenance of Black House was a wise policy was a subject of disagreement within the Movement. It was very expensive, it attracted an element of layabouts who were useless as Fascists and it tended to concentrate activity on a central point at Chelsea instead of encouraging members to win new recruits in their own localities. On the other hand, the Fascist atmosphere at Black House gave the new recruit an impression of strength, of a powerful Fascist community, which he would not have received if his training had been with half a dozen zealots in a suburb. Black House created a distinctively Fascist way of life and left a permanent stamp on the Movement. Above all, there was the convenience of Black House as a fortress and rallying point in the event of Communist revolution, which among themselves the Fascists really thought likely.

What very few people knew was where the money came from. By the end of 1933 the youthful BUF was not only running the costly Black House establishment but was also financing propaganda on a scale at least as large as that of the wealthy Conservative Central Office and probably larger. BUF propaganda expenditure far exceeded that of the Labour Party, the ILP, the Liberals or the Communists. The scale of BUF expenditure cannot have been less than £100,000 a year and was probably a good deal higher, for Mosley paid his officials on quite a generous scale. The highest salary was Forgan's, who received £600 a year as Director of Organization and £700 when he was promoted Deputy Leader. The journalists had the prevailing Fleet Street minimum rate of about £450 a year; other officials were paid on the same kind of scale, Joyce in charge of the relatively small Propaganda Department receiving £300, which was

less than he thought he deserved. The salaries were not high enough
to bribe a man to sacrifice his convictions but they provided a fair
living* at a time when jobs were not easy to find. For purposes of
comparison, it may be observed that Ernest Bevin received £650 a
year as General Secretary on the formation of the Transport and
General Workers' Union with 300,000 members.

At the most generous estimate, the paid-up membership of the
BUF in December 1933 cannot have been more than 5,000, and the
ordinary subscription income at a shilling a month cannot have
been worth more than £3,000 a year. The balance, amounting to very
large sums, came from Mosley himself, from wealthy commercial
concerns and private individuals and, possibly, from Mussolini.
Whether Hitler contributed is difficult to prove; certainly nothing
came from Germany in the early days and if anything came in the
immediate pre-war period it was well concealed.

Mosley's own fortune in 1933 has been estimated at £300,000, and
as the last heir to the family entail he was free to use it as he liked.
Cynthia Mosley in her lifetime had a trust income of £28,000 a year
which, on her death, passed not to Mosley but to her three children, of whom her sister, Baroness Ravensdale, became guardian.
Mosley gave generously to the BUF but, having a practical head in
money matters, did not impoverish himself. In *My Answer*, published
in 1946, he declared that up to the war he had spent £100,000 on
the political causes in which he had believed. Assuming that the
lion's share went to the BUF, it would seem that Mosley personally
financed about one-tenth of the Movement's work.

Conclusive evidence about the other British contributors is hard
to obtain. The BUF ran its finances through the BUF Trust, Ltd.,
a private company which never published a balance sheet. Mosley
himself (1961) takes the attitude that contributions were given in
confidence that cannot now be broken. From rumours and reports
that have appeared over the years it is possible to compile a list of
probable contributors, but it would be unfair to publish it. A list
based on rumour could omit some of the most important contributors and include the names of people who gave little or nothing.
Perhaps the most interesting of the rumours is in connection with a
millionaire who, bitten with a momentary enthusiasm for Fascism,
gave £40,000 to the Movement and collected a further £50,000 for it
from his friends. He quickly became disillusioned and regretted his

---

* The salaries would have to be multiplied by three to give their value in 1961
terms.

generosity. He was later created a peer and served as a Conservative minister.

What is clear is that the BUF did get substantial financial backing in its early days and that fear of Communism was a major factor in attracting money to its funds. Apart from the 'big business' donations, which provided the Movement with capital, there was a subsidiary source of revenue from the minor landed gentry who liked Mosley's plans for developing agriculture. There were dozens of subscriptions of around £100 from people of this type; in at least one case a donor continued his twenty-five-guinea subscription to Conservative Central Office while also supporting the BUF.

Mosley exerted his charm and persuasive ability to attract money but he did not appear to regard finance as a matter of overriding importance. He claimed – with justification – that he never planned his policy or tactics with a view to pleasing his subscribers. In 1934 his relaxed attitude and determination to call his own tune lost him a prospective donation of £200,000 from the millionairess Lady Houston.

Lady Houston owned the *Saturday Review* which had given some publicity to the BUF. Her main interest was aviation and she had financed an aircraft to win the world speed record for Britain – the aircraft was later redeveloped as the Spitfire fighter. She was very worried about the danger of aerial attack on Britain in the event of war and she campaigned for a stronger RAF and for air defences, causes also espoused by Rothermere and the BUF. In December 1933 she embarrassed the Government by offering a gift of £200,000 to improve the air defences of London. To her fury the Government procrastinated and three months later she withdrew the offer. She then thought of giving the money to the BUF but at the critical moment *Blackshirt* published a faintly derisive paragraph about her. She sent her editor, Warner Allen, to see Mosley and demand an apology. Mosley treated the matter too lightly for her satisfaction and she decided to keep the £200,000 to herself.*

Within the Movement it was widely assumed, even taken for granted, that subsidies were coming from Mussolini. Forgan admits that in the autumn of 1932 he went as an emissary to Rome where he saw Mussolini and presented him with a copy of *The Greater Britain*. He also solicited Italian interest and financial support, receiving non-committal replies. He did not know whether later emissaries

* *Lucy Houston, D.B.E.* by Warner Allen (1947).

repeated the request for money or whether Mosley – when in Rome the following year – himself made a direct request. At any rate, Forgan states that in the late spring of 1933, and thereafter at irregular intervals, the BUF received parcels of mixed European currencies, each the equivalent of some £5,000. He had no direct knowledge of the source of the parcels but at the time he and other senior officials believed that they came from the Italian Embassy.* The BUF finances certainly fluctuated wildly. Some weeks there would be insufficient money to pay the salaries. At other times the Movement was flush with funds and, until Mosley instituted a strict method of control, some officials were said to be lining their personal nests by drawing excessive sums for expenses. There was even outright peculation, one official of the Organization Department disappearing with £500. This uneven financial picture would appear to harmonize with the idea of parcels of money arriving irregularly.

In Parliament there were several references to foreign subsidies for the BUF. In November 1936, for example, John Simon, Home Secretary, said that Fascist – and Communist – funds were 'supplemented from abroad'. On these and other occasions the Fascists and the Communists issued prompt denials. The most circumstantial Parliamentary statement came just after the war when Chuter Ede was Home Secretary. It is worth quoting in full:

Lt.-Col. Sharp asked the Secretary of State for the Home Department whether he will make a statement on the evidence found in documents captured from the enemy that a foreign government was subsidizing the British Union of Fascists.

MR. EDE: Yes, Sir. Letters from Count Grandi, the Italian Ambassador in London, to Mussolini have been found among the latter's papers. The relevant portion of one such letter, dated 30 January 1934, is as follows: 'Mosley has asked me to express his gratitude to you for sending him the considerable sum which I arranged to hand over to him today. . . . He also spoke with gratitude of the simple generosity with which you accepted as a future commitment his requests for material aid. . . .' The relevant portion of a further letter, dated 1 March 1935, is as follows: 'At the moment you are spending a great deal of money in England. At any rate until a few days ago, you were giving Mosley about 3,500,000 in monthly instalments of about 300,000 lire. All this money, believe me Duce, even on the best supposition simply goes down the drain. At the

---

* Personal statement by Dr. Robert Forgan to the author (1961).

present time we should concentrate our efforts in a different direction. With a tenth of what you give Mosley, that is, with a monthly allowance to the Embassy of 35,000 lire, I feel that I could produce a result ten times better.'

LT.-COL. SHARP: Using the 1935 rates of exchange, can my Right Honourable Friend say what that payment represents in terms of British money?

MR. EDE: On 1st March 1935 the rate of exchange was $56\frac{9}{16}$ to 57 lire to the pound. At this rate, 3,500,000 lire is equivalent to £60,403.

MR. H. HYND: May I ask what action the Home Secretary proposes to take in view of this startling exposure?

MR. EDE: Unfortunately, it was not illegal for Sir Oswald Mosley to receive this sum of money. I can only hope that this will be an instructive foreword to the book he proposes to publish.

MR. WARBEY: Would my Right Honourable Friend say, humorous as this subject appears to be to some honourable Members, that there is evidence here of traitorous activities?

MR. WILSON HARRIS: Does the Right Honourable Gentleman know of any other sums of money being paid by other foreign Governments to any other parties in this country?

MR. EDE: No, Sir. If I come across anything like that – and I am not compelled to disclose the source of my information in certain cases – I will certainly acquaint the House. . . .

Chuter Ede's statement would appear to fit other known facts.

Towards the end of 1935 the BUF ran into serious financial difficulty. The first thing to go was the Black House, of which Mosley sold the lease to make way for a block of flats. In mid-1936 there were Draconic cuts in staff, the number of headquarters employees being reduced from 143 to thirty. The explanation could be that Mussolini acted on Grandi's advice in 1935 and cut off the £60,000-a-year subsidy.

Mosley claimed that the Grandi correspondence was a forgery and challenged Ede to repeat the statement in public, outside the protection of Parliamentary Privilege. Ede did not accept the challenge.

The difficulty with the forgery theory is that if the British Government or anybody else had wished to discredit Mosley they would surely have 'found' in the captured German and Italian archives evidence more detailed and more circumstantial than that of the Grandi correspondence. More convincing is the claim by Mosley that the financial crisis of 1935–36 can easily be explained in terms other than the cessation of a subsidy from Mussolini. By then Mosley was campaigning against the Jews, which certainly lost him subscribers. In any case, the 1931 crisis had faded into the past and businessmen were less eager to finance Mosley as a bulwark against Communism. They might have thought, too, that Mosley was proving a not particularly strong bulwark.

The full story of BUF finance will probably never be known. Mosley was the only man to know all the facts and he is unlikely ever to divulge them. Since he is the best witness and since he regards the charges that he received money from abroad as a serious insult, it is fair to give him the last word, which comes from *My Answer* (1946):

The extraordinary results of our movement were achieved by the self-dedication and financial sacrifices of thousands of ordinary British people who carried on the work, and maintained the finances, of British Union's network of branches, which covered the country on an entirely self-supporting basis. Our headquarters, also, was financed by the sacrifices of individuals and, in this connection I have before me a Chartered Accountant's certificate, concerning the origin of our funds for a considerable period before the war, which shews each subscriber to be British. . . . This certificate can be shewn to any Chartered Accountant whom anyone cares to pay to examine it under professional pledges not to reveal the names of the subscribers, or any detail beyond ascertaining that they were British.

CHAPTER 7

'Hurrah for the Blackshirts!'

FOR the first time since the Chartist riots almost a century earlier, the first half of 1934 saw a possibility of fast, revolutionary changes in the British Constitution and social system. The activists of the left, disillusioned by the 1929–31 failure, were rallying to the Socialist League under Stafford Cripps, which, on the election of a Labour majority in the Commons, proposed to abrogate the ordinary legislative processes in favour of socialization by decree. Even Attlee thought that such a process might become necessary. For a moment it looked as if Cripps and Mosley were the rival candidates for a dictatorship which must surely come. In personality the two men had some characteristics in common. They were both Wykehamists who had come to the working-class movement from outside. They both had an inner, unshakable conviction of their own rectitude. Both were first-class orators who adopted theatrical methods at their mass rallies.

At Westminster the MacDonald National Government was in deep trouble. Its vast Parliamentary majority had owed more to a momentary wave of panic than to any deep-seated popularity, and subsequently it had failed to win general confidence. Lloyd George and Churchill were both out of office and used their powers against the administration, Churchill leading seventy Conservative MPs against the Government's proposals for granting partial self-government for India. By-election results foreshadowed a possible defeat of the National Government in the next general election. The Labour Party being in the hands of what were considered left-wing extremists, the prospect, in Conservative eyes, was most alarming.

Might not Fascism prove a safer alternative than Labour? On the left there had been disillusionment with the Labour Party's record between 1929 and 1931, disillusionment which expressed itself mainly in a drift towards Communism but in some cases made former Labour supporters speculate on the possibility that Mosley might offer a more reliable road to social reform.

The mood of the moment was epitomized in 1934 by the astonishing sales of a memoir by Lord Lytton of his MP son Antony, Viscount Knebworth, who died in an air crash at the age of twenty-nine. There were popular editions at sixpence and readers appeared most attracted by quotations from the young politician's diaries. One written by Knebworth on entering Parliament in 1931 ran: 'The world appears to be shaking off the yoke of democracy . . . the hour is so ripe everywhere for a man, and a drive and a policy. I hope the great National Government is the last of the ancient regime.'

On the Continent the hour indeed appeared ripe. Hitler, at the end of his first year of office, had achieved absolute mastery of Germany. In February 1934 Dollfuss subdued a powerful and historic Social Democrat movement and set up a neo-Fascist regime in Austria. In the Balkans, Poland, Hungary, Rumania, Bulgaria and Portugal there were autocratic, neo-Fascist rulers. In the Netherlands, Belgium, France and Spain there were strong Fascist movements; even the Irish Free State had its Blueshirts under General O'Duffy. Across the Atlantic Roosevelt's New Deal was controlling the United States' economy with neo-Fascist methods of energetic government direction of a private-enterprise economy. Mosley watched Roosevelt with special interest, seeing the New Deal as the American equivalent of the 'modern movement' but doubting whether it would succeed in a democratic context and without the support of a disciplined Fascist Party.

In this context the prospects for Fascism in Britain looked bright at the start of 1934. There persisted a bitter hatred of Mosley on the extreme left, but elsewhere there was a wide disposition to look at Fascism, at least to see what it had to offer. Moreover, in January 1934 the BUF acquired a very influential new supporter, the Press magnate Lord Rothermere, a man who delighted in running newspaper campaigns and who, for six months, believed that Mosley had emerged at a moment when the hour was indeed ripe for a man, and a drive and a policy.

Rothermere opened his campaign on 8th January with a leader-page article in the *Daily Mail* from his own pen. Headlined 'Hurrah for the Blackshirts!' it claimed that Mosley's aim was to bring Britain 'up to date'. Italy and Germany were 'beyond all doubt the best-governed nations in Europe today'. Mosley could do the same for Britain, replacing the 'inertia and indecision' of the National Government.

'At this next, vital election,' wrote Rothermere, 'Britain's survival as a Great Power will depend on the existence of a well-organized Party of the Right, ready to take over responsibility for national affairs with the same directness of purpose and energy of method as Mussolini and Hitler have displayed.'

The article concluded with a list of addresses at which readers could enrol in the BUF. Alongside it ran a leading article which went to the heart of the matter. 'Above all,' it proclaimed, 'they [the BUF] offer the British people an alternative at the next general election to rule by Sir Stafford Cripps.'

The idea of an alternative to Sir Stafford Cripps seems to have obsessed Rothermere. His political perception was never particularly deep and his articles at the time displayed an almost hysterical fear of Red Revolution. His aim seems to have been to tame Mosley into co-operating with the Conservatives. Whether he can even have read *The Greater Britain* or the current BUF publications appears doubtful. In the *Daily Mail* the references were to the 'Blackshirt Movement', rarely to the Fascists; the words 'corporate state' appeared only in reports of Mosley's speeches and then deep down in the text.

Daily Mail support took the form of generous space on the news pages for reports of Fascist meetings, free 'puffs' for announcements of forthcoming BUF events, and occasional leading articles and feature articles extolling the BUF. When Mosley addressed a big meeting the report would occupy either the lead or second-lead position on the principal news page, complete with pictures, and continue for two or three columns on a subsidiary news page. The Rothermere Sunday papers, the *Sunday Pictorial* and the *Sunday Dispatch*, carried feature articles which were usually reproduced in the following morning's *Daily Mail*. The *Pictorial* carried a double-page 'spread' of pictures on activities at the Black House. The *Evening News* had a competition in which readers were invited to send post-cards giving reasons 'Why I like the Blackshirts' with free tickets for the BUF Albert Hall rally of April 1934 as prizes for the 250 best entries.

Many of Rothermere's employees disliked the new policy. Geoffrey Swaffer, for example, resigned his post as a senior editorial executive on the *Evening News*, declaring that he would not work for a Fascist paper. G. Ward Price, the *Daily Mail* star reporter, was, on the other hand, keenly attracted to Mosley and acted as the main intermediary between Rothermere and the BUF. Describing a rally attended by 8,000 people at the Bingley Hall, Birmingham, Price wrote: 'The aisles were lined with sturdy and efficient Blackshirt stewards – lithe, athletic, vigorous young men in the prime of manhood. In their simple, close-fitting modern uniform, standing rigidly to attention, they were themselves a visible expression of the businesslike but straightforward spirit which marks this up-to-date movement.'

Randolph Churchill, then working for the *Daily Mail*, struck a more detached note which contrasted sharply with Ward Price's enthusiasm. Churchill would praise Mosley's skill as a speaker but not Mosley's policy. Covering a meeting at York, he wrote:

> There is no doubt that Sir Oswald Mosley is today the most accomplished speaker in the country. His eloquence has often been compared to that of the leaders of Fascism in other countries. Personally I find him more attractive than any of them. He does not thunder like Mussolini. He has most in common with Dr. Goebbels. Both possess a voice with a real ring of conviction which carries a thrill to the audience.

The BUF at Oxford University had, in fact, attempted to avenge the defeat Randolph Churchill suffered in debate with the erstwhile New Party member C. E. M. Joad on the famous King and Country motion. Members of the University Fascist Association stalked into the Union and tore the offending record from the minute book. It was one of William Joyce's duties to organize Fascist groups at the universities; he kindled a certain amount of interest, especially at Oxford and Cambridge, but the groups had a fitful existence, bursts of activity being followed by long periods of abeyance.

In the fortnight following Rothermere's first article, the *Daily Mail* printed twenty-six readers' letters on Fascism, all of them in favour of it. The new editorial policy seems, however, to have aroused disquiet among some readers. At any rate Rothermere's next article was defensive in tone. Headlined 'Give the Blackshirts a Helping Hand', it appeared in the *Sunday Pictorial* of 21st January and the *Daily Mail* of 22nd January. Rothermere said that the Blackshirts had been subjected to 'hysterical abuse and misrepresentation'. He denied that Hitler was running 'a reign of terror in Germany'. It was time for the young men to take over in Britain, the 'elderly statesmen' having outlived their usefulness. He denied that the Blackshirts would be unconstitutional. '. . . Nor is there the slightest ground for supposing that the Blackshirts are, or ever will be, antagonistic to the Jews, the Trade Unions or the Freemasons'.

The Rothermere campaign helped to swell the flood of recruits now pouring in. There was much publicity for the thirty-three-year-old Earl of Erroll, Lord High Constable of Scotland, who was appointed BUF 'delegate' for Kenya but not afterwards heard of in the Movement. Another Scottish aristocrat, the Hon. H. M. Upton, was a prominent member at Motherwell. Carlyon Bellairs, a former Conservative MP, came in as an active speaker and writer. At least two Conservative members of local authorities came in – Gordon Kitchen at Liverpool and T. W. Mainwaring Hughes at Swansea. Kitchen wore his black shirt in the council chamber. Mary Richardson, who had served a total of three years in prison for suffragette activities, came in to organize the Women's Section. The aviation pioneer Sir Alliot Verdon-Roe joined in Hampshire. On a humbler level there was a staff of ten at Black House working full time at signing on new members and fitting them with shirts. The great majority of the newcomers had slight conception of what Fascism entailed and very few became permanent members. They did, however, help to provide an audience for the first of the big BUF rallies, which was held at the Albert Hall under Risdon's direction on 22nd April 1934.

The party rally was a vital part of Fascist technique, brought to the highest pitch of efficiency by Hitler. 'Mass demonstrations,' he wrote in *Mein Kampf*, 'must burn into the little man's soul the proud conviction that, though a little worm, he is nevertheless part of a great dragon.' The semi-mystical Fascist doctrine of the Leader as the embodiment of the people's will required an emotional communion between the Leader on the platform and the followers on the floor.

By nature Mosley is not a demagogue. His speeches tend to contain a stiff content of reasoned argument, demanding attention from the mind rather than surrender of the will. His style of the mid-1930's does, however, show signs of a studied attempt to add to his natural power of persuading an audience the added, Hitlerian, power of hypnotizing it. Couched in dramatic language, flying always to verbal extremes, he backed his speeches with theatrical methods of presentation, and exerted every resource of his willpower and capacity for leadership to put them across to his audience. The whole, perhaps, had a whiff of the midnight oil, but this was more discernible in the printed reports than in the speeches when these were delivered.

This speaking technique was not fully developed at the time of the first Albert Hall rally, but the Fascist pageantry was already mature. The great silver fasces hung over the organ. While waiting for the meeting to begin the audience sang the BUF songs, 'Britain Awake!' and 'Mosley'. Punctually at eight o'clock there was a fanfare of trumpets. Through the door in double file came a procession of Blackshirts carrying Union Jacks and Fascist standards. They marched through the hall and positioned themselves round the rostrum. Then, after an electrically tense pause, Mosley appeared – alone. From head to foot he was in black, the only relief being a silver fasces shining in the buckle of his belt. The 10,000 audience stood up, many of them raising their right arm in the Roman salute. Through a tunnel of arms Mosley limped across the length of the hall to the rostrum; his chin was high and his face, deathly pale, wore a relaxed, confident expression.

He spoke for an hour and forty minutes, outlining the basis of the BUF creed.

'The present system, not only by its whole structure and methods, makes action impossible; more than that, it produces a type of man to whom action and decision are impossible even if he had the power,' he said. 'We seek to establish a new ideal of public service and a new system of authority which rests on merit.'

At the end almost the whole audience rose to its feet, cheering and saluting. Above the noise the Blackshirts chanted over and over again in deep unison: 'M-O-S-L-E-Y – Mosley! We want Mosley! We want Mosley!'

Ward Price, too, was enthusiastic. The *Daily Mail* led its main news page with his account which began:

Mosley proved himself last night the paramount political personality in Britain. At his great meeting in the Albert Hall the Blackshirt movement was caught up on such a wave of deep-seated emotion as must sweep it on to victory. . . . If he can win so completely the support of such an audience as faced him last night, he can win the country.'

The detailed report of the speech filled an entire page.

A leader-page article the next day by Thomas Moore, Conservative MP for Ayr, gave a more political appreciation. It was headlined

'The Blackshirts Have What the Conservatives Need' and started
with a description of what the Blackshirts looked like:

> What is there [asked Moore] in a black shirt that gives
> apparent dignity and intelligence to its wearer? For certainly
> some inward feeling, or it may be the outward covering, does
> give an air of self-respect and assurance to all these young
> people. The men were fine examples of a healthy and intelligent
> mind in a healthy and well-made body; the girls, straight-eyed,
> vivacious and comely, well matched their male comrades.

Getting down to politics, Moore claimed that Fascist ideals were
'largely derived from the Conservative Party'. There could not be
any fundamental difference of outlook between 'the Blackshirts and
their parents, the Conservatives'. The difference was the Blackshirt
will to action.

Others on the Conservative right took a directly opposite view.
Winston Churchill – in spite of India – refused to have anything to
do with Mosley. Beaverbrook, who had worked with Rothermere
three years earlier in the attempt to form a United Empire Party,
not only refused to co-operate with Mosley but also permitted the
left-wing members of his staff to publish bitter, anti-Fascist attacks.

Thomas Moore had slight reward for his praise of the Blackshirts.
A BUF contingent under Joyce packed an Empire Union meeting at
the Caxton Hall with the result that Moore and Admiral Taylor,
Conservative MP for South Paddington, found themselves the only
dissentients against a pro-Fascist resolution.

Robert Forgan had by this time relinquished the post of Director
of Organization of the BUF to F. M. Box, a former Conservative
agent who had worked for the New Party. Box was criticized within
the Movement for having a narrow, bureaucratic approach, but he
did succeed in averting the administrative chaos which threatened
almost daily with the inflow of hundreds of new members and the
outflow of a number almost as great. Forgan, with the new title of
Deputy Leader, concentrated on trying to infiltrate what today
would be called the 'establishment'. His aim was to make Fascism
respectable and familiar in a wide influential circle. A series of private
dinner parties led, in December 1933, to the decision to form a club
for 'intellectuals' which would have as its object 'to inquire upon
modern methods of Government'. The qualification for membership was to be interest in, rather than support for, Fascism, and it was

given the neutral title of the January Club, the first meeting being held in January 1934. Two non-Fascists, Sir John C. Squire and Captain H. W. Luttman-Johnson, became chairman and secretary but it was definitely a 'front' organization, controlled by Forgan. Since Forgan was himself becoming lukewarm to the BUF he probably found the atmosphere of the January Club congenial.

The January Club lasted about two years, its main activity being a monthly dinner at which Mosley, Forgan, Joyce or a non-Fascist speaker would make a speech and answer questions. On one occasion there was a debate between Joyce and a Jewish MP, H. L. Nathan, who had just left the Liberals to join Labour. There were catcalls when Nathan criticized Hitler. Another Labour speaker was Geoffrey de Freitas, President of the Cambridge Union. At its zenith the January Club attracted an attendance of 200 more or less influential people including Lord Rothermere, Lord Lloyd, the Spanish Ambassador, Lord Iddesleigh, Professor Rushbrook Williams and others whose names were not given in the official reports. Sir Charles Petrie who spoke at the May 1934 meeting recorded his impressions sixteen years later in his autobiography:

. . . Not the least important result of the reaction against Baldwinism was a remarkable, if temporary, upsurging of Fascism [wrote Petrie]. It is true that very few people of note actually joined Sir Oswald Mosley, but a considerable number were sympathetically inclined towards him, as the membership of the January Club proved. They were not enamoured of Fascism as such, but they were so weary of the drabness of the Baldwin regime that they were prepared to embrace almost any alternative. Whether, had Mosley succeeded, they would have liked what they would then have got is another matter. . . . Mosley failed because of his methods, not because of his ends. His continued flirtation with Hitler and Mussolini caused his movement to be regarded as something not far removed from a foreign conspiracy: had he put his followers into blue pullovers instead of black shirts much would have been forgiven him. Then, again, there was grave distrust among the more sober-minded of the implications of his anti-Semitic policy. . . . Finally, when war came Fascism was felt to be unpatriotic, and that sealed its fate. All this, however, cannot blind us to the fact that at one moment it was a very considerable force indeed.

The anti-Semitism mentioned by Petrie was not an official part of BUF policy in the first half of 1934. Jews, however, were already refused membership and the few Jews who had joined in the early days, including 'Kid' Lewis, had been frozen out. In practice many of the most active Blackshirts were anti-Semitic, including most of the recruits from the British Fascists and the Imperial Fascist League. Francis-Hawkins, Joyce, Chesterton, Raven Thomson and others close to Mosley were, in varying degrees, inclined to lay at least a share of the blame for the world's troubles on 'international Jewry'.

The drift towards anti-Semitism worried the *Daily Mail*. Rothermere, it was rumoured, warned Mosley that an anti-Semitic policy acted like a pair of blinkers; once a politician had donned it he could see nothing but Jews. A *Daily Mail* leading article of June 1934 referred to the 'utterly baseless fiction that the Blackshirt movement is anti-Jewish'. It continued: 'Had they any such purpose, they would not be receiving the support of the *Daily Mail*.' As described in the next chapter, anti-Semitism was a principal cause of the breach between Mosley and Rothermere.

Anti-Semitism had no part in official Fascist propaganda which was slanted violently towards a jingoistic patriotism calculated, perhaps, to have a special appeal to the *Daily Mail* and its readers. The BUF plastered the country with posters carrying the slogan 'For King and Empire' and a picture of Mosley standing before the Union Jack. The Movement's badge changed from a simple fasces to a fasces with a Union Jack background. Chesterton's articles in *Fascist Week* carried a fervent message of loyalty to the Crown and defence of the British Empire. There was a note of deep respect for King George V. For the Prince of Wales there was high adulation with the implication that one day he would prove the ideal monarch for a Fascist Britain. Some Fascist branches used 'Land of Hope and Glory' as their official anthem but this was, surprisingly, banned by National Headquarters on the ground that the song represented an outdated and over-sentimental form of imperialism.

At the same time Mosley was at pains to keep his movement distinct from Conservatism. The former ILP-er, W. J. Leaper, wrote blazing attacks on monopoly capitalism in *Fascist Week*, of which he was Assistant Editor. 'You will,' he announced on the front page,

see the Tory monument on the banks of the Clyde, on Tyneside, in derelict Lancashire, in the Midlands, in the vast agricultural communities now stirring in revolt. These are the fruits of Toryism, and if this is the measure of their efficiency, then the sooner Britain is rid of them for ever, the better for Britain. . . . Let us get this clear once and for all. Oswald Mosley has no intention of winning elections for the Tory Party.

Over the London County Council elections of the spring of 1934, when Labour won control, there was a divergence between the *Daily Mail* and *Fascist Week*. Throughout the campaign the *Daily Mail* campaigned violently against Labour and, on polling day, had a leading article pleading for every anti-Socialist to vote. *Fascist Week* hardly mentioned the election and dismissed the result with the remark: 'At least the Socialists may actually accomplish something.'

That the BUF was capable of attracting recruits from the left was shown by the arrival in March 1934 of John Beckett, the former Labour MP for Peckham, who at once became a full-time official. Beckett, a tall, red-faced, handsome man, with a tendency to lose his temper, was among the most interesting figures who attached themselves to Mosley. His career inside and outside politics has been marked by a combination of recklessness and an intelligent instinct for self-preservation. Over a somewhat arrogant belief in his own abilities lies a jovial charm and a boyish delight in elaborating an anecdote. His native ability might have carried him to a leading place in the Labour Movement, but, like Mosley, he was a casualty of the 1929–31 Parliament. Born in the same year as Mosley, he started life as a shop assistant and served with the King's Shropshire Light Infantry in the First World War. Invalided out in 1917, he contacted Ramsay MacDonald and other ILP leaders, forming with their support the National Union of Ex-Servicemen, a left-wing predecessor of the British Legion. It was refused affiliation to the Labour Party and, on the formation of the British Legion in 1921, dissolved after a referendum of its members. Beckett qualified as a Labour agent and went to work with Attlee, then MP for Limehouse. The Becketts and the Attlees shared a house and formed the nucleus of an ILP ginger group which also included Fenner Brockway and Clifford Allen, who ended as a peer and a supporter of the Mac-Donald National Labour Party. Beckett left Attlee in 1923 to fight unsuccessfully as Labour candidate for North Newcastle. At the following election he won Gateshead and, with a move to Peckham in 1929, remained in Parliament until 1931.

During the 1929–31 Parliament Beckett acted as whip for the rebel

ILP group but had little contact with Mosley. He attracted news-paper publicity with a sensational Gretna Green marriage to the widow of the actor-manager Arthur Bourchier just three days after his divorce from his first wife became absolute. Even more publicity came with the adventure which was to label him for the rest of his life 'the man who stole the mace'. It happened in the summer of 1930. Fenner Brockway, wishing to make a dramatic demonstration to Indian opinion, courted suspension by persistently questioning the Government about political prisoners in Indian gaols. He disobeyed the Speaker's order to resume his seat and the motion was moved for his suspension. Beckett and W. J. Brown were the ILP tellers in the ensuing division. When the Government whip read the voting figures Beckett, standing in the tellers' place before the clerks' table, exclaimed: 'It's a damned shame, Mr. Speaker!' He seized the mace and, as *Hansard* put it, 'proceeded to carry it out of the Chamber'. At the door the Serjeant-at-Arms and five MPs intervened and, after a slight tussle, Beckett surrendered the mace. He afterwards joked: 'I would have left it in the cloakroom.' He was apparently irked that whereas the Conservatives tended to treat the episode as a joke the Labour MPs took it seriously and told Beckett he had lowered the dignity of the Party.

Beckett fought the 1931 election as Independent Labour, forcing to the bottom of the poll the official Labour candidate who inter-vened against him but losing his seat to the Conservatives. He then retired from politics into the management of the Strand Theatre. His conversion to Fascism came from independent study of Musso-lini's system in Italy, but William Joyce, too, was an influence. Shortly before joining the BUF Beckett went to a Fascist meeting at Padding-ton Baths where Joyce substituted for Mosley as the principal speaker. Beckett at once decided that 'Here was one of the dozen finest orators in the country. Snowden's close reasoning and unerring instinct for words were allied to Maxton's humour and Churchill's daring. . . . After that meeting I joined the British Union of Fascists.'*

Within the BUF Beckett and Joyce became close friends and collaborators. Beckett threw himself into his new career with gigantic enthusiasm, addressing 100 meetings in his first six months, leading his stewards in two-fisted battles against violent opposition. He ventured even to his old constituency where he met a roar of

---

* *National Socialism Now* by William Joyce, introduced by John Beckett (1937).

'Traitor Beckett!' To a violent, emotional method of self-expression he added a rough humour. In his first statement on joining the BUF he explained: 'During my life I have roamed a good deal. I have lived in Limehouse and Mayfair, have known intimately dockers and big-business men, Boers, Indians, Australians and English Tommies, all sorts and conditions. In the Parliamentary Labour Party I discovered a new low level.'

He had a mature Fascist attitude. In the same statement he said: 'Fifteen years in the working-class movement have taught me that the workmen want security. They do not want to govern. . . . Manliness, courage, thought and discipline are weapons with which security, peace and comfort can be obtained.'

Beckett was especially useful for carrying the message to the provinces. The Movement's winter campaign of 1933–34 had been interrupted for three months while Mosley was incapacitated with phlebitis; he was able to continue his administrative work at Headquarters but could not travel to meetings. Joyce deputized for Mosley on a number of occasions, including a big rally at Liverpool, but had too many engagements of his own to carry out Mosley's full programme. At the time Chesterton was confined mainly to the Midlands while Raven Thomson was still little known in the Movement. A Streatham schoolmaster, Leonard Gueroult, was temporarily among the most active speakers, travelling widely in the south and Midlands, but he never held an official position higher than that of Area Administrative Organizer for South London, and by 1935 apparently became disillusioned and dropped out.

The policy in the provinces was always to present a show of strength. For a first meeting in new territory the speaker would arrive with a coachload of Blackshirts who, often accompanied by a band, would march through the streets to advertise the meeting. Afterwards there would be another march, with new recruits encouraged to fall in behind. A full-time official from National Headquarters would stay in the town for three or four weeks, instruct the new recruits and organize them into a branch. The aim was then to find a local leader capable of taking over as Branch Officer. The outstanding practitioner in the inauguration of branches was 'Tommy' Moran, ex-miner and a former cruiserweight boxing champion of the Royal Navy, who resigned a local Labour Party secretaryship to join the BUF in July 1933. Moran was variously at Merthyr, Swansea, Newcastle, Manchester, Northampton, Birmingham and London. He had a reputation for toughness and courage;

legendary in the Movement was a story of how he tackled single-handed twenty Communists and knocked them all out. He married an intelligent, ambitious wife and himself had ambitions to be an intellectual rather than a strong-arm man.

The arrival of Blackshirts in a town generally caused a stir which on many occasions turned to violence. Nervous Chief Constables attempted to ban the marches but the Fascists protested vigorously that they had the right to free speech and free assembly and claimed that the 'Government' was trying to suppress them. One of the biggest upsets was at Bristol on 29th March 1934. Mosley was involved himself and the post mortem eventually reached the floor of the House of Commons. At the request of the police the Blackshirts assembled inside the Colston Hall where the meeting was being held instead of marching there. While Mosley was speaking an angry crowd gathered outside. This was the kind of challenge the Fascists delighted to accept and at the end of the meeting Mosley decided to march his men through the town. Violent scuffles broke out and the situation turned to near riot. Answering questions by Bristol Members of Parliament, Sir John Gilmour, the Home Secretary, complained that Mosley with his semi-military evolutions had provoked the trouble. Mosley indignantly replied: 'Two Negroes attempted to attack me and were knocked down by Fascists. One of these men carried and raised a knife in his hand. If it is provocative to defend ourselves from being knifed by Negroes in the streets of an English city, we must plead guilty to that charge.' He affirmed the Fascists' undoubted right to demonstrate in public and thus began the campaign by anti-Fascists for a change in the law which eventually produced the 1936 Public Order Act.* A Home Office official, in a letter to Mosley, said the Bristol police had observed nobody with a knife although they had seen 'a very excitable half-caste Communist'.

Beckett was involved in disorder at Newcastle where, for some time, the weekly Fascist open-air meeting at Cowan's Monument had turned into a weekly riot as Blackshirt stewards attempted to silence the hecklers, who arrived ready for battle, often armed. The police decided that the Fascist uniforms were to blame and on his arrival in the city Beckett agreed to try the experiment of speaking at Cowan's Monument in plain clothes and without uniformed stewards. Beckett failed to get a hearing and a free fight developed as Piercy and a group of plain-clothed Fascists tried to prevent the

* See Chapter 10.

opposition rushing the platform. Police closed the meeting and the Fascists returned to their headquarters, occasionally sallying out to fight the anti-Fascists jeering outside. A full-scale street-battle developed when about twenty Blackshirts came out to avenge, they said, a stone thrown at a Fascist girl. Two Fascists were arrested and convicted for assaulting plain-clothed policemen.

The BUF was also conducting an energetic campaign in the countryside. The *Greater Britain* policy of providing a fair price and a market for everything the British farmer could produce was an ideal propaganda point. In addition the Fascists cherished the hope, common in new political movements, that if only they could pierce the farmworkers' stubborn regard for tradition they could, without difficulty, win the countryside from the Conservatives. Accordingly the BUF muscled into the 'tithe war' in which the farmers, suffering desperately from failure to sell their crops, were refusing to pay tithes and were having their machinery distrained by orders of the county courts. Mosley, declaring that he opposed not the principle of State support for the Church of England but only the method of providing support through tithes, sent his men to the countryside with instructions to obstruct the county-court bailiffs. The main activity was in East Anglia. Richard Plathen, a tall Scot with the rank of National Political Officer, ran the operation, showing ingenuity in designing obstacles and ditches to prevent the bailiffs executing their warrants. Whether or not the Fascists were breaking the law was a moot point until nineteen Blackshirts, headed by Plathen, were arrested in Suffolk and eventually pleaded guilty to the unusual charge that they had 'conducted themselves as an apparently organized force so as to cause alarm to His Majesty's subjects; to cause a public mischief by diverting the constables of the East Suffolk force from all ordinary duties; and by their action inciting to the commission of crime and a breach of the peace'. The Attorney General prosecuted and Sir Patrick Hastings appeared for the defence. Mr. Justice Hawke bound over all the defendants to keep the peace and Mosley called off the campaign.

Addresses of the defendants given in court showed six as living at Black House, two as living at the BUF Bayswater headquarters at Pembridge Villas, three as coming from other parts of London and the remainder from various parts of East Anglia.

By the summer of 1934 the BUF had over a hundred branches. Their main strength was still in London but they also had strong-points in Manchester, Liverpool and Stoke. The *Daily Mail* list of offices where recruits could join gave addresses at Manchester, Liverpool, Birmingham, Leeds, Bristol, Edinburgh, Newcastle, Plymouth, Southampton, Cardiff, Worthing and Durham.

The most difficult area was Scotland where, throughout its existence, the BUF found it impossible to make headway. The Movement's activities tended to degenerate into squabbles with Scottish Nationalists and with a pocket-sized Scottish Fascist Democratic Party founded by William Weir Gilmour who had been New Party candidate for Coatbridge in 1931. Glasgow had been one of the strongest New Party areas but support for the BUF was almost nil. A man called Angus Baxter did try to run a Glasgow movement but aroused violent opposition, the ILP and the Communists chalking on pavements the slogan 'Keep Baxter off the streets'. Both Baxter and the daubings faded away and Glasgow was the only major British city unvisited by Mosley between 1932 and 1940. The position was slightly more encouraging for the BUF in Edinburgh which Mosley visited for the first time in June 1934, receiving a rough welcome. Crowds surged round the Fascist motor coaches, hurling stones at the windows. Plathen remained behind as Scottish Organizer and formed a tiny branch which persisted on a small scale until the war. The real centre of Scottish Fascism was Aberdeen, where W. E. A. Chambers-Hunter, a former planter from Ceylon who had lost an arm in the war, ran a keen, lively group.

In England, however, the Movement had attracted a core of enthusiastic supporters who believed that the day of Fascism was about to dawn. Fascism was the bright novelty which was to solve every problem. The mood was one of high purpose and dedication. As Chesterton wrote at that time in *Blackshirt*:

Fascism tolerates no whining about 'rights'. The highest privilege it grants is the renunciation of 'rights'. All but the right to serve, to suffer, to sacrifice. . . . Those who serve Fascism must lay aside creature comforts and security. . . . Civilization in its crisis calls for decisions in black and white. . . . Victory shall come to us because, by ruthless discipline, we have surrendered these pernicious pleasures and surrendered our ego utterly to the cause we serve.

CHAPTER 8

Olympia and the Jews

D ELIGHTED with the success of their Albert Hall rally of March 1934, the Fascists decided to repeat it on an even bigger scale. Fascist oratory and Fascist pageantry should appear in the heart of London on the scale of the largest political meetings ever held by any party. They booked Olympia for 7th June and confidently advertised 13,000 seats for sale through theatre agencies at prices between one shilling and seven shillings and sixpence. 'Do not delay your application or it may be too late,' fussed the *Daily Mail* on 15th May. A further 2,000 seats were to be free. The rally was intended to mark an important step in the inexorable stride of the BUF to power and, in addition, would yield a cash profit for the Movement's funds.

Anti-Fascists, too, were impressed. London Trades Council had already called conferences to seek ways of stopping Fascism but the BUF was still advancing. If Mosley could get away with Olympia, could he not get away with anything? With the *Daily Worker* agitating urgently on the sidelines, trade-union, Labour Party, ILP and Communist branches planned to attend Olympia in force in a counter-demonstration, to show that the forces of the left were stronger than those of Mosley.

Tension mounted on both sides as the day of the rally approached. Mosley's audience at Olympia was to be strong, not only in numbers but also in influence, including MPs, peers, diplomats, big-business men and leading journalists, who were regarding the rally as their opportunity to assess Fascist strength. It would be a shattering blow to Fascist prestige if the anti-Fascists managed to seize the limelight. The Blackshirts, admirers of Hitler's storm troopers, were in any case eager to prove that they could be as efficient as the Germans in smashing left-wing opposition and, eager but tense, prepared for battle.

The result was not only one of the biggest indoor political meetings ever held in Britain but also the bloodiest. In a spotlight of glaring publicity the Blackshirts demonstrated their ability to smash opposition. But at the same time the BUF earned a reputation for brutality which, rightly or wrongly, was to prove indelible. There was a full-dress debate in the House of Commons, widespread newspaper comment and a special programme on the BBC.

A comparison of Fascist and anti-Fascist accounts of the meeting shows a surprising amount of agreement on the main facts, although the details of allegations against particular Blackshirt stewards remain neither proved nor disproved. Each side accused the other of using weapons – the anti-Fascists were said to have razors and coshes, the Blackshirts to have knuckledusters, rubber truncheons and, in one case, a walking stick. Mosley afterwards mounted an exhibition of the weapons he claimed his Blackshirts had confiscated from the 'Reds'. It seems clear, however, that the greater part of the fighting was with bare fists and that on neither side were weapons used to a significant extent.

On the night of the meeting the anti-Fascists, numbering about 10,000, marched to Olympia and formed a surging crowd around the hall, jeering at the ticket holders as they made their way inside. Dundas had earlier written to the police asking for permission for the Blackshirts to keep order outside as well as inside the hall. Had the permission been granted it is hard to see how the situation could have developed into anything less than a serious street riot. As it was a force of 760 foot and mounted police had difficulty in keeping the crowd in order, and during the evening some fifty people were arrested for obstruction or assaults on the police. In the entrances to the hall there were long queues as Blackshirts scrutinized tickets (some were forged) and 'frisked' many of the holders for weapons. Eventually, an hour after the advertised time, the lights went down inside the hall and Mosley, preceded by a procession of banners, limped to the rostrum; tall, black, intimidating in the glare of powerful spotlights.

His voice reinforced by a battery of twenty-four loudspeakers, Mosley started with his usual warning that he intended to have an orderly meeting – a warning which in the circumstances some took as a challenge. Interruptions began immediately and the prepared Fascist drill swung into operation. At each catcall Mosley stopped speaking and the spotlights swivelled from the platform to focus on the interrupter. The massed Blackshirts led the pro-Fascist section of the audience in a rhythmic roar of 'Mosley! Mosley! We want Mosley!' While this was going on a group of ten or a dozen Black-shirts pounced on the interrupter and, generally with punches, carried him out of the hall and threw him into the street.

For two hours Mosley spoke scarcely fifty words at a time, again and again falling silent while the ejection procedure was repeated. In some cases the anti-Fascists fought back and, as the evening wore on, both sides became very angry. The worst assaults took place on stairways and in corridors out of sight of the audience, where the 'Pansies' were on duty; the activity of the 'Pansies' in beating up people who had already been ejected from the hall caused some resentment among the Blackshirts inside who felt that the 'Pansies' were shirking the real fight. Rooms prepared in advance as dressing stations soon filled with a procession of bleeding and bruised Black-shirts. One Blackshirt girl, it was said, had a razor cut running across her cheek, neck and back. A few anti-Fascists were treated for injury inside the building but most were cared for outside. Doctors used cars as dressing stations. The injuries were mainly cuts, bruises, broken teeth and broken noses. The worst casualty was a student from Sheffield University who spent nine days in hospital with head wounds and concussion. That there was danger of much more serious consequences was proved when two anti-Fascists carrying pamphlets escaped from the Blackshirts by climbing from the balcony to the high girders supporting the roof. Francis-Hawkins led four Blackshirts after them and the audience had a view illumi-nated by spotlights of men fighting in a position where a fall would probably have been fatal. Francis-Hawkins managed to chase his opponents off the girder and they were seized by other Blackshirts and ejected.

In the audience was Giles Romilly, nephew of Winston Churchill, who as a schoolboy had supported the New Party. With his brother Esmond he was now running a left-wing 'revolt' of public school-boys. Their book *Out of Bounds* (1934) includes an account of Giles's reactions:

One of the things which most disgusted me [wrote Romilly] was the attitude of certain sections of the audience. Coming in

evening dress and Rolls-Royce cars, they gave every sign of
enjoying the spectacle of the brutal ejection of the interrupters.
Their spirit, indeed, I felt, was very much that of the Roman
aristocracy watching the early Christians being thrown to the
lions. . . . During the fighting I recognized a boy I had known
slightly at Wellington. He was wearing a black shirt . . . so as
he came towards me I punched hard with my fist into his face.
Recalling the incident half an hour later, I had an idea that
perhaps he might have been trying to shake hands with me.

Romilly's possibly unprovoked attack on a Blackshirt had its
counterpart on the other side. Short-tempered and anxious to nip
interruptions in the bud, towards the end of the fighting the Blackshirts began to pounce on peaceable members of the audience who
had risen from their seats either to protest against some case of
brutality or merely with the intention of walking out in disgust.

Among those who did walk out were three Conservative MPs:
W. J. Anstruther-Gray, J. Scrymgeour-Wedderburn (who had won
his seat from Forgan) and T. J. O'Connor. They hurried to *The
Times* office to compose a letter which appeared the following
morning:

> We think a protest is worth recording at once [they wrote]
> against the method by which it was sought to maintain order. We
> were involuntary witnesses of wholly unnecessary violence
> inflicted by uniformed Blackshirts on interrupters. Men and
> women were knocked down and were still assaulted and kicked
> on the floor. It will be a matter of surprise for us if there were
> no fatal injuries. These methods of securing freedom of speech
> may have been effective, but they are happily unusual in
> England, and constitute in our opinion a deplorable outrage on
> public order.

In a statement to the *Daily Telegraph* the following day Anstruther-
Gray was yet more specific:

> If anyone could have told me before I went to that meeting
> last night that I would ever be in sympathy with Communist
> interrupters, I would have called him a liar [he said]. But I
> had not been at that meeting for more than a few minutes before
> all my sympathies were with the men who were being handled

with such gross brutality. . . . I saw one man being set on by a gang of Blackshirts, who seized him on every side. He flung up his hands to show his willingness to surrender and allow himself to be escorted out of the hall. Despite his obvious reluctance to enter into an entirely unequal fight, he was thrown down by a ju-jitsu trick and kicked in the ribs while unable to move. Having yanked him up again the Blackshirts were not content with leading him away, but others ran behind him battering him on the head with their bare fists. . . . I fail to see the necessity for this brutality, which is so foreign to the British race. . . . Something must be done to prevent a recurrence of last night's disgusting behaviour.

Another Conservative witness was Geoffrey Lloyd, MP for Ladywood and Parliamentary Private Secretary to Stanley Baldwin. In a letter to the *Yorkshire Post* he wrote:

. . . I was appalled by the brutal conduct of the Fascists. . . . There seems little doubt that some of the later victims of the Blackshirt stewards were Conservatives endeavouring to make a protest at the unnecessary violence. . . . I saw with my own eyes case after case of single interrupters being attacked by ten to twenty Fascists. Again and again, as five or six Blackshirts carried out an interrupter by arms and legs, several other Blackshirts were engaged in kicking and hitting his helpless body. . . . I saw several respectable-looking people, who merely rose in their places and made no struggle, treated with the unmerciful brutality that I have described. . . . I wondered what further violence was inflicted when the Blackshirts had dragged their victims out of public view. . . . It was a deeply shocking scene for an Englishman to see in London. The Blackshirts behaved like bullies and cads.

Lloyd went on to accuse Mosley of having deliberately provoked the trouble. With the aid of his loudspeakers, Lloyd argued, Mosley could easily have drowned the unaided voices of the hecklers. Yet Mosley had stopped speaking even for one small interruption at the back of the hall.

His tactics [Lloyd continued] were calculated to exaggerate the effect of the most trivial interruptions and to provide an apparent excuse for the violence of the Blackshirts. . . . I could not help shuddering at the thought of this vile bitterness. I came to the conclusion that Mosley was a political maniac and that all decent people must combine to kill his movement.

The author Storm Jameson wrote to the *Daily Telegraph* to describe Blackshirt assaults on women interrupters. She saw

a young woman carried past me by five Blackshirts, her clothes half torn off and her mouth and nose closed by the large hand of one; her head was forced back by the pressure and she must have been in considerable pain. I mention her especially since I have seen a reference to the delicacy with which women interrupters were left to women Blackshirts. This is merely untrue. . . . Why train decent young men to indulge in such peculiarly nasty brutality?

T. J. O'Connor told the Commons on 14th June that he had seen a young man thrown down a flight of a dozen steel stairs. Ritchie Calder, reported in a Victor Gollancz pamphlet,* said he saw one Fascist using a walking stick and Blackshirts hitting their victims with rabbit punches. An anonymous doctor, also quoted in the Gollancz pamphlet, described 'a young woman who had received a violent blow in the stomach and as a result was bleeding from the vagina'.

The BUF version of Olympia was that there was a systematic attempt to break up the meeting and it would have succeeded if the Blackshirts had been any less determined in putting down opposition. Today (1961) some of the ex-Fascists who took part in the operation consider, in retrospect, that the violence was overdone and that there was indiscipline and loss of temper; they do, however, maintain that the anti-Fascists were principally to blame.†

Support for the BUF came from the *Daily Mail*. Ward Price in his report likened the Blackshirts to a rugby football team. 'The struggling rowdies,' he wrote, 'would find themselves outside with black eyes as the only practical result of their disturbance.' The BUF also had sympathy from some Conservative MPs. Thomas Moore wrote to the *Daily Telegraph*:

* *Fascists at Olympia* by 'Vindicator', published by Victor Gollancz, Ltd., in 1934. The BUF gave its version of the events in a rival pamphlet *Blue Lies and Red Violence*.
† Verbal statements to the author.

I imagine it will be generally agreed that when a listener – before questions are invited – persistently disturbs the continuity of the speaker's address he merits little consideration, and the stewards, in the interests of the audience, must do their duty. In those cases of ejection which I personally noted, the meddlers suffered more from resentful civilians than from the official Blackshirt stewards.

Another Conservative MP, M. W. Beaumont, wrote to *The Times* to protest against the Gray-Wedderburn-O'Connor letter:

The use of such methods [Beaumont wrote] is the only way in which those putting forward an unknown and controversial case can obtain a hearing. No one present can doubt that the interruptions which were dealt with were skilfully organized with the object of preventing Sir Oswald Mosley from speaking. . . . I was pleased to see the organized hooligans dealt with in the only manner that can be effective.

Sir Nicholas Grattan-Doyle, Conservative MP for Newcastle, also in a letter to *The Times*, wrote:

I have no use for Fascism or dictatorships but less sympathy for the views expressed in your columns of those who think that the Red hooligans who were present in their hundreds were not treated with sufficient leniency. . . . Was more force than was necessary used in ejecting the disturbers? Probably there was and probably also the organizers of the meeting were determined to give an object lesson to the gangs who were present for an illegal purpose. If so, and with a view to preventing the same tactics being employed at other meetings in the future, is not the Fascists' psychology understandable?

Grattan-Doyle's notion that the Blackshirt strategy was to give the opposition an 'object lesson' ties in with Geoffrey Lloyd's idea that the disturbances were deliberately provoked. It is a tenable theory that the BUF intended Olympia to be an opportunity to terrorize the anti-Fascists and to demonstrate clearly to Conservative opinion how effectively the Blackshirts could work. The BUF replied that it was ridiculous to suppose that they would go to all the trouble of hiring a hall and advertising a meeting merely for the pleasure of beating up the audience, but this hardly takes account of the view of Romilly and others that a substantial part of the audience might regard the beating up of Communists as a positive attraction.

Whatever were the rights and wrongs of Olympia, there was one unchallengeable consequence. Justly or unjustly the BUF became associated in the public mind with violence, the same kind of violence as described in early newspaper accounts of Hitler's Germany. Patriotic *Daily Mail* readers, who might have become its backbone, were repelled from the BUF. Into the BUF was attracted a small but influential element which gloried even in the Nazism described by anti-Nazis. Olympia was the decisive step in a rapid process which in three or four months demoted Mosley's popular status from that of a potential national leader to that of an eccentric ex-MP with delusions of grandeur.

Three weeks after Olympia came the 'night of the long knives' when Hitler summarily executed ninety Nazi veterans, including Roehm who had been his close friend. The purge came as a sickening shock to the substantial body of opinion in Britain which was still disposed to regard Hitler as a useful barrier against Bolshevism. The *Daily Mail* posed anxious questions in its leader column; the bulk of Conservative, Liberal and left-wing opinion swung decisively and finally to the view that the Nazi regime was arbitrary, cruel and based on a rejection of the values of Western civilization. The BUF swam desperately against the tide by pointing to the sensual and extravagant mode of life of the murdered men who, said *Black-shirt*, had committed 'the greatest Fascist crime of disloyalty to their leader'. Up to that point the BUF had managed to combine a policy of general sympathy for Hitler with a detached attitude towards the details of Nazi administration. The Roehm purge was too big to be ignored; it had either to be supported or denounced. In supporting it the BUF finally aligned itself with the Nazis and, with one minor exception in 1937, they were as faithful in supporting Hitler as the Communists were in supporting Stalin. Thus was weakened what should have been the Fascists' strongest propaganda appeal – the appeal to patriotism. Now this primarily nationalistic movement appeared to be siding with foreigners.

Olympia, the Roehm purge and, above all, the BUF's growing tendency towards anti-Semitism precipitated a breach between Mosley and Rothermere which in July 1934 led to a formal withdrawal of support by the Rothermere Press. From a correspondence between Mosley and Rothermere published in the *Daily Mail* of 19th July it is clear that Rothermere had been trying to secure important changes in BUF policy. He wanted Mosley to drop the name 'Fascist', to modify the corporate state to provide more freedom for private enterprise, to guarantee the continuance of Parliamentary government and to extirpate anti-Semitism from the Movement. In other words, Rothermere wanted the BUF to drop its distinctively Fascist principles and to become an ally of the Conservative Party. That Mosley would agree was inconceivable. At heavy damage to his political career he had broken away from the Parliamentary system to form a movement over which he could have complete control. Subsequently to surrender his independence would make a mockery of the whole venture. In a firm, polite letter he thanked Rothermere for past support and said the BUF would go ahead on its own.

The question remains as to why Rothermere supported Mosley in the first place. The best answer must be that Rothermere believed he could capture the Fascist Movement and turn it to his own political ends. Rothermere was basically a Conservative, alarmed at the prospect of Red Revolution. But he nursed grievances against an official Conservative Party which refused to accept his guidance. He still smarted from Baldwin's jibe of five years earlier that the Press Lords sought power without responsibility – 'the prerogative of the harlot throughout the ages'. Armed with a virile Fascist Movement Rothermere could finally defeat Baldwin and enthrone the *Daily Mail* in the seat of power. If this were Rothermere's plan it showed a basic failure to understand Mosley's character. The only alternative explanation is even less flattering to Rothermere. Could it be that he supported the BUF because of its anti-Socialism, its support for British rule in India and advocacy of a stronger air force, and yet did so without even reading *The Greater Britain* to discover the Movement's real principles? Then did he pull out as soon as he realized the truth? Either explanation would show Rothermere as a political amateur, his attitude contrasting with that of the more professional Lord Beaverbrook, ally of Rothermere in the United Empire Party of 1930, who from the start had no faith in Fascism and was bitterly attacked by the BUF.

The loss of Rothermere and of the sympathy of some Conservatives whose support was momentarily his in the first half of 1934 was a good illustration of Mosley's tactical dilemma. To win success he had to get support from authoritarians on the right and from radicals on the left. In appealing to one he lost the support of the other. His favourite notion of appealing simultaneously to two political extremes proved unacceptable in British conditions.

On the left there was quick, decisive action. The Labour Party and the Trade Union Congress opposed the BUF. In the muddled political conditions of 1933 and 1934 this was important; had the leaders of the left shown any hesitation Mosley might have had a much bigger impact on organized labour. As early as March 1933 the National Council of Labour, representing both Labour Party and trade unions, issued a firm statement: 'If the British working class . . . toy with the idea of Dictatorship, Fascist or Communist, they will go down to servitude such as they have never suffered.' The TUC Annual Report for 1933 insisted that the political freedoms which existed in capitalist society were safeguards of the workers' right to improve their conditions. 'The freedom and independence of the unions would not be worth a day's purchase if these safeguards were destroyed.' On the motion of the Locomotive Engineers and Firemen, and with the support of Ellis Smith who had been Labour candidate against Mosley in 1931 at Stoke, the 1933 Labour Party Conference pledged itself to resist Fascism at home and abroad. The following year the TUC and the Labour Party Conference passed identically worded resolutions against Fascism from Charles Dukes of the General and Municipal Workers and agreed to mount combined trade-union and Labour Party demonstrations throughout the country.

This, however, all took place before the BUF formally adopted a policy of anti-Semitism – although the anti-Semitic trends had obviously worried Rothermere. Fleet Street rumour was that the *Daily Mail*'s Jewish advertisers had threatened to stop buying space if the pro-Fascist campaign continued; there was a good deal of amusement among journalists when, shortly after the end of its pro-Fascist campaign, the *Daily Mail* ran two leading articles which praised the Jewish contribution to British life. While it was, perhaps, commercially dangerous for a national newspaper to back an anti-Semitic movement – or a movement attacking any other section of the community – there is no reason to suppose that Rothermere was other than sincere in opposing anti-Semitism. As it turned out, quite apart from the Jewish question, a pro-Fascist campaign would have tended to alienate readers.

From the autumn of 1934 onwards, the BUF conducted an intense campaign against the British Jewish community. Anti-Semitism became so much one of the Movement's main principles that it is necessary to go back to its infancy to see how it developed, with Mosley, for once, leading from behind.

Mosley had shown no tendency towards anti-Semitism in his pre-Fascist days. He mixed as freely with Jews as he did with anybody else and, while in the Labour Party, had a great respect for Harold Laski. He did take some pains to establish the ancestry of his wife's grandfather, Levi Leiter of Chicago, and established that he was of Dutch-Calvinist and not Jewish extraction. But this research appears to have been a genealogical rather than an anti-Semitic exercise. There was no anti-Semitism in the New Party nor in the early BUF. In the very early days there were some Jewish Fascists, including 'Kid' Lewis and a Jew of Central European origin called Cohen who gave voluntary clerical assistance. These were frozen out at about the time of the move to Black House and, in any case, cannot have felt at home in a movement which sympathized with Hitler. *The Greater Britain* uses the term 'alien financiers' but the word 'Jew' appears nowhere in its pages.

Early issues of *Blackshirt* contained articles which argued that Hitler was not anti-Semitic. Assaults by storm troopers on Jews had nothing to do with race or religion; Jews would suffer in so far as they were 'internationalists or pacifists', but no more than Gentiles in the same categories. But this was a difficult argument to sustain and by April 1933 *Blackshirt* moved to a different tack, quoting a statement by Goering: 'The German Government will not tolerate persecution of a person merely because he is a Jew.' *Blackshirt*, commenting on the Goering statement, observed: 'It is unfortunate that this policy was not maintained in the Nazi Movement from their early days. The issue of Fascism in Germany has been obscured by the irrelevant Jewish question.' Admitting that there had actually been anti-Semitic outrages in Germany, *Blackshirt* added: 'The disciplined movement of world Fascism looks to the Government to suppress them.... If we must look abroad ... let us recall the single-mindedness of the Italian Leader, who avoided conflict with Jews, with Church, with sectional interests of any kind.' The reference to Mussolini was correct; anti-Semitism formed no part of Italian Fascism until 1938 when, under German influence, it appeared in a relatively mild form. In 1933 the Chief Rabbi of Italy was a member of the Fascist Party.

W. E. D. Allen summed up the early BUF attitude to anti-Semitism in his book *Oswald Mosley, B.U.F. and British Fascism* which he published in the spring of 1934 under the pen-name of 'James Drennan'. He quoted Mosley as having said that 'national pride has no need of the delirium of race', and continued:

> The English, the French and the Italians are strong enough to ignore – and to absorb – the Jews, but in Germany they remain a constant intellectual provocation to a people always sensitive to the newness of their nationhood. . . . The Nazis can only turn upon the nearest aliens in the streets to find consolation for the past and assurance for the future. . . . Nevertheless such phases must be passing, for the new Fascist nations will justify their pride of nation within themselves and not in extrovert antagonisms.

Before the BUF adopted it, anti-Semitism in Britain was the creed of small groups of eccentrics who lacked powers of persuasion. As a coherent system of thought, British anti-Semitism can be traced back to a Rhodesian, Henry Hamilton Beamish, who in 1919 founded an anti-Semitic society in London called The Britons. Beamish was a bizarre figure. Socially well connected, and the son of an admiral, he fought in the First World War and thereafter devoted his life to a world-wide crusade against Jews. He went to Germany in the early days of the Nazi Movement and claimed that he had 'trained Hitler'; a notion which is hard to believe but which is borne out at least by the fact that when the Nazis achieved power Beamish was treated as a speaker and honoured guest at the Nuremberg rallies. Through the 1920's and 1930's Beamish's name bobbed up in various parts of Europe, Africa and South America, always as an anti-Jewish speaker. He even tried to persuade the Japanese to be anti-Semitic. Shortly before the Second World War he returned to Africa and was elected to the Southern Rhodesian Parliament as an Independent. During the war he was gaoled under local defence regulations. He died in 1948 aged seventy-six.

The creed of Beamish was simple. The Jews, he believed, had since the time of King Solomon engaged in a gigantic, secret conspiracy to gain mastery of the world and to make the remainder of the human race their slaves. Wars, revolutions and every social evil were the work of the Jews. Communism and capitalism were the twin manifestations of Jewish power, both having the same objective of concentrating the world's wealth into a small number of Jewish hands. The Jews also worked through Freemasonry, Black Magic and the Christian religion. The panacea for all the world's evils was permanently to segregate the Jews from the remainder of humanity. Needless to say, he defined the Jews as a race rather than a religious group.

The textbook for Beamish's creed, as for all extreme anti-Semitism, was *The Protocols of the Learned Elders of Zion*, a curious work which has had a world-wide circulation. It supposedly contains the instructions of the Jewish 'Elders' to their people, the Elders being a secret, self-perpetuating body appointed by King Solomon to rule the Jewish people. The book explains that the French Revolution, organized by the Jews, prepared the way for world-wide democracy, a form of government ideally suited for Jewish manipulation. Democracy, says the book, is

> a blind force which will never be in a position to move in any direction without the guidance of our agents. . . . God has granted to us, His Chosen People, the gift of dispersion, and from this which appears in all eyes to be our weakness, has come forth our strength, which has now brought us to the threshold of sovereignty over all the world.

The book goes on to describe Jewish techniques – digging tunnels to blow up cities, Jewish families masquerading for generations as Christians and acting as the Elders' secret agents, of the duty of Jewish men to pollute Gentile blood by seducing Gentile women thence producing half-Jewish children. This latter point of the supposed sexual prowess of Jewish men provides a link between anti-Semitism and other forms of racialist propaganda. At various times there have been popular superstitions that male Jews, Africans, Chinese and probably others have exceptionally large genital organs which make them especially attractive to women. Where anti-Semitism of the Beamish type differs from other forms of racialism is that it contained no suggestion that the Jews were inferior, but rather that they were intellectually superior to Gentiles; racialist propaganda based on skin colour has generally taken the line that the European races are superior to others.

The Protocols was first published in St Petersburg in 1905 by a Russian religious mystic, Sergei Nilus, who claimed that the text had been 'stealthily removed from the secret vaults of the Zionist headquarters which are at present situated in Paris'. A more common view is that the book was a forgery by the Tsarist police, who found it convenient to lump all liberal and Socialist opposition to the regime into a single category, smeared with the anti-Semitic brush. This view was accepted by a court of law at Berne in 1935. The first German edition appeared in 1919 and editions in English were published by The Britons in 1923 and 1932. The English translator was Victor E. Marsden who had been the *Morning Post* correspondent in St Petersburg during the Russian Revolution and who was convinced that Lenin was an agent of the 'Elders of Zion'.

Arnold Leese was the first in Britain to combine anti-Semitism with Fascism to produce a coherent political doctrine. Earlier there had been some anti-Semitism among members of the British Fascists, but it was anti-Semitism of the mild, non-doctrinaire type which excludes Jews from golf clubs, rather than the type which regards them as enemies of humanity. From the beginning Leese regarded himself as a 'Racial Fascist' and devoted about ninety per cent of his propaganda to 'exposures' of Jews and 'Jewish agents' in high positions in political, business and trade-union life. He took elaborate precautions to prevent secret Jews infiltrating the Imperial Fascist League. The infallible way of identifying a man of true 'Nordic' blood, Leese believed, was to measure his head. Leese personally examined the shapes of the skulls of his recruits. Some prospective crusaders against Jewry actually failed Leese's test and were sent away with contumely.

Mosley's anti-Semitism lacked any such clear doctrinal basis. Members of the BUF would glumly observe that the *The Protocols* was probably a fake but that the Jews behaved as if it were genuine. There was a vague notion that Jews were 'orientals' and therefore unsuited to the British way of life, and there were much stronger assertions that they were 'internationalists' and therefore inimical to Mosley's nationalist policy. By attacking international finance, it was said, Mosley unwittingly attacked the financial power of the Jews, a fact he did not realize until he found the Jews in the vanguard of anti-Fascism. The connection between the Jewish millionaire in the City of London and the Jewish Communist attacking Black-shirts in the streets was shadowy and unexplained. The Jewish 'oriental' mentality made them unscrupulous businessmen who by price-cutting and sweated labour were unfair competitors against 'British' enterprises. Above all, Mosley claimed that the Jews were trying to embroil Britain in war against Hitler's Germany.

The first signs of anti-Semitism appeared in the autumn of 1933 when the BUF was a year old. At about this time it became a formal rule that Jews could not be admitted to membership and there were 'warnings' to British Jews not to conduct campaigns against Hitler. There were criticisms of refugees who had arrived in Britain from Germany, *Blackshirt* in November 1933 proclaiming: 'We do not object to these refugees because they are Jews but because they are unwanted aliens taking advantage of public sentimentality. . . . Jews have always been well treated in this country. . . . They should be careful not to abuse this hospitality.'

Now, at every level in the BUF there was pressure in favour of an anti-Semitic line. Most of the Blackshirts were admirers of Hitler and they smarted at Leese's gibes of 'Kosher Fascism'. Within the inner leadership Joyce, Francis-Hawkins and others were, in varying degrees, anti-Semitic. The pressure mounted when it became clear that British Jews were playing a prominent part in anti-Fascism, identifying the BUF with Hitler. Stories circulated within the BUF of befurred Jewish women leaning from their cars to spit at Blackshirts, of Jewish employers victimizing Fascist employees. When a Jewish tailor in Manchester offered to supply the Blackshirts with black raincoats at bargain prices the Movement regarded it as a rich joke. The allegation that there was an organized plot by British Jewry to demolish the BUF seems improbable, if only for the reason that the Jews had no organization capable of mounting such a campaign. Not until 1936 did the Board of Deputies set up their 'Jewish Defence Committee'. With his emotional loyalty to his followers, and with his resentment of outside criticism, Mosley must have found it difficult to resist the pressure in favour of anti-Semitism. He may, moreover, have believed that Fascism would win popular support more effectively if it could hit at a personal enemy – the Jew – rather than against abstract evils of international finance. According to his sister-in-law, Baroness Ravensdale, Mosley 'argued . . . that a dynamic creed such as Fascism cannot flourish unless it has a scapegoat to hit out at, such as Jewry'.*

Mosley's nominal deputy, Forgan, was opposed to the idea of a campaign against the Jews, believing it would be tactically unwise. During the summer of 1934 he had private talks with Jewish leaders at the Savoy Hotel to try to thrash out a Jewish-Fascist agreement; the talks had no effective result and it is hard to see how there could have been one.

* *In Many Rhythms* by Baroness Ravensdale (1953).

It was largely on this Jewish question that Forgan resigned from the BUF in October 1934. He left quietly, publicly giving ill health as his reason, and there was a leading article in *Blackshirt* thanking him for his services, which in the early days of the Movement had been considerable. With a quiet Scottish charm, Forgan could move widely in non-Fascist circles and he had been an admirable public-relations officer. In the New Party period and at the start of the BUF he was very close to Mosley and, as a former MP, had a special status. Latterly new men of another type came to the fore and Forgan was left with little effective role. Later he tried to rejoin the Labour Party but was refused admission. His only subsequent venture into politics was to speak for Sir Richard Acland's Common Wealth Party during the 1945 general election.

The last big rally before the Movement became anti-Semitic was in September 1934 at Hyde Park. Following Olympia Mosley had booked the White City for a display of Fascist pageantry, gymnastics and oratory, but at the last moment the booking was cancelled on the grounds that the Fascists might damage the tracks which had been laid for the forthcoming Empire Games. As a substitute Mosley ordered a march to Hyde Park. Great pains were taken in organizing the biggest possible show of strength, with special trains provided to bring Blackshirts from the Midlands and the north to London. William Joyce was in charge of the arrangements and three days before the rally he unsuccessfully prosecuted the *Daily Worker* at Bow Street for 'incitement to violence' in urging anti-Fascists to counter-demonstrate. 'Despite the howls of the alien mob and the corrupt Press', as Mosley put it, some 2,500 Blackshirts were on parade, Mosley's mother leading the women's section. It was the biggest show of Fascist strength that London had seen and, apart from some minor scuffles, the occasion passed off relatively quietly. Police formed a human cordon right round the Blackshirts, insulating them from the general public. Kingsley Martin reported in the *New Statesman* that trying to see them was 'like trying to get near the cages at the Zoo on a Bank Holiday'. Loudspeakers being forbidden, the Fascist orators spoke simultaneously from half a dozen platforms, Mosley and Joyce attracting the biggest crowds. The Press was uniformly critical, especially the *Daily Express* which wrongly reported that Mosley arrived at Hyde Park by car instead of marching with the Blackshirts. Describing this error, *Blackshirt* called Beaverbrook 'the most loathsome little specimen that has yet crawled from the underworld of Financial-Democratic politics'.

Three weeks later the BUF held a rally for their northern members at Belle Vue, Manchester. The Chief Constable banned Fascist and anti-Fascist marches to the ground but neither this nor drizzling rain damped the spirits of the audience. Under the blare of the loud-speakers sounded 'We want Mosley' from the Blackshirts and 'We want Mosley – dead or alive' from the opposition. A riot squad of firemen used their hoses to separate the two sections of the crowd. Mosley spoke from the grandstand, around which was stationed a bodyguard of 900 Blackshirts. As he began speaking, several hundred voices broke unsteadily into 'The Red Flag'. Mosley apparently lost his temper and flung his voice harshly through the loud-speakers with what amounted to – a declaration of war against the Jews.

'The mention of the Empire makes the mob yell louder than ever!' he roared. 'Let them destroy it if they can, these Jewish rascals! The Red mob howls that we shall put them down. They are right. We shall put them down but we shall put the nation up.

'What they call today the will of the people is nothing but the organized corruption of Press, cinema and Parliament, which is called democracy but which is ruled by Jewish finance – the same finance which has hired alien mobs to yell here tonight!'

The following issue of *Blackshirt* vigorously supported the new line: 'No more is needed than the sight of the Jewish sub-men on parade to rouse this land to the full knowledge of the tyranny which it has been, for so long, patiently bearing in Christian silence,' it remarked.

Mosley followed up his Belle Vue statement a week later at a meeting in Millbank Drill Hall, Plymouth. This, too, was a noisy meeting with Mosley leaving the platform to supervise a force of 100 Blackshirt stewards. It ended in riot with the police entering the hall to restore order. Mosley did not mention the Jews during his main speech, but answering a question afterwards he said: 'We tell the Jews straight that they have to put the interests of Britain before the interests of Jewry. They have fought Fascism; they have asked for it; now they will get it.'

At this stage Mosley could still have held back. His remarks at Manchester and Plymouth were spoken in the heat of the moment, and he could have reverted to the formal position that there was no Jewish problem in Britain requiring Fascist action. But wherever he turned for advice within the Movement the officials he most trusted were urging him to attack the Jews, who, they explained, were attacking Fascism. Mosley hesitated. To attack the Jewish community would be a bigger break with his ideals of the past than any he had yet made. Exactly what went on in his mind is impossible to fathom, but, after long deliberation, he decided he would go ahead. His zest for novelty, at once a strength and a weakness, may have combined with the conviction that the 'modern movement' would prove its independence of outside support by leading the common people in a great crusade against their 'racial' enemies. There could, too, have been a hunger for the applause from the Movement that he knew anti-Semitism would bring.

The second of the BUF Albert Hall rallies, held on 28th October 1934, provided the occasion for Mosley formally to launch the new policy. The Albert Hall management, remembering Olympia, had insisted that the police should steward the meeting, but their services were little required, the audience consisting largely of the Fascist faithful. Rumour spread beforehand that the Leader was going to attack the 'Yids' and there was an electric tension as Mosley, to an accompaniment of drums and trumpets, limped to the rostrum. The tension mounted through the opening passages of the speech until he reached the section for which nearly everyone was waiting:

'I find,' said Mosley, 'that as I have proceeded in Fascism I have encountered forces which I did not dream existed in Britain. . . . One of them is the power of organized Jewry which is today mobilized against Fascism. They have thrown down their challenge to Fascism and I am not in the habit of ignoring challenges. Now they seek to howl over the length and breadth of the land that we are bent on racial or religious persecution. . . . That charge is utterly untrue. . . . From the very outset we have preserved the principle of no racial or religious persecution. . . . Our Empire is composed of numerous races, a great conglomeration of races of the earth, bound together in a mighty unity, and any suggestion of racial or religious discrimination strikes a blow at the conception of the British Empire. . . .

'Today we do not attack the Jews on racial or religious grounds. We take up the challenge that they have thrown down because they fight against Fascism and against Britain!'

At this point the tension in the hall snapped and great sections of the audience rose to their feet waving and cheering. Mosley's voice broke through the applause with the ringing words: 'They have dared in their great folly to challenge the conquering force of the modern age! Tonight they will begin to have their answer!'

More quietly Mosley recited figures to allege that although the Jews constituted only six per cent of the population they had been responsible for fifty per cent of the attacks on Fascists. He spoke of Fascists being victimized by Jewish employers and of potential Fascist supporters – including newspaper proprietors – being black-mailed by Jews into opposing the BUF.

There were, said Mosley, two kinds of Jews – big Jews working in secret and little Jews in the streets. 'Little people who can hardly speak English at all. . . . That is not really so serious. That is due to the fact that the Liberal Government before the war opened the floodgates . . . and admitted the sweepings of foreign Ghettos to Great Britain. It is not so much these people as the big men who are the real menace to this country. Though, heaven knows, the big men are nasty enough! Let me hasten to add that I do not say for one moment that every nasty bit of work who has found a happy refuge in Great Britain is Jewish. It would be impolite of any Fascist ever to forget Lord Beaverbrook. . . .

'In other countries,' Mosley continued, 'the problem is more obvious than it is here because it is a problem of little Jews. In Britain it is the big Jews who are the real danger. . . . They oppose us by every reason of their tradition and their character. We stand for bringing to an end the system of international usury by which they live. . . . Then again they fight a movement of national revival because they owe allegiance – and admit they owe allegiance – not in the first place to this Empire, but to their own relatives and to their own race and kith and kin in nations beyond our frontiers. There, not on grounds of race or religion but on the fundamental principle of Fascism, we declare that we will not tolerate an organized community within the State which owes allegiance not to Britain but to another race in foreign countries. . . . We fought Germany once in our British quarrel. We shall not fight Germany again in a Jewish quarrel.'

Again the speech was halted by tumultuous cheering and dis-ciplined Blackshirt shouts of 'Hail Mosley!' When it died down Mosley went on to describe how the Jews, through ownership and advertising, held the Press in their hands, how the cinema was 'Jewish from beginning to end'. What he did not do was to explain why Fascism could not control the abuses it disliked on a basis of blaming individual offenders rather than on the basis of blaming a whole community; the omission was the more glaring because he had admitted that there were non-Jewish culprits like Lord Beaverbrook who, in his view, were as bad as the Jews. The audience did not appear to notice any gap in logic but heard with rapt attention a peroration which, better than anything else of the same length, sums up the gist of the Fascist creed – the cult of youth versus the old men; the urge to destroy and rebuild; the belief in the power of science.

'This is the generation,' said Mosley, 'which faced 1914, which in four years made an effort which staggered the world with a display of manhood, of courage, and of sacrifice, that mankind had not previously witnessed. The story of our generation is an epic of the human race that has gone on from victory to victory, from triumph to triumph. In the laboratories of science it has conjured up the wonders that are transforming the modern world; in the field and in the upper spheres it challenges the very dominion of nature with the triumphant mind of man.

'THIS IS OUR GENERATION NOT THEIRS. We have fought and conquered while they muddled and destroyed.*

'This Movement of our generation, of New Britain, of the New World, raises itself to challenge, to sweep away, to destroy, and THEN TO BUILD AGAIN!'

Stiffly Mosley smiled, nodded and saluted as for fifteen minutes he received the ovation of his life. He looked like a Leader who had won a great war. What he could not have realized was that those cheers were the effective death-knell of British Fascism.

Blackshirt's editorial the following week summed up the new situation with clinical precision: 'The Movement is now untrammelled with outside support that never understood our objective and our spirit. . . . Fascists must be prepared to fight tooth and nail for every inch of the advancement of their cause against the solid enmity of the whole world.'

---

* The capitalization follows that in the report of the speech in *Blackshirt* of 2nd November 1934. 'They', of course, refers to the older generation of politicians.

CHAPTER 9

'Mosley Says Peace'

BY THE end of 1934 the British economy had reached a condition which in the context of the inter-war period could pass for prosperity. Unemployment was at its highest at the start of 1933 and thereafter fell steadily. Standards of living, especially in the lower middle class, were rising and the consumer-goods industries of the London area and the Midlands swung back to full production. The terms of international trade moved heavily in Britain's favour to the benefit of the majority of the population. But they moved to the detriment of the old, heavy industries of the north, Clydeside and South Wales which could not find foreign markets for their products and consequently remained in continued depression. A pattern developed of wealth and poverty existing side by side. When Jarrow had an unemployment rate of sixty-seven per cent Birmingham's was only six per cent; Merthyr Tydfil had sixty-one per cent unemployed and St. Albans three per cent. There was little communication between the 'two nations', and the Baldwin-Mac-Donald skill at soothing the prosperous majority postponed indefi-nitely the violent changes which had seemed so possible in the period between 1931 and 1934. There was no repetition of the great strikes of the 1920's. Trade-union leaders like Citrine and Bevin now negotiated with a new generation of employers on something like equal terms. A political lethargy settled over the land, broken only in the depressed areas and by excitement among a relatively small number of intellectuals.

Even if the BUF had not forfeited potential support by its reputa-tion for violence, by its apparent imitation of foreign movements and by its anti-Semitism, the social context was hardly one in which it could look for easy success. Classically, Fascism grows from a discontented lower middle class. But in the mid-1930's the bulk of the British lower middle classes was in a heyday of prosperity. White-collar workers in the £250–£750 a year salary range were too busy with their baby cars and their new red houses, which ribboned into the countryside from every great city, to worry about politics. The only potential revolutionaries were the unemployed in the depressed areas and the young intellectuals, both of which groups were firmly anti-Fascist.

Membership figures of the BUF were always a close secret, never being known to more than two or three people at a time. Mosley is still (1961) unwilling to give exact figures of the support he received, his argument being that if you are weak you are unwise to reveal your weakness to your enemies, and if you are strong you are unwise to warn your enemies. It is generally agreed, however, that the turnover in membership was very considerable. This was especially so in the *Daily Mail* period, when a BUF branch could count itself fortunate if one recruit in ten became a permanent member. What Mosley does claim – with justice – is that nearly all ex-Fascists (except *Daily Mail* ones who never understood the Movement) continued to believe in fundamental Fascist principles and would, in time of crisis, rally back to the cause. Being an active Blackshirt was an arduous life. The Movement not only expected heavy duties – some members working five or six nights a week – but also exposed them to ridicule and active persecution. To a few, such a life of sacrifice had positive attractions; especially in the provinces Fascism had a semi-religious air, with the glory of a Fascist state and Blackshirts enthroned in power as the reward for martyrdom. But to the apathetic recruit such attitudes among dedicated Fascists were insufferable.

A major difficulty in measuring BUF strength is the lack of a definite yardstick by which to define whether a person was or was not a member. Most political parties have elections to choose officers and a test, based mainly on payment of subscriptions, of who is entitled to vote. The Fascists, based on the principle of authority, had no elections and therefore no qualified voters. Even the official membership records, therefore, can rarely have shown a true picture. A man who, in a moment of enthusiasm after a Mosley meeting, had paid one week's subscription might remain on the books for months or years, although he paid no more money and played no active role. Depending on the attitude of local leaders, there would be periodic purges in which membership figures were drastically reduced by mass expulsions of the ineffectives.

During 1934 the *News Chronicle* conducted an investigation of the BUF and established a membership figure of 17,000. The *Daily Herald*, in a similar investigation, hazarded a guess of 35,000. In the same year Ellen Wilkinson and Edward Conze wrote a generally well-informed book called *Why Fascism?* in which they estimated the membership at 20,000. BUF propaganda talked vaguely of 'tens of thousands of supporters'.

The true figures were much lower. Robert Forgan declares (1960) that when he resigned the deputy leadership in October 1934 the active membership was 'nearer 5,000 than 10,000'. This bears out estimates for later periods by Beckett, Chesterton, Risdon and others, who in their day-to-day work in the heart of the Movement gained a clear idea of what was happening. Chesterton, for instance, estimates (1960) the membership in 1938 at 3,000 active and 15,000 inactive, 100,000 people having passed through the Movement by then. These figures may appear ridiculously small at first sight and it is strange to recall that Aneurin Bevan and Jennie Lee were so alarmed at the prospect of a Fascist revolution that they had standing arrangements for going into hiding.* On the other hand, the Communists, who during the 1930's made at least as much noise as the Fascists, had an officially declared membership of about the same size. In 1930 the Communist Party of Great Britain had 1,376 members. By 1938, after steady growth, it had reached 15,570. The quality of Communist members was higher than that of the Fascists; J. R. Campbell could claim in a speech at Moscow in 1935† that out of 7,700 British Communists 600 held trade-union office. The number of Fascists who could claim such influence outside their own organization was very small.

A method of cross-checking the estimates of Fascist membership from ex-officials is to examine the numbers of branches. In the autumn of 1934, according to figures given by Mosley two years later, the BUF had 180 branches. From internal evidence it is clear that most of them were small. The average Blackshirt group in the country was lucky if it had two dozen active members. Allowing an average of twenty members for each of 160 smaller branches produces a total of 3,200, to which may be added a further 2,000 or 3,000

---

* *Nye, The Beloved Patrician* by David Llewellyn (1960).
† Quoted in *The Life and Times of Ernest Bevin, Volume One* by Alan Bullock (1960).

from the twenty big branches to produce Forgan's figure. After 1934 the number of branches tended to increase but this was more by rallying small groups of the existing faithful than by any kind of mass conversion, except in the East End of London where there was substantial progress. From 1938 onwards the membership steeply and continuously declined; during the summer of 1940 there were arrests of about 1,000 Mosley Fascists under the Defence Regulations, representing almost the whole active strength of the Movement and including some very small fry.

Examination of the branches gives, too, a fair idea of the Movement's geographical distribution. A sample survey of *Blackshirt* for the months of September and October 1934 yields the names of seventy-nine branches, a generous proportion of the whole. Of these seventy-nine branches, fifty-six were south of a line drawn immediately below Birmingham and seventeen were within fifteen miles of Charing Cross. Outside London the major concentration of strength was a chain of branches in the seaside resorts of the south coast – Margate, Ramsgate, Deal, Dover, Folkestone, Seaford, Brighton, Littlehampton, Chichester, Portsmouth, the Isle of Wight, Southampton, Bournemouth, Plymouth. Of the small number of twenty-three branches in Birmingham and farther north, nine were in essentially non-industrial places like Blackpool, Southport and Harrogate. In the industrial Midlands and north, mainly the biggest centres were covered – Birmingham, Manchester, Leeds, Newcastle, Sheffield, Liverpool, Glasgow and Edinburgh.

Up to 1934 the Fascist advance was breathtakingly rapid, so rapid that during the period of Rothermere support there was a possibility that it would gather enough momentum to take Mosley to 10 Downing Street. As, however, the public attitude hardened, and the Movement became associated with violence and with developments in Germany, the Movement's path after 1934 was uphill with every step a battle. To check the leakages the BUF had to soft-pedal its main, national campaign and concentrate its propaganda on a series of appeals to special interests. During 1935 there was an energetic campaign in Lancashire to enlist cotton workers for Fascism on the promise that a Mosley Government would close competing cotton mills in India, exclude Japanese cotton goods from Empire markets and deal with the 'Jewish' capitalists of the City who produced cheap cotton with sweated labour abroad instead of investing their money in Lancashire mills. The BUF opened about a score of propaganda centres in the cotton towns which, under Risdon's direction, enrolled new members by the thousand and were so successful as seriously to worry the Labour Party. The campaign had no lasting effect; when the propaganda eased off in 1936, probably through lack of funds, Fascist support melted away entirely. Another important propaganda target was the small shop-keeper, whose livelihood was being threatened by expansions of the 'Jewish' chain-stores. Mosley pledged that on gaining office he would make chain-stores illegal, giving local managers the option of running as proprietors the shops they had managed for the 'Jews'. Appeals were directed, too, to occupations where trade unionism was weak – to clerks, insurance salesmen, shop assistants, cinema staffs and others – with the promise that the corporate state would secure higher wages and shorter hours.

Such campaigns did no more than enable the Movement to hold its own against the constant leakages of members, who left through apathy or because of the internal quarrels that riddled the Movement at every level – quarrels that were the more serious because there was no safety valve of internal elections. On Mosley's shoulders fell a burden which was heavier in its way than that borne by any other politician in the country. He was the Movement's chief propagandist, sole policy-maker and only source of authority. He embodied the Movement in his own person and could show no sign of weakness. It was his massive burden to rally the faithful by assuring them that the supreme crisis of the nation would soon come and that meanwhile they must be patient and work hard. For those who had struggled in the days of adversity there would be high honour when the great day came.

Power within the Movement fell into the hands of those most willing to believe in the dream-world that Mosley created. Neil Francis-Hawkins achieved rapid promotion, until by 1936 he was Director-General, ranking second only to Mosley. Tactically this was a mistake. A politician of Mosley's stamp needed a strong man at his elbow, capable of questioning decisions and acting as devil's advocate – the role which Strachey once had filled. In matters of organization Francis-Hawkins was competent though bureaucratic, but he had no ambition to influence the Movement's basic policy; he seemed to regard Mosley as infallible. Mosley himself had self-conscious ideas of how he should behave as Leader. He believed in a clear-cut delegation of responsibility and reserved for himself as

Leader absolute control of policy and propaganda, a staggering burden for a movement so active as the BUF. Equally clearly, he believed it was no part of a leader's function to worry about day-to-day administrative details and in Francis-Hawkins he found a competent man to look after them. The mistake was that on the day-to-day details depended the morale of the Movement, and there was irritation at the absolute authority held by so non-political a man as Francis-Hawkins. The 'political' leaders – men like Beckett, Chesterton and Joyce – were irritated at having to beg Francis-Hawkins's permission for petty items of expenditure, and quarrelled with Francis-Hawkins's selection of men for junior posts. As Francis-Hawkins gathered his own aides – B. D. E. Donovan, a school-master, and U. A. Hick, a retired army officer – a state of near civil war broke out at National Headquarters. Within the Movement there were rumours of favouritism and of promotions based on homosexual friendships.

The secret of Francis-Hawkins's influence must have been his unquestioning loyalty, a quality to which Mosley attached high value when so many were leaving him. Mosley received adulation and expected it. Blackshirts even saluted him when he went into the sea to bathe at the Movement's summer camps at Selsey. On ceremonial occasions he had an escort of twelve motor-cyclists round his car. The rank and file whispered his name in religious awe and every Fascist speech had its quota of praise for the Leader, who was presented to the public as a superman. Criticism was totally taboo and humour nearly so.

Beckett tells an anecdote about an influential Catholic who had shown interest in Fascism. Beckett went to see him and argued that the BUF should be especially attractive to Catholics because it re-produced in secular form the hierarchy of the Church. 'Look here,' replied the Catholic, 'I don't object to the Pope laying down a dogma once in a hundred years, but I'm damned if I'm going to put up with Tom Mosley making one every ten minutes.' According to Beckett, Mosley gave the story a chilly reception when it was retailed to him.

'Tom Mosley' was in any case an expression out of place. To his face Mosley was called 'Sir' and behind his back the rank and file referred to him as 'The Leader'. Officials spoke together of 'O.M.' or 'the old man'.

Even those not fully hypnotized by Mosley's personality were not ashamed to express a fervent hero-worship. In *Portrait of a Leader*, a

biography of Mosley accurate in matters of fact, A. K. Chesterton
wrote a eulogy such as few politicians can have received:

'. . . Now he moves forward to a still greater destiny, an implac-
able figure looming ever more immense against the background of
his times; through his own eager spirit, so full of aspiration and
boldness, symbolizing the immortal spirit of his race,' runs the
book's closing passage.

> Through his own example he has restored the heroic thing
> which is the spirit of Britain. If the hearts of his followers prove
> one-tenth as great as Mosley's heart, their courage one-tenth as
> high as his courage, they will not relinquish the struggle until
> the heights of Fascist power be won; until Britain's great
> revolutionary leader, sprung from one thousand years' contact
> with British soil, achieves power to act for and with the British
> people, in the name of their ancient sanity and splendour, that
> there may be built up in their peerless land a corporate life,
> which shall ensure that her million hero-sons did not die to make
> a mock for history. Their battle shout sounds above the discords
> and semi-tones of a fading age: Hail, Mosley, patriot, revolu-
> tionary, and leader of men!

On leaving the Movement two years later Chesterton wrote a
pamphlet showing some more of what he saw in Mosley's character:

> . . . In order to back up his favourites, there is no affront
> which he will refuse to offer to common sense and no specious
> excuse he will hesitate to advance. If a leader shows himself
> unable to maintain even the pretence of a judicial attitude in
> dealing with his own organization, he can plead with no con-
> vincing justification for the sacrifices which service to him
> imposes . . . .

The adulation was a two-way process, with Mosley having as high
an opinion of his followers as they had of him. Although he was on
occasion very kind-hearted, he showed little sign of personal feeling
towards them. Cinematographic records show him inspecting serried
ranks of Blackshirts at high speed with never a glance at their faces.
If they were loyal they were, to Mosley, the sacred instruments of
Fascism and therefore fit to rule. He expressed his devotion to his
followers in *Tomorrow We Live* (1938):

They who lead the people to a higher civilization are ever those who are capable of supreme self-dedication. The authority of leadership carries with it the responsibility of such a life. Thus our new leaders of the people, in every area of the land, have been discovered, tried and tested in the actual ordeal of struggle. Their sacrifice during a struggle, harder and fiercer in its whole nature than any movement has known before in this country, is the guarantee to the people that they will not again be betrayed. A Fascist who, in power after such a struggle, betrayed his cause, would betray his own life blood. Thus the struggle of the National Socialist Movement is a necessary preliminary to the exercise of power, because the bitter character of that struggle gives to the people an absolute guarantee that those who have passed through that test unbroken will not betray their people or their country. Thus alone is forged the 'instrument of steel' to save and then to serve the people.

CHAPTER 10

'The Future Is With Us'

DURING 1935 Mosley carried through an extensive reorganization, centralizing the control of branches through a system
of headquarters inspectors, inaugurating strict financial con-
trols and turning the bias of the Movement away from semi-military
training, designed to suppress Communist revolution, towards a
more conventional plan for winning power at a general election.

In its early days the Movement centred largely on Fascist clubs,
of which Black House, Chelsea, was the exemplar. There were about
a score of such clubs in provincial centres, elaborately equipped with
bars, gymnasia, lounges, dining-halls and suites of administrative
offices. The Newcastle club filled a four-storey house. The clubs were
a useful means of attracting the unemployed to membership of the
Movement, but from a propaganda point of view it was better to
have Blackshirts selling papers in the streets than engaging in boxing
matches in the gymnasium.

Headquarters inspectors embarked on tours of the country to reorganize the branches, purge the non-workers from the membership lists and to replace the clubs with small, administrative offices
with, where possible, bookshops attached.

The inspector for the Midlands was Chesterton, who was alarmed
to discover the extent to which Blackshirts passively waited in their
clubs for the revolution instead of sallying outside to propagate the
Fascist cause. At Smethwick he found a snug social club with separate
bars marked 'Officers' and 'Blackshirts'. Along the counters ran lines
of tankards, each bearing its owner's name. Of political activity

there was no sign. The apparition of the tense, eager Chesterton must have been a great shock. He quickly closed the club and dismissed the Branch Officer. Moving on to Stoke, Chesterton found an even more unsatisfactory situation. Stoke branch, which dated back to the foundation of the New Party in 1930, was recorded as the biggest in the country, with 400 members, but the level of political activity had fallen very low. The club had a sinister reputation locally for being part thieves' kitchen and part bawdy house. Chesterton closed the club on the spot and carried out the biggest purge in the Movement's history, expelling 300 members in one go.

In the autumn of 1935 Black House itself closed down. Mosley sold the lease for a substantial sum – rumour put it at £50,000 – and a development company pulled the house down and replaced it with a block of flats. The closure showed that the easy financial situation of 1933 and 1934 had given way to some stringency and, possibly, that the Movement had begun to live on its capital. The anti-Semitic policy certainly cost the Movement a good deal of financial support, and in the smoother political atmosphere there was less disposition to finance Fascism as a bulwark against Communism. The new offices in Sanctuary Buildings, Westminster, were run as an ordinary administrative unit with no residential quarters; the semi-military atmosphere remained, with a good deal of saluting and heel-clicking which impressed visitors. Dudley Barker described in the *Evening Standard* how some of the Blackshirts saluted even when answering the telephone.

Under Beckett, Box and Risdon plans were drawn up for training election agents against the day when the Movement would try its strength at the polls. The aim was for every branch to have a Political Officer to supervise electoral work and a Propaganda Officer to take charge of public speaking. Fascist discipline, *Blackshirt* boasted, would enable the Movement to build the most efficient electoral machine the country had ever seen. The political and propaganda officers inevitably formed a separate hierarchy in the Movement and were inclined, as 'intellectuals', to come into conflict with the autocratic officials appointed by Francis-Hawkins, who tended to pay more regard to reliability than to intelligence. These innumerable disputes were generally settled by Mosley in accordance with Francis-Hawkins's advice.

To encourage team spirit, Blackshirts were divided into units of six, each commanded by a Unit Leader. The idea was that the members of each unit should work together, the Branch Officer assigning tasks to complete units rather than to individuals. Where possible the members of a unit were urged to relax together as well as work together, and Mosley noted with approval a unit diary which, after recording five nights' political work, had for Saturday night the entry: 'Unit went to the cinema.' The Unit Leader was to be a miniature Mosley, entitled to unquestioning obedience. *Blackshirt* explained: 'Betrayal of the group is betrayal of Fascism; disloyalty to the group leader is disloyalty to the Leader of Fascism. The man who creates discord among his five comrades is a bad Fascist, no matter how loud the protestations of his own good faith.'

At the same time the specialized Fascist Defence Force ceased to exist and its members were ordered to general political duties. Under the new system any Blackshirt was to be available for stewarding meetings or acting as a bodyguard, but there was a distinction between Division I Blackshirts who undertook to give three nights' service a week and Division II Blackshirts who were required to give only one night's. To Division I was confined the privilege of wearing breeches and jackboots; Division II had to be content with ordinary trousers. A third division of membership was for people who joined the Fascists as they would any ordinary political party and gave no pledge of obedience to orders. They were to be 'invited', not 'instructed', to perform political duties and were allowed no uniform beyond the 'undress' black shirt worn with collar and tie under a suit. It was in Division III that Mosley hoped to build up a mass following for the day when he would fight a general election.

The reorganization reached its climax at the beginning of 1936 with a change in the Movement's name. From 'British Union of Fascists' it became 'British Union of Fascists and National Socialists'. But the new title was rarely used in full and for practical purposes the Movement became known as 'British Union'. The use of 'Fascist' or 'Fascism' dropped out of the Movement's literature and was replaced by 'National Socialism'. A favourite campaign slogan was: 'If you love your country you are National, if you love her people you are Socialist – Be a National Socialist.' There was opposition to the change when Mosley announced it to the Policy Committee, Beckett and others complaining that the Movement's work in familiarizing the public with Fascism was being wasted. But Mosley had no difficulty in carrying the majority, which now took much more inspiration from Germany than it did from Italy. In any case, the change had tactical advantages. 'National Socialism' was an easier term to explain than 'Fascism' and might be expected to have an appeal to the left. 'British Union' was a simple, patriotic title.

Much of the detailed drafting of the new constitution and rules was the work of Major-General J. F. C. Fuller, who had joined in 1934. A military historian of note, and a world expert on tank warfare, Fuller was a valuable acquisition. He was never a full-time official but as a member of the Policy Committee he gave shrewd, detached advice on tactics and organization. He also wrote pamphlets and articles. In his time he had been a student of the occult and had known Aleister Crowley, to which bizarre interest he added a *recherché* form of anti-Semitism. In political matters he had a belief in the need for strong leadership. There was friction between Fuller and Joyce, who in theory admired the officer class but in practice disliked most individual members of it. Fuller had a more original mind than the ordinary ex-officer Fascist and introduced fresh air into what was becoming a stifling atmosphere.

Mosley, meanwhile, was continuing his tremendous programme of speaking tours. Accompanied by coachloads of Blackshirts he attracted massive audiences to Fascist rallies in every part of the country. With Mussolini's invasion of Abyssinia he turned his propaganda sharply in favour of non-intervention, declaring that the Abyssinians needed the civilizing influence of Italy. *Blackshirt* published pictures of alleged atrocities by the Abyssinians, defended the use of mustard gas by the Italians and mocked Haile Selassie. Although there was never a serious likelihood of war between Britain and Italy, British public opinion was sympathetic to Abyssinia and, as the Peace Ballot showed, was prepared to back League of Nations action to halt the invasion.

The Fascists ran a vigorous 'Peace Campaign', introducing the lightning-flash symbol to replace the fasces as their main symbol. With chalk and whitewash they painted 'Mosley Says Peace' on walls all over Britain and even on the doorstep of 10 Downing Street. The whole was a preview of the desperate peace campaigns with which Mosley tried to persuade British public opinion to acquiesce in German expansion and in Franco's capture of Spain. At least in the case of Germany, the campaigns were against the mainstream of public opinion and further weakened the Movement.

Arnold Leese's Imperial Fascist League had a different policy. Leese opposed the Italians over Abyssinia and declared that the invasion was a Jewish plot. He gave general support to Franco but was suspicious of the Jewish influence he detected in the Falange.

His advocacy of Hitler went a good deal further than Mosley's. Leese's campaign was not so much for 'peace' as for a fighting alliance of the 'Nordic' peoples against everyone else.

For his peace campaigns Mosley tried to enlist the support of religious opinion but, apart from a few Catholics who came in on the matter of Spain, he had little success. Mosley was at pains to conciliate the Catholics and adopted a policy of complete State support for church schools. His weekly *Action*, refounded in 1936, went so far as mildly to criticize Hitler's attacks on the Roman Catholic Church and the pagan rites which were fashionable among the Nazis – the only criticisms of Nazi Germany which ever appeared in official BUF publications. Catholics were, perhaps, slightly over-represented in Fascism – a census in 1935 showed that twelve per cent of the officials were Catholics – but no form of religion was really significant in the Movement. A little clerical support came from the Church of England and the Free Churches. Among the regular contributors to Fascist publications were the Reverend Ellis G. Roberts – 'Israel has rejected God, and now, for the last time God rejects Israel'; and the Reverend M. Yate Allen – 'It is because I am a padre and firmly believe in the Christian religion that I welcome and thank God for what has already been achieved by Mussolini and Hitler and look forward to the time when Mosley may be equally successful.'

The Reverend Geoffrey Dymock, Vicar of St. Bede, Bristol, was an active Fascist propagandist and during the summer of 1935 toured West Country seaside resorts with a propaganda van called 'Black Prince' from which he addressed holidaymakers and distributed BUF pamphlets. When Dr. Bell, Bishop of Chichester, criticized Hitler, Dymock sprang to the Fuehrer's defence with an open letter to the Bishop published in *Blackshirt*. 'Undeterred by the ominous signs of approaching Armageddon, definitely fomented and encouraged by Bolshevik Jewry, you have decided that the present hour is the time to insult one of the great races of Europe which has succeeded in extricating itself from the Laocoon toils of a foul slavery to international finance.' Joyce, in the same issue of *Blackshirt*, referred to the Bishop more succinctly as 'a mitred buffoon'.

Mosley himself insisted that the Movement should take no sides in religious issues. In 1935 he described his own faith as a synthesis of the creeds of Christianity and Nietzsche – the self-sacrifice of Christianity combined with the Nietzschian 'challenge to all existing things'. The detachment from religion was, on the whole, successful, and there is little evidence to justify charges by contemporary opponents that the BUF was simultaneously pro-Catholic in Liverpool and anti-Catholic in East Anglia, although there was a definite attempt to woo the Irish Catholics of the East End of London.

Apart from his public-speaking activities Mosley and the Movement were at this time much engaged in appearances in the law courts. Mosley was a first-class witness and showed great skill in the courtroom. He would have made an excellent barrister. The contrast between his flamboyant manner on the public platform and his courteous, persuasive manner in the courtroom suggests another similarity between Mosley and Stafford Cripps.

The first big case was a criminal prosecution at Lewes Assizes, involving Mosley, Joyce, Charles Bentinck-Budd and Bernard Mullens. They were charged with a 'riotous assembly' following a Fascist public meeting at Worthing Town Hall. According to John Flowers, KC, prosecuting at the three-day preliminary hearing before Worthing magistrates, Mosley and his companions left the hall after the meeting and struck out with their fists against a crowd of anti-Fascists outside. Under cross-examination by St. John Hutchinson, defending, the police witnesses agreed that the crowd had been exploding fireworks and singing 'Poor old Mosley's got the wind up'. The Fascists pleaded that they had acted only in self-defence, but they were committed for trial. The Assize hearing was very brief, the jury acquitting all the defendants without hearing their defence.

A piquant feature of the Worthing 'riot' was that Charles Bentinck-Budd was a prominent local figure. When he joined the Fascists in 1933 he was a member of Worthing Town Council and of West Sussex County Council. Despite protests from his opponents, he asserted his right to wear a black shirt in the council chamber and, furthermore, secured an unopposed return to both authorities at the next elections. At the time of the trial he was BUF Area Officer for West Sussex, but shortly afterwards he moved to Birmingham to become Midlands Inspector and from 1937 onwards worked at National Headquarters. On resigning from the county council in order to go to Birmingham he said that there were 'several other members of our organization on the council', a claim which is difficult to substantiate. A man of moderate means, in 1935 he was aged thirty-seven, and had an artificial leg resulting from war wounds at Loos.

At almost the same time, Mosley won his biggest legal triumph – an award of £5,000 damages and costs in a libel action against the *Star*, the London evening newspaper of radical views. The action was of key importance for it established once and for all that the BUF was a constitutional movement. It arose from a leading article which quoted Mosley as having said that he 'would be ready to take over the Government with Fascist machine guns when the moment arrived' and that the Communist, Tom Mann, had been imprisoned 'on the mere suspicion that he might say something ten times less provocative than Sir Oswald's words'. The *Star* decided vigorously to fight the action and engaged Norman Birkett, KC, and Valentine Holmes to conduct their defence. On Mosley's side there was an equally bright array of counsel, Sir Patrick Hastings, KC, leading St. John Hutchinson and Gerald Gardiner.

The decisive moment of the trial was Mosley's own evidence in the witness-box. He insisted that the Fascists would use force only if the Communists tried to take over the Government, a proposition from which Birkett, in a three-hour cross-examination, failed to shake him.

BIRKETT: Suppose a Communist Government were in power with the consent of the King?

MOSLEY: A Communist Government?

BIRKETT: Yes: would you face them still with guns?

MOSLEY: That is a hypothetical question on a wild hypothesis that I have never seen.

BIRKETT: If a Communist Government is called to power with the consent of the King would you shoot them down?

MOSLEY: It is possible to put a question on ever-increasing hypotheses which lead at last to an absurdity. You might as well say that if His Majesty the King of England enacted the law of Herod that every first-born shall be slain, would you, in those circumstances be a revolutionary? The question you have put is a hypothetical absurdity.

BIRKETT: Can you answer it?

MOSLEY: You cannot answer questions which are by their very nature absurd.

BIRKETT: You are not going to shoot the Old Gang, by any chance?

MOSLEY: What a very foolish and unnecessary thing to do.

BIRKETT: It is now conceded that the Fascist Movement in this country is organized in two ways, one to capture power in normality, as you term it, in the ordinary way, public meetings, voting, and so on; secondly it is an organization to meet force in the State by force. Is that right?

MOSLEY: When it is used against the State.

BIRKETT: Who is to be the judge – you?

MOSLEY: When there is a condition of anarchy it does not require much judgment. If you were shot in the streets, it would not require any great condition of judgment to know that you had been shot.

BIRKETT: Let me put this, and press it. Who are you to interfere with the forces of law and order which are in the country to maintain order against all revolution?

MOSLEY: Good heavens, no. I never suggested interfering with the forces of law and order. You will find in this book,* from which you have been quoting extensively, a phrase to the effect that under no circumstances should we ever use force against the forces of the Crown.

BIRKETT: It is the first time in this country, is it not, in our peaceful evolution of late years that a political leader has used language saying: 'I am going to judge the moment when I use guns in the street'?

MOSLEY: No. Lord Carson said hundreds of things far worse than that at a time when he was a leader at the Bar.

BIRKETT: It is the first time in this country, is it not, in the government of our own country, that any leader has said: 'I will judge when the guns will shoot'?

MOSLEY: When did I say I should be the judge?

BIRKETT: Well, who is?

MOSLEY: It does not require much judgment. If I saw a policeman knocked down with two toughs stamping on him, it does not require the exercise of judgment to know whether one ought to intervene or not . . .

Other lawsuits had, for the Fascists, less satisfactory results. Beckett won £1,000 for slander by an ephemeral anti-Fascist group, but the group dissolved without paying the money. The eight members of the executive committee of the Amalgamated Engineering Union won seventy-five pounds each and costs for libellous imputations in an article by Beckett in *Fascist Quarterly*, reprinted as a pamphlet. The kernel of the libel was that the members of the executive were 'elected for three years, and in the meantime, provided

* *The Greater Britain.*

(Associated Press)

3rd October 1937

(*above*) A barricade, surmounted by a red flag, in Long Lane, Bermondsey.
below) The head of the South London march. Neil Francis-Hawkins and
3. D. E. Donovan are marching on either side of Sir Oswald Mosley. March-
ng side by side on the extreme left are A. K. Chesterton (in dark suit, looking
traight ahead) and A. Raven Thomson (with moustache, looking towards the
camera)

(*Daily Herald*)

Sir Oswald Mosley i
1944, soon after his
release from prison
(*Daily Herald*)

Sir Oswald and
Lady Mosley in 196
(*Evening Standard*)

they scratch each other's backs, there is no reasonable limit to the comfort they may enjoy or the expenses they may incur'. BUF Publications, Ltd., publishers of *Fascist Quarterly* and the pamphlet, shortly afterwards went into compulsory liquidation with liabilities of £5,255 and assets of £65. The liabilities included £3,438 owed to the BUF Trust, Ltd. and £1,600 damages and costs outstanding from the AEU action.

A slander action by Mosley against John Marchbanks, General Secretary of the National Union of Railwaymen, again involved the imputation that the Fascists were planning an armed revolution but the result was less clear-cut than the *Star* case. It originated in a speech at Newcastle during 1934 by Marchbanks in which he said: 'I hold a document which represents secret instructions issued by Sir Oswald Mosley and his supporters to their adherents. They are also active in the armed forces of the Crown. They have to mingle with officers and find out how many will join the Party on the promise of jobs in the Fascist Party, and ultimately in the Government when the Fascist regime is established. Weapons recommended to members of the Fascist Movement include corrugated rubber clubs filled with shot, knuckledusters (not to be used by members in uniform), knives (not to be used by members in uniform), potatoes containing razor blades, and a miniature breastplate of cardboard studded with drawing pins. . . . We strongly object to any particular party assembling in the guise of a military machine with the object of over-throwing by force the constitutional government of this country.' Patrick Hastings and Gerald Gardiner again appeared for the Fascists and D. N. Pritt, KC, G. J. Lynskey, KC, and Walter Frampton appeared for Marchbanks.

With the *Star* verdict behind him, Mosley had little difficulty in establishing that he was not bent on armed revolution. Most of the five-day hearing centred around the charge that Fascists used weapons. Mosley, in the witness-box, said that weapons were generally banned but admitted that rubber truncheons had on one occasion been used in Manchester Free Trade Hall.

The 'document' to which Marchbanks had referred in his speech turned out to be a copy of a statement by Charles McEwan Dolan, a Methodist pastor at Goldthorpe. Dolan, aged forty-four, said in evidence that he had left the Communist Party to join the Fascists in 1933 and had been engaged by Forgan and Plathen as a paid speaker. At National Headquarters he was issued with black shirt, rubber truncheon and collapsible platform and sent out to propagate

the cause. The Communists stole the truncheon from his lodgings at
Reading and embarrassed him by producing it at one of his meetings.
In the armoury at National Headquarters he had seen truncheons,
knuckledusters, a loaded walking stick and a sword-stick. While
working for the Fascists he had been converted to Christianity and
was now working for the Methodists.

The jury awarded Mosley damages of one farthing and made no
order as to costs.

The lawsuits did not interrupt Mosley's speaking tours. During
the three weeks following the Marchbanks case, for example, he
spoke at Newport (Mon.), Hastings, Leeds, Bethnal Green, Clee-
thorpes, Durham, Lancaster, Skipton and Streatham. At Leeds he
took part in a march headed by the 'Northern Command drum and
Trumpet Band'. From Bethnal Green to Bow he led a march of
Blackshirts and drummers which took two hours.

He was suffering increasing difficulties in getting halls, local
authorities being especially shy of accepting Fascist bookings.
Birmingham, Bournemouth and Oxford town halls were refused to
the BUF in quick succession. The refusals were doubtless in part due
to distaste for Fascism but the ostensible reason, for which there
was plenty of backing, was that Fascist meetings were apt to lead to
violence. Four men were fined and one gaoled after a Mosley meeting
at Stratford Town Hall in the East End of London. Two were fined
at Sunderland. At Hull a bullet-hole was found in a window of
Mosley's car. At the Mound, Edinburgh, the Fascist speakers' stand
was demolished by an angry crowd. There was a riot at Leicester.
Frank Pakenham, then an Oxford don, wrote to *The Times* to complain that he had been beaten up by Blackshirt stewards when he
attempted to rescue some of his undergraduates who were being
manhandled at an Oxford meeting.

Although the Blackshirts looked provocative, and were very quick
to eject interrupters, there is little evidence that they started fights
without reason. The challenge always came from the militant left,
especially the Communists. Nor was violence the invariable consequence of a Fascist meeting; the more level-headed members of the
Labour Party believed it more effective to ignore the Fascists than
to provide free advertisement by provoking fights. Over great areas
of the provinces where the militants of the left were weak the Blackshirt meetings took place in order, marred only by the aggressive
attitude of a few Fascist stewards. During a very orderly meeting
addressed by Mosley at Cheltenham, for example, the respectable,

middle-class audience were willing peacefully to hear the Fascist case. There was only one interrupter, a weedy-looking man with spectacles, who shouted in high-pitched tones: 'The Jews are cleverer than you.' Mosley ignored the interruption but two massive stewards from London called to each other across the hall to decide when to 'do' him. Eventually they tramped over the feet of innocent members of the audience, plucked the interrupter from the middle of a row of seats, frogmarched him down the aisle and flung him into the street, smashing his spectacles. So far as that audience was concerned the conduct of the bullying stewards must have made a stronger impression than Mosley's oratory.

As the main relaxation in his strenuous life, Mosley was a keen fencer. He was runner-up in the British épée championships in 1932, and in 1935 was a member of the British fencing team in the Empire Games. Fencing was a popular sport within the Movement – part of the opening ceremony of a headquarters at Hull was a fencing match between Mosley and the local leader, Captain R. Piper.

The general election of November 1935, called by Baldwin with less than a month's notice, brought a problem for Mosley which must have temporarily banished everything else from his mind. It was a nice dilemma. Fascism had proclaimed itself as a consti-tutional creed which aimed at the annihilation of all other political parties. To stand aside from the general election would be invidious. On the other hand, Mosley must have well remembered the New Party débâcle of 1931. If he fought the election there was not one constituency in the country where he could expect to better the New Party result and the 'infinite majesty' of Fascism would be turned to ridicule.

Three weeks before polling day he resolved the dilemma. The Fascists would fight a campaign but would put up no candidates. The slogan would be 'Fascism next time' and supporters were advised not to vote.

'My advice,' said Mosley, 'is not to waste a vote for a farce. Wait for the real battle. . . . This election is a sham battle which at the next election will be followed by the real battle, for not until Fascist candidates enter the field as challengers for power will any reality be introduced into British politics.'

The election was apathetic. Meetings were dull. Polls were low. Leading Fascists were as active as the leaders of other parties in touring the country to address election rallies, Mosley alone speaking in sixteen towns. Rank-and-file Blackshirts happily daubed the

'Fascism next time' slogan in whitewash on every available wall. The result trebled the Labour representation in the Commons from fifty-two to 154, but the National (effectively Conservative) Government of Baldwin retained a comfortable majority. Mosley used the apathy as the basis of a brilliant rationalization to stimulate the hopes of his followers.

'Nearly ten million did not vote,' he wrote in *Blackshirt*.

It was the lowest poll of the last thirty years with the single exception of 1918 when the men had not returned from France. . . . The old parties and the old system are a dying force in Britain. . . . Conservatism declines despite the suicide of its opponents; Socialism recedes despite immense opportunities, by reason of its inherent ineptitude. Communism is driven by sheer funk of Fascism to support its enemies just when at last it has a chance to destroy them.

Fascism alone emerges as the triumphant challenger. . . .

The future is with us.

CHAPTER 11

The Battle of Cable Street

I T WAS in the East End of London, principally in Bethnal Green, Shoreditch and Stepney, that British Union from 1936 onwards at last found a mass following. This was the old East End, shortly to receive a mortal blow in the air raids of 1940 and 1941 and to be essentially destroyed in the massive post-war building schemes, when council flats rose high over the sites of the old tenements. Between 1935 and 1955 the combined population of Bethnal Green, Shoreditch and Stepney fell by half, continuing a century-old tradition of emigration by the prosperous East Ender to more attractive quarters. Poplar, the Hams and the outer suburbs of modern London have, successively, been the new homes of the Cockney moving up the social scale. Rarely has the Cockney gone south of the Thames, the frontier which divides London so decisively into two worlds. The Thames, too, was the frontier of British Union power. While Mosley attracted followers by the thousand in Stepney he made as slight an impact in Bermondsey, just across the river, as he did in any other Labour-controlled working-class area.

Despite the exodus of Cockneys, the East End, up to 1940, remained overcrowded. Into it came big immigrant communities, mainly Irish and Jewish. The main Jewish immigrations were between 1880 and 1900, representing the backwash of pogroms in Russia and Eastern Europe. Whole streets and districts of the East End acquired a Jewish flavour with Kosher shops, elderly Jews talking in Yiddish and a flattening silence on Friday nights and Saturday mornings as the Jews repaired to their synagogues. The

Irish, too, maintained a community life with a strong religious background but, despite Saturday fights in the public houses, they integrated better with the Cockneys.

About the Cockneys who remained it is difficult to generalize. It must be remembered, however, that many of the more energetic Cockney families had, both through insular distaste of foreigners and a general desire to better themselves, moved elsewhere. Among the Cockneys who remained there was a feckless element, lacking ambition itself and resenting it in others. This element maintained a fierce local patriotism which helped to make tolerable an otherwise drab existence.

The Jews stood apart from Cockneys and Irish as a community of quite a different kind. The Jews tended to be hard workers who, with serious minds, would make it a lifetime's aim to improve their lot. Behind the scrubbed doorsteps of Whitechapel many a Jewish family would live in poverty simply to give its children the best education. Jews who achieved prosperity continued to live in their old neighbourhoods instead of moving out like the well-to-do Gentiles, creating an impression of Jewish wealth which irked their non-Jewish neighbours. The suspicion was that the Jews had made their money at the Gentiles' expense. Self-righteous, proud of their community, perhaps a little snobbish, some Jews, in their turn, felt a certain scorn for the complacent Gentile. Between Jews and Gentiles there was little social contact. Inter-marriage was abhorred on both sides. A non-political form of anti-Semitism existed in the East End long before Mosley appeared there, although the most open manifestations had been before the First World War.

Another East End characteristic was lack of large-scale industry. The area was a hotbed of small businesses, mainly tailoring and furniture-making, conducted in backyards and front rooms. Trade-union organization was weak and the Labour Party, while it won elections, never built up an industrial-political machine of the kind which guaranteed its power in other 'safe' Labour areas. The East End was never, in the sense of a Jarrow or a Merthyr Tydfil, a depressed area, but the proliferation of small businesses tended to lead to a continuous chain of small bankruptcies and a sense of insecurity. Conditions were such as to encourage the sweating of labour; for each Jewish employer sweater the whole Jewish community tended to get the blame.

Mosley's proposals for planned rises in wages within the structure of the corporate state had an obvious appeal. So did his militant patriotism, his attacks on foreigners who were taking work from British hands. There was, too, the excitement of the bands, the British Union uniforms, the processions, which relieved the drabness of East End life. London's glamour usually shone so brightly in the City and westwards as to plunge the East End into comparative darkness. The East Ender felt a forgotten man. Mosley was a politician from 'up West' who regarded the East End as important. Above all, Mosley was prepared to use the latent anti-Semitism as a political instrument.

British Union never actually captured the East End. There the forces of anti-Fascism always remained stronger than those of Fascism. But what Mosley did do was to capture, especially among the young, enough support to become a serious contender for local power. His success was the more impressive against the background of the fact that a quarter of the population was Jewish and implacably opposed to him. And he achieved it in a relatively short time. How Mosley would have fared had there been no war is a matter for speculation. If there is some evidence to suggest that support for British Union was passing its peak by 1939, on the other hand, a comparatively small accession of support would have been enough to give Mosley political control.

That the East End would prove the most fruitful area for its activities does not appear to have been foreseen by British Union. Fascism arrived comparatively late, the first Bethnal Green branch being formed towards the end of 1934 and the first Shoreditch branch a few months later. There was no Stepney branch until July 1936, when one was formed at Limehouse.

Two Irishmen, Owen Burke and E. G. 'Mick' Clarke, pioneered the first East End meetings, often being rescued from angry anti-Fascists by squads of Blackshirts rushed by van from Black House. Burke was officially in charge but Clarke speedily became more important. Within the Movement Clarke was called 'the Idol of Bethnal Green', a description which had some truth. With a violent, abusive manner, Clarke established himself as an effective open-air speaker, never afraid to express British Union policy on the Jews. So strongly did he become entrenched in the East End that when in 1938 he was transferred to National Headquarters there were rumours that Mosley was jealous of him and wished to remove him from the limelight.

Raven Thomson was the first of the national speakers to enter the East End, being joined later by Joyce. As the snowball of support began to grow, Francis-Hawkins and Donovan stepped in to organize the branches and to direct a series of special campaigns. By the spring of 1936 it was apparently the policy to build up the East End as the central stronghold of British Union and a springboard from which the rest of the country could be converted. Mosley's visits became more frequent; he delighted especially in the surprise visit to a Fascist pitch or headquarters. Through the narrow streets he would stride of an evening, surrounded by forests of hundreds of arms raised in salute. There would be jeers as well, but the shouts of 'Hail Mosley! We want Mosley!' predominated. In the drab East End Mosley could figure as nowhere else as the working-class Leader, beloved of the faithful.

The East End successes changed the bias of the whole Movement. In the public estimation British Union tended to acquire a reputation as troublemakers in the East End rather than as challengers for national power. The strongly anti-Semitic flavour of the East End campaign did not suit the British Union provincial branches, for even in Leeds anti-Semitism was an embarrassment rather than a means of winning support. At British Union headquarters Mosley's critics complained that he was concentrating on the East End to the neglect of the rest of the country. There were whispers that Mosley liked the East End for reasons of vanity; that in the East End he could pretend that he was already the idolized Leader of the people.

It was certainly in the early East End period that British Union anti-Semitism cohered into a firm policy. Mosley set it out in his book *One Hundred Questions Answered*, published in 1936, and explained it further in *Tomorrow We Live*, two years later. The programme, briefly, was that Jews who could be proved to have worked against British interests should be deported. Other Jews would be allowed to remain but would be treated as foreigners, losing their rights of citizenship. The final solution would be for the Jews to be given a national home, not in Palestine but in one of the 'many waste places of the earth possessing great potential fertility'. On the details of the programme British Union was uncharacteristically vague. There was, for example, little attempt to define who was and who was not a Jew. What would happen to the 'anti-British' Jews before they were deported was not explained.

Arnold Leese and his Imperial Fascist League had been more specific. The possession of one Jewish grandparent was enough, in Leese's eyes, to make a person a Jew. Nor did Leese shrink from the methods that the Third Reich was later to adopt. He wrote the following words in the February 1935 issue of his paper *The Fascist*:

It must be admitted that the most certain and permanent way of disposing of the Jews would be to exterminate them by some humane method such as the lethal chamber. It is quite practicable but (some would say unfortunately) in our time it is unlikely that the world will demand the adoption of that drastic procedure.

As an alternative to the lethal chamber, Leese proposed to send everybody of Jewish extraction to Madagascar. The island's existing inhabitants would be moved out and compensated with property confiscated from the Jews. Around Madagascar the world's navies would maintain a perpetual patrol to ensure that no Jew ever got out. In *The Fascist* Leese published a jubilant cartoon showing mile-long lines of men, women and children embarking on a fleet of ships which was to take them from England for ever.

Imperial Fascist League propaganda methods were more violent than those of British Union. Mosley himself tried, against the tide, to keep anti-Semitism in proportion and rarely allowed it to fill more than about ten minutes of a speech lasting an hour. *Notes for Speakers*, issued from National Headquarters, laid it down that 'Speakers will not devote a disproportionate amount of their speech to the Jewish question, the effect of which is to flatter the Jews' sense of self-importance. They should be treated as a problem with which Fascism will deal faithfully, but by no means the only problem which confronts us.' In the East End the instruction was honoured more in the breach than the observance, although it did serve as a standard of conduct elsewhere. Printed propaganda centred on the allegation that the Jews were unscrupulous businessmen, that 'Communism is Jewish' and that the Jews were trying to make war between Britain and Germany.

Leese, a proud disciple of Julius Streicher, was quite uninhibited. It was his positive aim to inflate the importance of the Jews and his leaflets claimed that Britain had a Jewish population of 3,000,000,* all of whom were bad. British Union maintained at least a formal *caveat* that there were good Jews as well as bad Jews, a notion which to Leese was ridiculous. Copying Streicher's paper *Der Stuermer*, he claimed that the Jews were the seducers of Gentile women and the murderers of Gentile children. For their Passover Feast the Jews

* The true figure was under half a million.

kidnapped Gentile children, killed them and drained off their blood
to mix with the ceremonial bread. That the Jews were bad was, to
Leese, self-evident and he wasted little time in attempting to argue
the matter. A high proportion of the space in his monthly paper
The Fascist was given over to lists of the names of Jews and
alleged Jews in the Government, Parliament, big business and the
aristocracy.

British Union's propaganda was the more effective and by 1936
had obviously made a big impact. The pro-Fascist crowds chanted
'Yids, Yids, we gotta get rid of the Yids'. Huge scrawlings of P.J.
(Perish Judah) appeared on the walls of synagogues and Jewish
shops and, with the example of Germany in their minds, the East
End Jewish population reached a state of mind bordering on panic.
Dudley Barker, who conducted an investigation for the *Evening
Standard* in November 1936, wrote that 'the visitor's first impression
is that of an atmosphere of sullen excitement, of some tension'.

The effort British Union put into the East End was on a scale
unprecedented in British politics. With open-air meetings every
night, rallies every week-end, it was like a perpetual general election.
The loudspeaker vans, manned by Clarke, 'Panther' Moir, 'Mick'
Goulding and other regular speakers, poured out anti-Semitic
propaganda even in the solely Jewish streets where there was no hope
of making converts – an action which is difficult to explain save in
terms of deliberate provocation. Jewish parents trying to settle their
children to sleep against the roar of Fascist amplifiers outside the
bedroom windows conceived a cold hatred of Mosley such as no
British politician ever before had earned. The East End split into
warring camps. In 1936 the Jewish Board of Deputies started a
Jewish Defence Committee which provided speakers every night to
answer the Fascist charges. The Association of Jewish Ex-Servicemen built up its own strong-arm equivalent of the Blackshirts for
the protection of the Jewish people. The Communists moved in on
a big scale, like the Fascists drawing into the East End supporters
from other parts of London. On an unofficial level a state of gang
warfare developed, with hooligans on both sides joining in simply
for the sake of the fighting and the petty robberies that became
possible. Jewish shop windows were smashed for mercenary as well
as ideological reasons. Whole areas of the East End were marked off
as 'Jewish' or 'Fascist' and at night it was as dangerous for a Blackshirt to venture unaccompanied into some Jewish streets as it was
for a Jew to linger near a Fascist headquarters. Even the children

joined in, Mosley forming Blackshirt cadets for youths aged between fifteen and eighteen and a Fascist Youth for children from eleven upwards. Gangs of Jewish and anti-Jewish children fought each other in school playgrounds, Joyce commenting with satisfaction in *Action* how 'Jews and Blackshirts' had replaced 'Cowboys and Indians' as the favourite game.

Only one of the regular *Action* contributors kept clear of the pervading anti-Semitism. This was John Scanlon, a former miner and shipyard worker, who had been prominent in the Glasgow ILP in the early 1920's. He came to London to work as private secretary to Sir Patrick Hastings and was afterwards a journalist and writer closely in touch with the Labour Movement. For Mosley he conceived a high admiration and praised him in his sardonic, informative book *The Decline and Fall of the Labour Party* (1932). Scanlon was never a member of British Union but it is clear from his writings that he regarded it as the legitimate heir to the Socialist tradition. Until 1939 he wrote a weekly industrial article for *Action* under the pen-name 'John Emery', attacking employers and trade unions alike. 'I do not know what Sir Oswald Mosley means by National Socialism,' he wrote in July 1936. 'Apart from the anti-Jewish side I see nothing different from what Keir Hardie preached.' British Union liked the parallel between Mosley and Keir Hardie and took to publishing Hardie's picture under the caption 'The first National Socialist'. In three years of weekly articles Scanlon never attacked the Jews. He could, for example, devote an entire article to abusing Emanuel Shinwell without mentioning Shinwell's Jewish background – a feat which any other *Action* contributor of that time would have found impossible.

By German standards the British Union anti-Semitic campaign was on a small scale and the violence was comparatively modest. Nobody died in clashes with the Blackshirts and there was none of the shooting in the streets which had punctuated the years of Hitler's rise to power. There was never a prolonged breakdown in public order; the police were under strain but they always had the situation under control. The Army was never called in. The Metropolitan Police Commissioner was Sir Philip Game. Until 1935 Game had been Governor of New South Wales where, by an odd coincidence, his most difficult problem had been to handle the local Fascist Movement, the New Guard, which had campaigned vigorously for him to dismiss his Labour Government. Game's policy was firstly to maintain order and secondly to protect freedom of speech, including freedom of speech for the Fascists. The charge that the police favoured the Fascists was a result of this policy and is discussed more fully in the next chapter.

Broadly speaking, the Fascists were acting within their legal rights in attacking the Jews. Mosley summarized the position in a letter to Sir John Simon, Home Secretary, who had attacked anti-Semitism during a Parliamentary debate on the East End:

> We have as much right to attack Jews in public speech as Mr. Lloyd George had the right to attack landlords when Chancellor of the Exchequer in the pre-war Liberal Government of which you were Home Secretary. We have as much right to attack Jews as members of the Labour Party have the right to attack anybody who possesses capital. . . . You appeared to suggest in your speech that Jews are the only people in this country immune from criticism or attack in public speech.

Two court cases did, however, put a limit on the right to propagate anti-Semitism.

The first was a prosecution of Arnold Leese for his allegations that the Jews indulged in ritual murder. He was charged at the Old Bailey on two counts, one of seditious libel and one of 'inciting a Public Mischief by rendering His Majesty's subjects of the Jewish faith liable to suspicion, affront and boycott'. The Attorney-General prosecuted and Leese, alleging that all lawyers were in the pay of the Jews, conducted his own defence. He secured an acquittal on the charge of seditious libel but was found guilty of public mischief and, having refused to pay a fine, was sentenced to six months' imprisonment.

The sentence had no deterrent effect on Leese. His followers met him outside Wandsworth Prison on his release and drove him in triumph, swastikas fluttering from their cars, to a celebration party. Leese then elaborated the ritual-murder allegations into a full-length book, against which there was no prosecution.

The second case revolved round the question of whether or not it was libellous falsely to describe a man as a Jew. It arose from an article by Beckett in *Action* in which he bitterly attacked the first Lord Camrose, proprietor of the *Daily Telegraph*, saying that 'the Berry family is of Jewish extraction and has intimate contacts with international Jewish interests'. Camrose's case, presented by Roland

Oliver, KC, Valentine Holmes and John Seaton, was that within the context of Fascist propaganda the word 'Jew' was clearly defamatory. Gerald Gardiner, for *Action*, conceded that Camrose was not a Jew but said that there could be nothing derogatory in so describing him. Acting on his clients' instructions, Gardiner went on to try to prove up to the hilt the remaining allegations about Camrose's links with 'international finance'. Beckett, appearing in person, said the article could be justified only if Camrose were in fact a Jew; he had written the article on the basis of information given him by the British Union Research Department. (Beckett had left the Movement by the time of the trial.) The printers made no attempt at justification. After a three-day trial the jury awarded a total of £20,000 damages which, of course, neither *Action* nor Beckett was able to pay. Camrose proceeded to judgment against the printers who, in their turn, failed to recover anything from the co-defendants. During the hearing it was revealed that Action Press, Ltd., had a capital of £100 and, shortly before the trial began, had issued a £1,000 debenture on all its assets.

Commented *Action*: 'The company laws of this system were devised by the capitalists for use against the people. None can complain if the people now use the company law for their own purposes.'

During the long, summer evenings the East End situation grew more tense, with British Union acquiring a closer resemblance to the German Nazis by dressing its most active members in a uniform which, with peaked cap, black jacket and black breeches, looked much like that of the S.S. British Union described the new dress as a 'police style' uniform but its introduction led to more disputes within the Policy Committee. Beckett, Risdon and others argued that the simple black shirt had been in use long enough to be generally recognized and accepted. The new uniform would arouse unnecessary hostility. The argument the other way was that the rank and file wanted the new uniform and, since they received little reward for their work, they should be allowed to have it. The resemblance to the Nazis became yet closer with the adoption of an armlet, bearing the lightning-flash emblem in red, white and blue, for wear with both old and new uniforms – from a distance it looked like the swastika armband of the Nazis. Whatever the motives, the result was to heighten the tension even further in the East End.

Mosley's final public appearance in a black shirt at a large-scale rally was in March 1936. It was at the Albert Hall, and it was to be the last time he would appear there. The trustees refused to allow the

Fascists to hire it again. Inside there were the usual scenes of ceremony; outside the police broke up an angry anti-Fascist demonstration.

Four young women tried to unfurl from a balcony a banner protesting at Hitler's treatment of German Catholics. From left-wing interrupters came shouts of 'Fascism means war.' It was noticed in both cases that the Blackshirt chuckers-out had acquired an efficient and relatively humane technique.

'The great and powerful were afraid when our Fascist Movement opened its crusade against Jewry,' Mosley declared. 'What has been the result? When we began that struggle we possessed 160 branches in Britain. Today we possess 500. . . . Up to three years ago anti-Semitism was unknown as a strong force in Britain. Today, in any audience in Britain, the strongest passion that can be aroused is the passion against the corruption of Jewish power. . . .'

[The peroration showed Mosley's exalted style of oratory continuing as strongly as ever. Perhaps, if he had won, words like these would now be committed to heart by British schoolchildren as Americans learn the Gettysburg address.]

'We count it a privilege to live in an age when England demands that great things shall be done, a privilege to be of the generation which learns to say: "What can we give?" instead of: "What can we take?"

'For thus our generation learns that there are greater things than slothful ease; greater things than safety; more terrible things than death.

'For this shall be the epic generation which scales again the heights of time and history to see once more the immortal lights – the lights of sacrifice and high endeavour summoning through the ordeal the soul of humanity to the sublime and eternal. The alternatives of our age are heroism or oblivion. There are no lesser paths in the history of great nations. Can we, therefore, doubt which path to choose?

'Let us tonight at this great meeting give the answer.

'Hold high the head of England! Lift strong the voice of Empire! Let us to Europe and the world proclaim that the heart of this great people is undaunted and invincible. This flag still challenges the winds of destiny. This flame still burns. This glory shall not die.

'The soul of Empire is alive and England again dares to be great!'

Four months later Mosley appeared in spanking new uniform,

jackboots shining, cap at a rakish angle, to review his forces in the East End. He had a jerky way of giving the Fascist salute with bended elbow and palm upright, like a policeman stopping traffic. After the review there was a big open-air rally in Victoria Park, Bow, at which British Union estimated there was an attendance of 100,000. (Sir Philip Game put it at 5,000 in his annual report.) The LCC retaliated by forbidding the use of loudspeakers in its parks.

The new uniforms, the Victoria Park rally and the growth of hooliganism brought renewed interest in Parliament, and in the first six months of 1936 there were two debates on the Home Office vote. Mosley decided to answer the complaints by fighting the next LCC election in order to prove the existence of a local, East End demand for National Socialism.

'East London,' declared Mosley, 'will be asked to choose between us and the parties of Jewry. . . . The charges against British Union relate in particular to East London. So we shall take the opportunity of the LCC elections to ask for the verdict of the people of East London.'

This was a break with the principle which British Union had hitherto upheld – that it was a waste of energy to fight local elections, Fascism being capable of implementation only at national level. The principle was, however, maintained inasmuch as British Union made no attempt to fight the LCC election on a local, London policy. The campaign, which started immediately after Mosley's announcement with the distribution of leaflets to 50,000 houses, was fought on British Union's national policy with special emphasis on the Jews. Mosley himself was out of the fight for the first two months through an appendicitis operation but he returned in time for the climax of all the East End disorders – the so-called Battle of Cable Street.

The battle arose from a march which the Blackshirts planned to make on Sunday, 5th October 1936, through the East End, and including the Jewish areas. It was to be the biggest show of Fascist strength the East End had ever seen. At four points the column would halt to hear speeches by Mosley. The Jews feared that the march would be the prelude to a real pogrom. The left saw it in terms of Fascist aggression. The Spanish Civil War had just broken out to arouse intense emotional passion among Socialists and Communists. They at once saw Mosley's march as the British equivalent of Franco's rebellion.

Using the Spanish Republican motto 'They shall not pass', the Communists rallied their supporters physically to stop British

Union. The more pacific ILP planned a form of passive resistance and instructed their members to form human barriers in the streets. The East End Labour parties joined in the preparations. For a week before the scheduled date the area of the march seethed with excitement, fear and anger.

Attlee, Morrison and other Labour Party leaders visited Sir John Simon, Home Secretary, to warn him that if the march took place there would be bloodshed and violence. On the Saturday night the *Star* carried warnings under the glaring headline 'STOP MOSLEY'.

Game made preparations as if for a battle. Into the East End he drafted 6,000 constables – a third of his entire force – together with the whole mounted division. He arranged an elaborate system of communications with wireless and an autogiro flying overhead. In the London suburbs the Special Constabulary took the place of regulars called to the East End.

The Blackshirts, expecting the battle of their lives, paraded in threes in Royal Mint Street near the Tower of London with a strong force of police to protect them from the crowd. Mosley and Francis-Hawkins with stern, white faces arrived in open cars, motor-cycle escorts roaring beside them. As Mosley inspected his men – between 2,000 and 3,000 were on parade – stones flew over the police cordon, one smashing the window of Mosley's car, another striking him in the face.

Farther in the East End a riot had already developed. Thousands of demonstrators jammed the streets, the sheer physical pressure of human bodies smashing shop windows. The centre of the trouble was Cable Street, where crowds attempted to erect barricades, ripping doors and furniture from houses and pulling up paving stones. The police strategy was to try to clear a passage for traffic – including the Mosley procession – to pass. Again and again the foot and mounted police charged with drawn batons but failed to make headway against the surging demonstrators. As the day wore on tempers on both sides worsened, and there was a clear danger of serious bloodshed. Some of the policemen were hitting out indiscriminately with their truncheons and it would have taken only a slight shift in mood for the crowd to have turned really ugly and lynched the overwhelmingly outnumbered police.

The ILP Secretary, Fenner Brockway, had been trampled on by police horses. Forcing his way to a telephone box he warned the Home Office that if the march were not called off there would be bloodshed. Game, coming to the same conclusion, consulted Simon, who was week-ending in the country, and ordered Mosley, still at Royal Mint Street, to disperse his Blackshirts. Great waves of cheering rose in the air as the news spread through the crowd. The workers had triumphed! Mosley had not passed!

Before dismissing his men Mosley made a short speech. 'The Government,' he said, 'surrenders to Red violence and Jewish corruption. *We* never surrender. We shall triumph over the parties of corruption because our faith is greater than their faith, our will is stronger than their will, and within us is the flame that shall light this country and light this world.'

A week later the pro-Fascists took their revenge. While the police were concentrating their forces on a Communist victory demonstration, a gang of about a hundred youths burst into the Mile End Road, smashing windows of Jewish shops and houses and assaulting everyone in sight they thought Jewish. One Jew, a hairdresser, was picked up and hurled through a plate-glass window; after him the pro-Fascists threw a four year-old girl. It was the most violent anti-Semitic outbreak the East End had seen. British Union denied responsibility.

The Battle of Cable Street and the Mile End Road pogrom led directly to the Government decision to announce the Public Order Bill in the King's Speech at the opening of Parliament the following month. The Bill had four main provisions: (1) It banned the wearing of political uniforms save with the permission of the police on private, ceremonial occasions. (2) It forbade the use of stewards at open-air meetings. (3) It strengthened the existing law which made it a criminal offence to use insulting words likely to lead to a breach of the peace. (4) It gave the police power to ban marches and processions if, in the opinion of the Commissioner, they were likely to lead to a breach of the peace. The ban, if applied, was to cover all political parties in a specified area for a specified time. The Bill passed quickly through all its stages and became law on 1st January 1937.

There was opposition to the Bill from several directions. Communists, Socialists and trade unionists feared that the power to ban political processions would interfere with their traditional liberties. Among the Conservatives there was some doubt about the wisdom of banning uniforms; that British Union uniforms were provocative was generally agreed, but there was sympathy for the green-shirted Social Credit Party which had worn uniform long before Mosley. British Union opposed the whole Bill.

A few days after the Cable Street battle, Mosley went to Berlin for talks with Hitler. This was his second meeting with the Fuehrer; the first had been in the spring of 1935. During the second visit the German Government provided facilities for Mosley secretly to marry Mrs. Bryan Guinness, secret marriage being permissible under the local law of Prussia. The marriage took place before a registrar in a house near the Reichs Chancellery with everyone present sworn to secrecy. The gathering consisted of the bride and groom; Josef Goebbels, the German Propaganda Minister; Frau Goebbels and two British witnesses. A few hours later Hitler marked the occasion by entertaining the newly married couple to dinner, with the Goebbelses and other members of the Nazi hierarchy among the guests.*

The new Lady Mosley, whose first marriage had ended in divorce in 1934, was (and is) a woman of character and beauty. She was born Diana Freeman-Mitford, one of the six remarkable Mitford sisters, daughters of Lord Redesdale. She and her younger sister Unity Mitford joined the BUF in its early days and both were keenly interested in the German Nazi Movement. Hitler called them 'perfect specimens of Aryan womanhood'. Others of her sisters went in different political directions. Jessica Mitford favoured the extreme left. Nancy Mitford, the novelist and arbiter of 'U' and 'non-U', published a novel in 1935 called *Wigs on the Green* in which she satirized the BUF. Another sister, Deborah Mitford, became Duchess of Devonshire. In the mid-1930's Unity was the best-known, having attracted a good deal of newspaper publicity by her association with the Nazis.

Wigs on the Green and Jessica Mitford's autobiographical book *Hons and Rebels* (1960) vividly portray how the backwash of Fascism reached rural England.

Unity Mitford appears in *Wigs on the Green* thinly disguised as Eugenia Malmains, a peer's daughter who tries to convert her village to the militant new creed of 'Captain Jack' and the 'Union Jack-shirts'. It opens with Eugenia addressing a public meeting:

'Britons, awake! Arise! oh British lion,' cried Eugenia Malmains in thrilling tone. She stood on an overturned washtub on Chalford village green and harangued about a dozen aged yokels. Her straight hair, cut in a fringe, large, pale-blue eyes, dark skin, well-proportioned limbs and classical features,

* Verbal account by Sir Oswald Mosley to the author (1960).

combined with a fanaticism of gesture to give her the aspect of a modern Joan of Arc. . . .

'The Union Jack Movement is a Youth Movement,' Eugenia cried passionately. 'We are tired of the old. We see things through their eyes no longer. We see nothing admirable in the debating society of aged and corrupt men which muddles our great Empire into wars or treaties, dropping one by one the jewels from its crown, casting away its glorious Colonies, its hitherto undenied supremacy at sea, its prestige abroad, its prosperity at home, and all according to each vacillating whim of some octogenarian statesman's mistress——'

At this point a very old lady came up to the crowd, pushed her way through it and began twitching at Eugenia's skirt. 'Eugenia, my child,' she said brokenly, 'do get off that tub, pray, please get down at once. Oh! when her ladyship hears of this I don't know what will happen.'

'Go away, Nanny,' said Eugenia, who in the rising tide of oratory seemed scarcely aware that she had been interrupted. '. . . Britons I beseech you to take action. Oh! British lion, shake off the nets that bind you.' Here the old lady again plucked at Eugenia's skirt. This time, however, Eugenia turned round and roared at her, 'Get out, you filthy Pacifist, get out, I say, and take your yellow razor gang with you. I will have free speech at my meetings. Now will you go of your own accord or must I tell the Comrades to fling you out? Where are my Union Jackshirts?' Two hobbledehoys . . . dressed in red, white and blue shirts here came forward, saluted Eugenia and each taking one of Nanny's hands they led her to a neighbouring bench. . . .

'We Union Jackshirts,' remarked Eugenia to the company at large, 'insist upon the right to be heard without interruption at our own meetings. Let the Pacifists' – and here she gave her Nanny a very nasty look – 'hold their own meetings, we shall not interfere with them at all, but if they try to break up our meetings they do so at their own risk.'

Hons and Rebels tells of Fascist Unity and pro-left Jessica scratching the swastika and hammer-and-sickle emblems with diamonds on the windows of the Mitford Gloucestershire home; of Unity and Diana singing Nazi songs and Jessica trying to shout them down by singing Communist words to the same tune. All took their creeds very seriously. Jessica eloped to Spain and thence to America with

Esmond Romilly, left-wing nephew of Winston Churchill. Unity, devoted to Hitler, tried to commit suicide on the outbreak of war in 1939. Hitler shipped her home via Switzerland and she lived the rest of her life in seclusion, dying of meningitis in 1948.

Mosley kept his marriage a close secret, denying even to the children of his first marriage that it had taken place.* During 1937 rumours of the event appeared in *Paris Soir*, the *Daily Mail* and other newspapers but there was no official disclosure until December 1938, on the birth of the first son. In a long statement to *Action* Mosley denied a current rumour that he had been married in Munich but gave no details of the true circumstances. The reason for secrecy, he explained, was that 'certain special risks are attached to my life and it was my strong desire that no woman should share them'.

Mosley returned from Berlin to plunge almost at once into the Abdication Crisis of December 1936. British Union threw all its resources into a campaign on behalf of King Edward VIII, advocating that he should be allowed to marry Mrs. Wallis Simpson and to keep his throne. The campaign had deep roots, the Movement having long regarded Edward as an ideal King for a Fascist Britain. Mosley himself had links with the Royal Family. His grandfather, the fourth baronet, had been a close friend of Edward VII. In the 1920's the Mosleys had moved in some of the same social circles as the Prince of Wales, and Cynthia Mosley's sister married 'Fruity' Metcalfe, the Prince's closest friend. That Edward favoured a Fascist revolution is unlikely, but British Union was convinced that he would make a good Fascist monarch and, long before he came to the throne, had devoted a good deal of space in its publications to praising him.

Fervent support for the Crown had been a Fascist characteristic from the start. It reached its height with the death of George V in January 1936, when *Blackshirt* devoted two of its eight pages to pictures and obituaries. (Another full page in the same issue was devoted to the death of Kipling.) Fascist writers hailed Edward's accession with enthusiasm: 'This steel-true King who now comes to the throne is destined to lend no weight to Britain's decline, but to throw the whole influence of his brave spirit into Britain's resurgence and triumph,' wrote Chesterton. Even more enthusiastic was Joyce, who in an article describing Edward's first broadcast, wrote: 'Soldierly brevity, youthful energy, deep filial affection and a royal

* *In Many Rhythms* by Baroness Ravensdale (1953).

dignity were the immediate impressions created; but beyond these qualities was something suggestive of whipcord – the buoyant and invincible confidence of a man who knows himself to be fit for enormous responsibilities which it has become his duty to bear. It was a speech which could appropriately have been made only at the beginning of a great and successful reign.'

When the news broke of the King's wish to marry Mrs. Simpson, Mosley coined the slogan 'Stand by the King!' and seemed seriously to consider the possibility of being called to form a pro-King government. Joyce took a whole page in *Action* to explain that the real authors of the crisis were 'the party manager, the odious minions of Finance, the parasites of Mayfair, the ecclesiastical cult of Selassie and Thaelmann, that with monstrous arrogance pretend to represent the people and the dominions'.

Mosley's speeches, his own secret marriage just accomplished, had a personal flavour.

'The King,' he declared, 'has been loyal and true to us. My simple demand is that we should be loyal and true to him. . . . The recompense of his country for twenty-five years' faithful service is the denial of every man's right to live in private happiness with the woman he loves. Let the man or woman who has never loved be the first to cast the stone. . . .'

Edward paid scant attention to Mosley's appeals and did not even ask to see the list of ministers which, Fascist rumour said, Mosley had already prepared. So far as the general public was concerned, the only available candidate as pro-King Prime Minister was Mosley's old opponent, Winston Churchill. The pro-King newspapers, the *Daily Express* and *Daily Mail*, considered the British Union campaign hardly worth noticing.

'I regret,' said Mosley at Limehouse the day after the Abdication, 'that the King did not see fit to stay and fight his battle, which is the battle of the people, because I know the battle could have been won.'

After the Abdication British Union pledged loyalty to George VI, but the heart had gone out of its monarchism. From 1937 onwards the references to the Crown were few and impersonal and in redeveloping his policy after the war Mosley paid almost no attention to the role of the monarchy.

From the King's crisis British Union, now in plain clothes, turned its attention to the LCC election, in which it decided to fight three double-member constituencies. For Bethnal Green North-East the candidates were Raven Thomson and 'Mick' Clarke; for Limehouse Mosley chose Anne Brock Griggs, architect's wife and British Union's Chief Women's Organizer, and Charles Wegg-Prosser, a young Catholic lawyer whose religion was calculated to appeal to the Irish vote. For Shoreditch the candidates were William Joyce and J. A. 'Bill' Bailey, a local man who worked in the furniture trade. Had he been elected Joyce, the secret American citizen, would have been debarred from sitting on the council. The nomination paper at that time, however, contained no provision for a candidate to state his nationality.

For British Union the big issue was anti-Semitism. Joyce's election address, for example, consisted of fifteen paragraphs, of which nine attacked the Jews. British Union used the Union Jack as an election favour and conducted a vigorous campaign with over 150 meetings, Mosley speaking six times in each constituency. The campaign was also the first occcasion on which British Union made a public appeal for funds. A series of appeals in *Action* produced a total of £632 14s. 2d., the subscription list showing some 700 contributions, about half of them anonymous. *Action* and *Blackshirt* deepened their anti-Semitic campaigns until they covered even the film reviews. There was an attack on the film star Elizabeth Bergner for 'the collection of nods and grimaces which go to make up the Bergner personality'. There was a similar attack on Merle Oberon, *Action* apologizing a week later on being told that she was not Jewish.

The results, declared on 6th March 1937, fell far short of the victory for which British Union had hoped but did prove the existence of a substantial body of support for Fascism. At Bethnal Green the British Union candidates actually came second, pushing the Liberals to the bottom of the poll. The full results, with approximate percentages, were as follows:

Bethnal Green North-East

T. Dawson (Labour)	7,777
Mrs. R. S. Keeling (Labour)	7,756
A. Raven Thomson (British Union)	3,028
E. G. Clarke (British Union)	3,022
A. J. Irvine (Liberal)	2,328
H. K. Sadler (Liberal)	2,298

(Labour 59 per cent, British Union 23 per cent, Liberal 18 per cent.)

Stepney (Limehouse)

R. Coppock (Labour)	8,272
Miss H. M. Whately (Labour)	8,042
V. G. Weeple (Municipal Reform)	2,542
G. E. Abrahams (Municipal Reform)	2,431
Mrs. A. Brock Griggs (British Union)	2,086
C. Wegg-Prosser (British Union)	2,086

(Labour 54 per cent, Municipal Reform 27 per cent, British Union 19 per cent.)

Shoreditch

Mrs. H. Girling (Labour)	11,098
S. W. Jeger (Labour)	11,069
S. L. Price (Municipal Progressive)	3,303
R. S. Falk (Municipal Progressive)	3,217
William Joyce (British Union)	2,564
J. A. Bailey (British Union)	2,492
C. E. Taylor (Independent Labour)	385

(Labour 63 per cent, Municipal Progressive 22 per cent, British Union 14 per cent, Independent Labour 1 per cent.)

These results were the high-water mark of British Union success. The young movement had secured nearly a fifth of the vote, despite the opposition of the large Jewish community and despite the fact that many of its most active supporters, not being ratepayers, were debarred from voting. On hearing the results Mosley is said to have smashed his fist into his palm and exclaimed: 'Better than Hitler!' and to have gone on to explain that four years before achieving power Hitler had polled under twenty per cent. The difference was that Hitler had won his votes over the whole of Germany whereas British Union was fighting the three constituencies which in the whole of Britain offered the best prospects of success. At the rate of progress shown in the LCC election it would have taken half a century for British Union to come within reaching distance of national power.

Six months later British Union fought borough elections, in London contesting all the areas where the police had banned marches under the Public Order Act and in the provinces fighting according to the energy of local branches.

In Bethnal Green, Limehouse and Shoreditch the borough results were about the same as those in the LCC six months earlier. The highest British Union poll was twenty-two per cent in Bethnal Green East. Altogether, British Union fought forty-eight seats in five London boroughs, its candidates polling an average of 560 votes each, compared with an average of 2,252 by Labour in the same seats. In Bethnal Green East, Bethnal Green North, Shoreditch Haggerston, Shoreditch Whitmore, Stepney Mile End and Stepney Limehouse, British Union secured second place, but nowhere came within reaching distance of victory.

The provincial results were disastrous. British Union put up candidates in Edinburgh, Leeds, Sheffield and Southampton. All came hopelessly at the bottom of the poll. Leeds, with its large Jewish population, was particularly interesting, the two British Union candidates polling 106 and 74 votes respectively and coming below even the Social Credit candidate. In Edinburgh the candidates polled 51 and 41, in Sheffield 98 and 97, and in Southampton only 29.

CHAPTER 12

Decline

IMMEDIATELY after the LCC election of March 1937 British Union plunged into a series of internal crises from which it was never to recover. Three main causes can be traced. In the first place a shortage of money was reflected in every sector of the Movement's activities. Mosley valiantly announced that in future he would give his whole income to the Movement, but this was far from enough to maintain the proliferation of salaried posts in the upper reaches of the Fascist hierarchy. Secondly there were the quarrelsome personal relationships between the 'politicals' like Beckett and the administrators like Francis-Hawkins. The shortage of money tended to sharpen the personal quarrels. Thirdly there was a widening divergence in policy and methods between the powerful East End movement and the isolated, idealistic Fascist branches in the provinces and the countryside. The East End branches with memberships running into hundreds, with their virile anti-Semitic propaganda, their adulation of the German National Socialists and their nightly conflicts with the militant anti-Fascists, had little in common with the tiny Fascist groups in other parts of the country, groups where patriotism was the mainspring and anti-Semitism an embarrassment.

A fortnight after the LCC election Mosley summoned over a hundred of his salaried speakers and officials to National Headquarters. As he entered the room they snapped stiffly to attention and saluted. Rumours had circulated about Mosley's intentions but the truth was worse than most had feared. In curt sentences Mosley thanked them for their work and went on to say that British Union's

paid staff was to be cut immediately from 143 to thirty. The Northern
Command headquarters at Manchester was to be closed altogether.
The dismissed officers were to call at the office the next day to collect
their outstanding wages. In words that many at the time found
persuasive, Mosley insisted that the dismissed officials were still
needed for Fascism and he asked them in future to work in an
unpaid capacity.

In a public statement Mosley explained that the purpose of the
cuts was to 'place the finances of British Union on such a stable and
durable foundation that the Movement is assured of staying-power
whether the struggle be long or short'. Answering newspaper questions, Mosley further explained: 'In general our chief propagandists
are now in the same position as those of other movements and as are
a great number of voluntary speakers in our own movement – namely,
they maintain themselves in ordinary occupations and give voluntary
services.' A full-length article by Mosley in *Action* to explain the
economies was announced but never published.

The purge included two men who, after Mosley, were the best-
known personalities in the Movement – John Beckett, Director of
Publications, and William Joyce, Director of Propaganda. Between
them they had supervised the entire output of the Movement's
printed and verbal propaganda, and their abrupt dismissal is
inexplicable merely in terms of economy. The truth was that they
had proved a pair of round pegs failing to fit in the square holes of
the Francis-Hawkins hierarchy, and the purge provided a convenient
opportunity to get rid of them.

Self-confident of his own abilities, conscious of the special status
he and Mosley shared as ex-MPs, Beckett had in the early days been
a close colleague of Mosley, and very free with advice. By 1937 his
status had declined and Mosley was less receptive to advice from
Beckett than he was to advice from other quarters, notably from
Francis-Hawkins. That he should cease giving advice would not
occur to Beckett. Nor was he the kind of man to keep silent when he
had a grievance. His witty but sardonic tongue became a major
administrative inconvenience, a potential source of treason against
the Leader.

Joyce, a close friend of Beckett, was a somewhat different case. His
lack of status outside Fascism made him cherish all the more the
status he had won inside the Movement. Hard, dedicated, but sensitive
to slights, Joyce had an ambition to become a great political teacher.
Power in the conventional form of political authority interested him

comparatively little. He had no ambition to replace Mosley as Leader of British Fascism. The power he wanted was over other men's minds, to teach them the ideas he had devised. He cherished the personal following he gained within the Movement and worked to extend it, an action which caused jealousies, especially when it became known that he had a private income subscribed by two or three of his wealthier admirers. He was the kind of man who needed a hero as a focus for his admiration – just one hero. Even the dreamy, humourless Joyce could see that in terms of practical politics Mosley was not a man of power and instead he turned all the fervour of his hero worship to Adolf Hitler. The transfer of allegiance was the easier for Joyce because of his awareness of his lack of British citizenship, although he kept it a secret. To the Francis-Hawkins group Joyce was a disturbing influence, a vain little man who had ideas at variance with those of the Leader and was using the Movement for his own ends. Out he had to go. The pretext seems to have been the private income which, it was argued, Joyce should hand to British Union funds.

In a word, Beckett and Joyce were individualists and therefore bad Fascists.

They both immediately formed a rival organization, the National Socialist League, with headquarters at 109 Vauxhall Bridge Road, S.W.1. With them into the new organization went John Angus MacNab, a product of Rugby and Christ Church, who had been editor of Mosley's *Fascist Quarterly*. A round-faced man of thirty with thick spectacles, MacNab had been a schoolmaster at Leeds. He was strongly anti-Semitic and made his first appearance in *Blackshirt* as author of a weekly column called 'Jolly Judah' in which he somewhat laboriously tried to poke fun at Jews. The National Socialist League was, of course, violently anti-Semitic. It differed subtly from Arnold Leese's Imperial Fascists in that it presented the Jews as the main cause rather than the sole cause of the world's troubles. Its policy, apart from expelling Jews from Britain, was to set up a system of 'guilds', roughly equivalent to Mosley's corporations.

In a book *National Socialism Now* (1937) Joyce explained his new creed as one of 'revolutionary patriotism' and called for the deportation of 'oriental criminals' who propagated the doctrines of 'the verminous old Jew, Karl Marx'. He was especially keen on maintaining British rule over India and attacked 'the handful of babus and fakirs paid by the masters of Indian slave-labour to drive the British out of India'. The masters of the slave-labour were, naturally, the 'Shylocks in the City of London'.

In the final pages he wrote vividly of the love he felt for England. In view of his later decision to side with Hitler in the 1939-45 war, they read rather strangely. Did he express deep patriotism merely for propaganda? Or, as seems more likely, did he really mean it?

> We generally forget the spring morning with the splendid sun sparkling on the dew in the green fields, the white lanes with their shining hedges in summer, the rich tint of leaves in the declining autumn afternoon . . . but if it ever happens to us to see the chalk cliffs receding for the last time as the water widens between us and our homeland, then the memories will come in a choking flood. . . . This is the land for which better than we have died.

The National Socialist League was never a serious political force but it attracted enough support to give Joyce a living. About a hundred British Union members joined, some of them being dismissed officials, but it was really a one-man show which allowed Joyce to stand on a soap-box every night and say exactly what he wanted. Beckett dropped out at the time of Munich, when Joyce said that in the event of war he would go to Germany to fight for Hitler. The war, Joyce believed, was fundamentally a struggle between Hitler and the Jews. In fighting for Hitler he would be serving Britain's highest interests. MacNab remained a member until the League was formally dissolved in September 1939.

After the first shock had passed, the loss of the Director of Publications and the Director of Propaganda and the formation of a splinter group did not damage British Union so much as might have been expected. The principal officials, Francis-Hawkins, Director-General, and Raven Thomson, Director of Policy, were unshakably loyal to Mosley and closed in to fill the gap. Chesterton's pen remained at the service of the Movement for a little while longer. More prominence went to Robert Gordon-Canning, Foreign Editor of *Action* and the Movement's expert on international affairs. A descendant of the Prime Minister Canning, he had served as a cavalry officer in Palestine and seemed to envisage himself as a latter-day Lawrence of Arabia, siding with the Arabs against the Jews. He took himself and Fascism very seriously, contributed generously to the Movement's funds and was industrious with a somewhat pompous pen. The editorship of *Action*, which Beckett had combined with his post of Director of Publications, went to Geoffrey Dorman, who had previously been Assistant Editor and aviation specialist.

Educated at Tonbridge and Downing College, Cambridge, Dorman had first met Mosley in 1915 when they had learned to fly together in the Royal Flying Corps at Shoreham. After the war he had worked for several years on the staff of the *Aeroplane* and also wrote adventure stories for boys. His sister, Pamela, had married Ian Dundas in 'the first Fascist wedding' in 1933. He was never within the inner circle of the leadership and during his periods as Editor was heavily chaperoned by Mosley and Raven Thomson.

A resignation of quite a different kind from that of Joyce and Beckett was that of Charles Wegg-Prosser, the Limehouse candidate in the LCC election. His was a rare, possibly unique, case of conversion from Fascism to militant anti-Fascism. Educated at Downside and Oriel College, Oxford, he first leaned towards Fascism while an undergraduate. For many with his background Fascism had a special attraction in that it combined a zeal for social reform with an apparent respectability that the left could not offer. He actually joined the Movement in 1934 at Hertford, where he went to work as a solicitor's articled clerk after leaving Oxford. He attracted some attention as a contributor to *Fascist Quarterly* and as a promising public speaker. When he came to work in London in 1936 he was chosen as an LCC candidate. Mosley had high hopes of him. For Wegg-Prosser, however, the contrast between the idealism of the tiny Hertford branch and the rough realism of East End Fascism brought total disillusionment. There had been a faint 'Communism is Jewish' trend in his writings but when he saw anti-Semitic propaganda in action in the East End he revised his views. Three months after the LCC election Mosley wrote him a letter inviting him to be a British Union Parliamentary candidate. Wegg-Prosser replied with a stinging denunciation of Mosley and all his works which came as a rude surprise to the Movement.

The letter, later printed as a pamphlet by the Jewish Board of Deputies, was especially bitter about anti-Semitism:

> Your methods [wrote Wegg-Prosser] have become increasingly dictatorial and un-English. You are side-tracking the whole issue of social betterment by the anti-Semitic campaign. Anti-Jewish propaganda, as you and Hitler use it, is a gigantic side-

tracking stunt, a smoke-screen to cloud thought and divert action with regard to our real problems. . . . Our people are fair, tolerant and humane. You introduce a movement imitating foreign dictators, you run it as a soulless despotism. You side-track the demand for social justice by attacking the Jew, you give the people a false answer and unloose the lowest mob passion.

The Labour Party admitted Wegg-Prosser to membership after a period of probation and he went on to become one of the most effective anti-Fascist speakers in the East End, on two occasions being physically attacked by his former British Union comrades. After war service and eight years after leaving British Union he was Labour Parliamentary candidate for South Paddington, which he fought again in 1950, 1951 and 1955.

Five months later J. A. Bailey, who had been Joyce's running mate at Shoreditch in the LCC election, withdrew from British Union and told the *News Chronicle* that he had become 'completely disillusioned'. The East End officials refused to accept his resignation and solemnly expelled him. Thus, before the year was out, three of the six candidates who had formed the spearhead of British Union's first election campaign had left the Movement.

Meanwhile the Public Order Act was proving effective in pacifying the East End. The abolition of uniforms made the Blackshirts look less impressive and less intimidating. Anti-Fascist newspapers tended henceforth to jibe at them as 'weedy-looking clerks' rather than to condemn them as 'Fascist bullies'. There were local attempts at Leeds and Hull to send uniformed Blackshirts into the streets to sell *Action*, the argument being that they were wearing the uniforms for commercial, not political, purposes. Magistrates in both places decided against British Union and there was no attempt to test the matter on appeal. Mosley himself wore the undress black shirt under a suit on public occasions, unsuccessfully challenging the police to prosecute. Generally, however, there was no serious attempt to evade the law and the only time the uniforms reappeared *en masse* was by police permission at the London Command annual dinner in the summer of 1937. The fashion grew within the Movement for members to wear dark or black polo-neck sweaters which, on a test case, were declared by at least one magistrates' court not to constitute uniform. There was also a fashion for heavy, belted raincoats in the style favoured by the Nazi hierarchy in Germany. Red armbands with the flash-and-circle emblem were within the law and continued in use.

The Police Commissioner, Philip Game, made generous use of his new powers to ban processions, bringing complaints from Communists, Socialists and trade unionists whose demonstrations were also affected. He also carried to a peak of efficiency the technique the police had previously developed for protecting outdoor meetings. The practice was to herd the Fascists close to the speaker's stand and to surround them with a police cordon. Anti-Fascists were unable to get at the Fascists and tended, therefore, to fight the police instead. Mounted police were held in reserve and if the foot cordon got into difficulties the mounted men would come in to disperse the crowd. Inevitably, the system gave rise to complaints that the police were siding with the Fascists.

That some individual police officers preferred Fascists to anti-Fascists seems beyond doubt. There was some evidence, too, of a strain of anti-Semitism in the police. The Fascists had a good record for co-operating with the police, Joyce being particularly well regarded in the East End for the disciplined way in which he marshalled his Blackshirts according to police instructions. Up to 1937 the Fascists rarely interfered with their opponents' meeting and so had little reason to clash with the police in that way. There is, however, no evidence to show that the police officially favoured the Fascists, or even that a majority of individual officers liked the Fascists. Most of the allegations of bias can be explained in terms of loss of temper or momentary misjudgments by the lower ranks in the heat of some very difficult situations.

The rule among newspaper journalists sent to cover Fascist meetings in the East End was always to wear their oldest clothes. From Fleet Street of an evening small groups of reporters would go out dressed as for gardening. This was not for disguise but because Fascist meetings tended to end in a rough-house in which little regard was paid to the rights of the Press. Arnold Turvey, Parliamentary Correspondent of the London *Evening News*, then a news-agency reporter, recalls how he and a colleague were caught in a charge by mounted police. It was in a narrow street with no means of escaping from the advancing horses. Turvey shinned up a lamp post, burning his gloves on the hot lamp. As he hung there, a mounted policeman rode past and attempted to hit him with a baton and nearly tumbled off his horse in the process. Turvey's colleague, sheltering in a shop doorway, was less fortunate. A group of foot policemen, running behind the mounted men, seized him and flung him into the gutter while he still fumbled in his pocket for his Press card.

In retrospect it may seem surprising that the police did not lose their tempers more often. The duty of controlling an angry crowd is a difficult one that in the ordinary way comes rarely to a British policeman. In the East End in 1936 and 1937 the police, working endless overtime, faced that duty three or four nights a week. The Communists saw the police as the workers' class enemies and had little hesitation in attacking them, a favourite trick being to roll marbles under the hoofs of the police horses.

When uniforms were abolished the Fascists announced that they no longer had the means of controlling their members and that they could no longer prevent indignant Blackshirts breaking up their opponents' meetings. By 1938 it was difficult for any non-Fascist to speak indoors or outdoors in the East End without being shouted down by organized Fascist barracking. Both Attlee, the Labour Leader, and Samuel, the Liberal Leader, failed to get hearings. Ernest Thurtle, Labour MP for Shoreditch, made a public appeal to Mosley to call off his men. 'As one man to another,' he wrote, 'I ask you if there are still limits of decency and humanity to which political antagonisms should be carried.' Mosley coldly replied: 'Our members have been attacked with razors, knives and every weapon known to the Ghettos of humanity. Yet I am unaware of a single word spoken by Labour leaders in condemnation of the violence of their supporters.'

A favourite way of interrupting non-Fascist meetings was by singing Blackshirt songs, of which the German *Horst Wessel Lied* was the unofficial favourite. The Movement tried hard to introduce its own British songs and back in 1932 Mosley had talked of persuading Osbert Sitwell to write Fascist words to Sousa's 'Stars and Stripes'.* The only home-grown product which did win favour was 'Song of Union' by E. D. Randall, sung to the tune of 'Sons of the Sea':

> Lift high the flag!
>   On with the fight!
> Strength is in Union;
>   Let the land unite!
> Fearless, faithful unto death,
>   All to dare and give!
> For the land that we love and the people's right!
>   For Britain yet shall live!

* *In Many Rhythms* by Baroness Ravensdale (1953).

Mosley's sister-in-law, Nancy Mitford, had her own ideas of what should constitute a Fascist song. In *Wigs on the Green* (1935) she provided an anthem to be sung to the tune of 'Onward Christian Soldiers' by her imaginary Jackshirts. The second verse ran:

> Fight with shell and bullet
> Fight with castor oil,
> Fight with pen and paper,
> Fight Oh Jackshirts loyal.
> Fight the loathly pacifist
> Fight the junket breast,
> Make them feel the Jackshirt's fist
> Make them howl for rest.
>
> Onward, Union Jackshirts
> Foreigners you'll whack.
> Fight and die for England
> And the Union Jack.

Whether it was by song or shouted insult, the Fascists became increasingly adept at interrupting their opponents' meetings and, for the first time, the London police found themselves seriously in action against Fascists as well as against anti-Fascists. This helped to answer the earlier accusations of pro-Fascist bias. The balance was further redressed by the energetic action Game took to implement the sections of the Public Order Act dealing with 'insulting words likely to lead to a breach of the peace'. Police shorthand writers regularly attended British Union meetings in search of insults and often found them.

The first conviction for insulting words was against a prominent East London speaker who had referred in an open-air speech to 'dirty, mongrel Russian Jews' and declared that 'Jews are the lice of the earth and must be exterminated from the national life'. Sir Philip Game, he had observed, was 'a damned old woman who has not the guts of a louse'. The magistrate bound over the speaker for six months in the sum of £50 and threatened imprisonment for the next offence. The result was a definite modification of Fascist propaganda with less provocation to Jews and other anti-Fascists.

By the summer of 1937 the worst disorders were already dying down. Mosley announced that the first Sunday in May should henceforth be 'National Socialist Day' and led a march to Victoria

Park Square at Bow. The National Socialists were insulated from the crowd by lines of police who marched on either side, reducing the spectacle to a farce. At a Trafalgar Square rally, two months later, so many police separated Mosley from the crowd and the anti-Fascists shouted so many catcalls that he was almost inaudible. *Action*, very angry, described the interrupters as 'a miserable collection of Orientals and of the garbage of Europe'.

The last big public disorder came in October 1937, just a year after the battle of Cable Street. Marches in East London were banned and Mosley decided to penetrate the hitherto peaceful areas south of the River Thames. For 3rd October he announced a propaganda march starting at Millbank and passing through the boroughs of Lambeth, Southwark and Bermondsey, the Labour mayors of which promptly appealed to the Home Secretary for it to be banned. The appeal failing, Jack Gibson, Mayor of Lambeth, announced that he and his council, wearing their robes of office, would stand in the street physically to bar the way to Mosley's men. On police advice he later changed his mind. The anti-Fascists of South London were, perhaps, a little frustrated at having so few Fascists to fight compared with the East End and they were anxious to show their mettle. Among moderate sections of opinion there was serious alarm lest the disorders of East London should spread south of the river. Again the slogan sounded 'Mosley Shall Not Pass' and the evening before the march there were street scuffles between anti-Fascists and Blackshirts who had arrived in force to sell *Action* and *Blackshirt*.

On the day, the fighting was almost entirely between police and anti-Fascists. It centred on the Jamaica Road where crowds of anti-Fascists, many of them visitors for the day from the East End, attempted to uproot trees and railings to form a barricade. The police handled the situation with considerable skill and foxed the Jamaica Road demonstrators by ordering Mosley to make a last-minute change of route. Limping badly at the end of the three-mile march, Mosley told his followers that it had been an 'historic adventure'.

There were 111 arrests, all of anti-Fascists. The following week's *Action* rejoiced with a big headline 'Mosley DID pass' and went on to explain that the trouble had been caused by old enemies from the East End – 'residents from the jewish Ghetto surrounding White-chapel'. (*Action* had temporarily adopted the Nazi habit of spelling 'jew' without a capital letter.)

On the wider, national front British Union's policy was now to press ahead with preparations for the next general election, expected in 1940. Between 1936 and 1938 Mosley selected eighty candidates for seventy-nine constituencies. (One candidate died after being selected, allegedly from the effects of a stone thrown by an anti-Fascist in Reading.) For a movement still young it was reasonable progress, but it was far short of the number needed for a serious bid for power. The choice of candidates was made entirely from National Headquarters and caused further dissensions and jealousies in the Movement. In a high proportion of the seats the candidates were imposed by National Headquarters simply as a means of spurring local organizations into greater activity. Nowhere outside East London did British Union have anything approaching an effective electioneering organization.

In a few instances the candidates were chosen more for their names than for their services to the Movement. For example, Vice-Admiral R. St. P. Parry, late of the India Defence League and candidate for Westminster (Abbey Division), made no apparent contribution beyond attending his adoption meeting.

Nevertheless a high proportion of candidates were full-time officials. Raven Thomson was candidate for South Hackney, 'Mick' Clarke for North-East Bethnal Green, Anne Brock Griggs for South Poplar and Bentinck-Budd for Birmingham Ladywood. Fuller challenged Duff Cooper, Secretary for War, at Westminster (St. George's). John MacNab, before leaving the Movement with Beckett and Joyce, was selected to fight South Leeds.

Candidates of social standing included Dorothy, Viscountess Downe, at North Norfolk; Lady Pearson (sister of Sir Henry Page-Croft, MP) at Canterbury; Sir Lionel Haworth (late Indian Civil Service) at Chelsea; and Ralph Gladwyn Jebb of Downton Manor, near Salisbury, who was candidate for Dorset West. Jebb was a friend of Mosley, worked actively for British Union and was the only person to receive the Movement's highest badge of honour, the 'Gold Distinction'.

Another category of candidates were the active local leaders, selected for their own districts, like Vice-Admiral G. B. Powell at Portsmouth Central; Mandeville Roe, the former British Fascist, at Balham; and Jorian Jenks, leading Fascist writer on agriculture, at Horsham. There was a mother-and-son partnership between Muriel Whinfield at Petersfield and Edward Whinfield at Stoke Newington.

The women candidates, numbering eleven among the eighty,

included two former suffragettes, Norah Elam (Mrs. Dacre-Fox) at Northampton and Mercédes Barrington at West Fulham. Miss Barrington was much alarmed at the splits in the Movement and wrote a fervent letter to *Action*: 'Stick by Mosley, as Mosley knows what he is doing. Loyalty must come first. Mosley will win. Hail Mosley!'

An analysis of the constituencies shows that the main strength of British Union was still in London and the south of England. Outposts of strength existed in East Anglia and Lancashire, the battle-grounds of old campaigns. For the whole of Scotland there was only one candidate, the one-armed veteran W. E. A. Chambers-Hunter at Aberdeen. Wales had only two candidates. Greater London had twenty-seven candidates, southern England and the West Country had seventeen, Lancashire had nine, the Midlands six and the north of England (apart from Lancashire) had nine.

From personal details of the candidates, given in *Action*, it is possible to get some idea of the kinds of people who were attracted to Fascism. The candidates were, on the whole, young. The ages of sixty-four of them were published, showing twenty-one in the age-group twenty-one to thirty, twenty-two in the age-group thirty-one to forty and twenty-one aged forty-one and over. Their occupations varied widely, the biggest categories being people engaged in 'business' (twelve), full-time British Union officials (ten), retired officers of the services (eight) and farmers, market gardeners and poultry farmers (six). There were two schoolmasters, two journalists, two railway clerks, two accountants, one barrister, one doctor, one actor, one commercial artist, one travel agent's courier, one miner, one bus-driver and one controller of the *Daily Mail*'s women canvassing staff.

Even without the steady exodus of members (including many of the Parliamentary candidates) during 1938 and 1939, it appears unlikely that British Union intervention in a general election in 1940 would have produced any Fascist MPs. Nor would it be fair to suppose that Mosley expected to win seats. He chose no constituency for himself, although rumour linked his name with Oliver Stanley's seat at Westmorland. His tactics were obviously to build up a framework of organization for the day when public opinion turned towards him in the economic crisis he freely predicted.

British Union's last pre-war electoral test was in the provincial borough elections of October 1938. The results were humiliating, the twenty-two candidates mustering a grand total of only 2,474 votes

– an average of 112 each. The lowest poll was in a Manchester ward where the Fascist candidate polled only twenty-three votes. A. J. Cummings wrote in the *News Chronicle*: 'In this country the Mosley brand of Fascism will soon be as dead as witchcraft.' *Action* retorted that the elections 'in nearly all cases showed a substantial advance on last year's results'.

Cummings's reference to 'the Mosley brand of Fascism' showed the shift that had come among anti-Fascist opinion. It was still widely expected, particularly by Marxists, that the contradictions of the existing social system would inevitably lead to an attempt by the capitalists to impose a dictatorship. As Aneurin Bevan put it: 'Poverty, great wealth and democracy are ultimately incompatible.' But the left no longer believed that the threat of dictatorship came from Mosley. The expectation was that in a crisis the Conservatives would adopt Fascist methods.

By this time it was the personal faith of Mosley that alone kept the Movement alive. He showed some signs of strain, especially in administrative matters, but he retained the old magnetism and the old power of grand oratory. That he should give up did not appear to enter his head. He retained his personal sense of destiny but he bore it in a gloomier manner than in the past. In April 1938 he issued a solemn warning to his opponents which in its very wording showed how he had changed from the high-spirited adventurer of six years earlier into something approaching a megalomaniac:

'The financial racketeer, the politician who has served not his country but his personal gain, the traitor in a hundred ways to the people's cause; all these shall meet justice at last.

'Clean courts of people's justice will be created to reveal all their foul transactions to the sterilizing light of day and to pass judgment upon them. . . .

'An honest opponent, who has fought us because he had different principles and has fought in manly and decent fashion for his beliefs, we can respect and can never injure. . . .

'But to the jackals of a putrescent system British Union will be relentless and merciless. . . . People's justice and people's law will deal with great and small alike. Then all things will be known and at last will be revealed to the people. Mighty on that day will be their wrath and justice shall be done. . . . So to the jackals of putrescence we say "Beware!". . . . The cleansing flame shall pursue you to the uttermost ends of the earth.'

CHAPTER 13

Fall

BRITISH FASCISM had few principles in foreign policy beyond an advocacy of strong national defences, a deep distrust of the League of Nations and a vague belief that the leaders of the 'modern movement' in the principal European countries should, in power, be capable of defining their individual spheres of influence – Britain in her empire, Hitler in Eastern Europe and Mussolini in the Balkans. Although in his Labour Party period Mosley had shown a detailed interest in foreign affairs, the early British Union of Fascists centred its policy almost entirely on Britain's internal politics.

The approach of the Second World War forced British Union into violent controversies about foreign affairs for which it was not suited and which more than any other cause led to its downfall.

The dress rehearsal for British Union, as for other British political parties, had been Mussolini's invasion of Abyssinia. For the Labour Party this was the moment to abandon its traditional pacifism, even at the loss of George Lansbury, and, through the League of Nations, to resist aggression even at the risk of war. British Union jumped the other way, supported Italy's 'civilizing mission' and ran a 'peace campaign' against League sanctions.

Franco's rising in Spain and Hitler's occupation of the Rhineland, both in 1936, marked the start of the campaign in earnest. On Spain the Fascists were far less aroused than the left and there was no attempt to recruit British volunteers to fight on Franco's side. The story goes that at its first meeting to consider the Spanish rising the British Union Policy Directorate, after long consideration, made the monumental misjudgment that the event was unlikely to have international repercussions. Mosley gave Franco general sympathy but declared: 'The whole of Spain is not worth one drop of British blood.' Although Hitler's occupation of the Rhineland was virtually the opening move of the Second World War, British public opinion was not inclined to fight Hitler just because he had 'walked into his own backyard'. But there was a general disposition in favour of rearmament. After 1937 even the Labour Opposition in the Commons abandoned its traditional opposition to the defence estimates. British Union took a different view, advocating an abandonment of the alliance between Britain and France in favour of a partnership between Britain and Germany. This would have entailed the return of her former colonies to Germany and a recognition of Germany's wish to expand eastwards. As early as January 1935 W. E. D. Allen, under his pen-name of James Drennan, wrote in *Fascist Quarterly* of 'the need for further lands geographically adjacent to Germany where the German peasant communities can spread themselves and develop that German corporate life in which the Nazis see the beginning and the end of all things'. In terms of power politics the British Union proposals were workable, but they took little account of the fact that the conflict between Britain and Germany was as much ideological as political. Fascism was a nationalistic creed in contrast to the internationalism of Communism, but, whatever the theoretical difference, in practice British Union echoed the voice of Berlin as readily as the Communist Party echoed the voice of Moscow.

Hitler was fascinated by the British Empire and right up to the summer of 1940 one of his principal aims was to secure his rear with an alliance with Britain. In the years before the war he encouraged a series of organizations to foster Anglo-German friendship, including the Anglo-German Fellowship, the 'Link', the anti-Semitic 'Right Club' under A. H. M. Ramsay, Conservative MP for Peebles, and, probably, the National Socialist League. With British Union his links were less direct. Mosley had no further meeting with Hitler after his marriage in 1936 and there is some reason for supposing that Hitler did not regard Mosley as an effective political force, but concentrated his propaganda instead on trying to influence the more orthodox sections of British public opinion. That he gave any money at all to Mosley is unlikely. If any did arrive it was such a small amount as to bring no relief to British Union's finances, which by 1938 were under obvious strain. The man most concerned with handling finance at this time was A. G. Findlay, a quiet young Aberdonian who had been in the New Party and resigned a post in a bank to become a full-time official in 1934.

In December 1937 a mysterious letter, typed on British Union's official writing paper, was circulated to Fleet Street newspapers. It purported to be a letter sent by Francis-Hawkins to one of the national inspectors. It ran:

> The Assistant Director-General of Organization (A) Northern Administration reports under confidential cover that you have been recently informing members that this Movement is financially supported by Italian and German funds.
>
> I must remind you of the Leader's conference, at which his statement to his Inspectors was given in the strictest confidence and not before he had bound everyone to their 'word of honour' regarding the entire proceedings.
>
> In view of Mr. Hone's report, it will be necessary for you to attend at these Headquarters at 10 a.m. on the 16th inst. when the whole matter will be investigated.
>
> N. Francis-Hawkins,
Director-General of Organization

How this letter got into anti-Fascist hands was not explained and British Union, while admitting that its paper had been used, denounced it as a forgery. Yet the Francis-Hawkins style rings true and some quite senior members of the British Union staff accepted it as genuine.* On the balance of probabilities it must be regarded as a forgery for the reason that it was simply not Mosley's habit to discuss financial details with his staff, although, to allay alarm, he might have given general assurances that funds were available to continue the Movement's work. The best explanation, again on balance of probabilities, is that the letter was forged by a member of the Movement wishing to pay off some grudge against Mosley, Francis-Hawkins or Hone.

One man who was definitely offered a paid post by the German Government was A. K. Chesterton, whose *Portrait of a Leader* was

---

* Statements to the author (1960).

published in a German edition in 1937. The offer was not for secret, under-cover work in Britain but of an open, salaried post as a propagandist in Berlin, and it came after he had resigned from British Union. He refused the offer.

In the autumn of 1937 Chesterton had taken over the editorship of *Action* from Dorman. He still admired many aspects of Mosley's personality and had a deep loyalty for his leader. He was, however, becoming increasingly disturbed at the way British Union was developing. Over and over again in his Fascist writings he had described British Union as a great purifying force which would cleanse what he regarded as the corruption of democratic politics. Now he wondered whether the purifying force had not itself become corrupt. He was particularly worried at the apparent lack of respect for truth in British Union propaganda. He was worried, too, that the close affinity between British Union and the Nazis was robbing the Movement of its patriotic character. Chesterton was by no means anti-Nazi. He expressed in his writings a qualified admiration of Hitler and, in his own mind, was prepared to accept German expansion in so far as it entailed the absorption into the Reich of Germanic minorities in other countries. He was not willing, however, to accept the incorporation of non-Germanic peoples which, he believed, would create rather than solve minority problems. Still less would he tolerate a German hegemony of Europe. Chesterton's attitude to these matters was significant in that it reflected the attitude of hundreds of lesser members of British Union, who hoped that Hitler would have no further territorial demands after he had united the German people.

In October 1937 the Movement's attention switched away from foreign affairs at the news that Mosley had been knocked unconscious by a brick while speaking at Queen's Drive, Walton, Liverpool. With his usual courage he had insisted on climbing to the top of the van to speak although the air was already full of brickbats. He uttered only two or three sentences before he fell unconscious and was rushed to hospital. The Liverpool mounted police cleared the ground just in time to prevent a serious riot. As *Action* put it: 'The Blackshirts, a glint of determination in their eyes and a desire to avenge this great outrage, were advancing in the direction of the rabble, and only the timely arrival of the mounted police prevented Queen's Drive being converted into a shambles.' An incidental result of this affair was to keep Chesterton in the Movement for an extra three months. He was sitting at home writing a letter of resignation when he turned on the wireless and heard what had happened at Liverpool. He felt that he could not desert an unconscious Mosley and tore up the letter. His wife, Doris Chesterton, never a member of the Movement, gathered the scraps and preserved them in a drawer against the day when they would be needed.

Action was anxious to avoid the impression that the Liverpool reception was typical and, as a contrast, gave in the same issue a lyrical account of Mosley in the East End where 'the people know Mosley and he returns their affection and love. You can see it in his every action, detect it in his every word. Soon that regard will spread beyond the boundaries of East London and will sweep over the whole of this land of ours.'

In March 1938 Chesterton finally resigned. He tried to go quietly. Before sending his last issue of *Action* to the printers he inserted a note: 'A. K. Chesterton wishes to announce that with the publication of this issue he resigns from the editorship of *Action* and from active membership of the British Union.' Within a fortnight, however, he had been critized by Mosley in a public speech, and he then resigned from the Movement altogether and issued a pamphlet setting out his grievances. He complained about Mosley's methods of leadership and of the nature of the Movement's propaganda:

> I have been amazed that a man so dynamic on the platform should prove so unimaginative, so timid, so lacking in initiative and resource. . . . The public aspect of this shows itself in his refusal to deal objectively with the Movement's fortunes. 'Flops' are written up as triumphs, and enormous pains are taken to titivate reports so as to give the impression of strength where there is weakness, growth where there is decline, of influence where there is only indifference. In a recent issue of his journal there were two major attacks on the veracity of the National Press, and yet in this very issue, to my knowledge, there were several statements which were sheer lies. National Socialism should have some nobler inspiration than to oppose one kind of corruption with another still less pleasing to the nostrils.*

That same week British Union was running noisy demonstrations in the West End in favour of Hitler's incorporation of Austria into

* See also page 135.

the Reich and limbering up for the much bigger battle over Czecho-slovakia. During the summer of 1938 Mosley led a 'Britain First' campaign and declared: 'Czech behaviour today is threatening the peace of the world.' At the same time the Movement stepped up its propaganda against the refugees from Germany who had settled in Britain, claiming that they were stealing work from Britons and that alien doctors represented a 'corruption of medicine'. The propaganda extended even to the Basque children brought to Britain as refugees from Spain. Mosley argued that there were British children in equal need and, with much publicity, wrote to the BBC with a demand that he should be allowed to broadcast on Christmas Day 1938 with an appeal on behalf of the poor people of Britain. The BBC refused, explaining that its Christmas charitable appeal was traditionally reserved for the Wireless for the Blind fund.

During the Munich crisis Mosley obviously expected war. The issue of *Action*, dated 1st October 1938, was prepared on the assump-tion that war had started. Mosley declared on the front page: 'British Union has declared against this war. . . . We oppose root and branch a war which sacrifices British lives in an alien quarrel.' What *Action* called Neville Chamberlain's 'act of courage and common sense' in forcing the Czechs to yield the Sudeten German areas changed the situation. The following week Mosley hailed the Munich agreement and in a speech at Manchester insisted that Hitler could be trusted to keep it. 'Hitler no more wants the Czechs than we want the aliens in our midst.' *Action* improved the moment with a new attack on the Jews, alleging that during the crisis they had bought country houses and let them to evacuees at inflated rents. The Jews had fled from London like 'a flowing river of grey slime'. It was soon afterwards that *Action* ceased to publish the names of contributors belonging to the headquarters staff, most of the articles thereafter appearing anonymously. This was probably an attempt to disguise the accelerating leakage. Among the many who left were Geoffrey Dorman and Chambers-Hunter, both in the spring of 1939. W. E. D. Allen had faded from the picture about eighteen months earlier. Of the New Party pioneers, Risdon – Mosley's colleague since the Birmingham ILP days – had dropped into the background.

The small number of Catholics who entered through motives connected with the Spanish Civil War were not plentiful enough to fill the empty places and few of them stayed long in the Movement. The *Catholic Herald*, in anxious mood, approached Mosley with

questions on anti-Semitism and compulsory sterilization of the
unfit, receiving answers which it considered unsatisfactory. It
described the anti-Semitism as 'frightening'.

On sterilization Mosley insisted that: 'There are certain cases
where the best scientific view is that it is ruinous for the State to
allow individuals to propagate. . . . I would therefore give a choice
to any individual of voluntary sterilization or of being in some way
segregated.'

The *Catholic Herald* pressed Mosley on the proposal to deport all
British Jews to a Jewish National Home.

> I asked Sir Oswald [wrote the interviewer] what would
> happen to Jews converted to the Church or to Jews who were
> entirely blameless. He insisted that it would not be feasible to
> differentiate between different types of Jews and that if such a
> measure bore hardly on the first generation it would not do so
> on the second. Any alternative would only perpetuate the
> problem.

Mosley's determination to ignore the decline in membership and
to present the picture of a British Union as strong as ever was well
reflected in his New Year message for 1939:

> 'This will be a year of decision. It is for such moments that Black-
> shirts live and struggle.
>
> 'For the first time this year, in electoral battle, British Union will
> face the Parliamentary machines of the old parties in all the panoply
> of their money power. They have the money, but we have the men
> and women.
>
> 'In this struggle will be developed the young strength that in gather-
> ing storm will sweep their old and corrupt power from the pages
> of a glorious history that it has disgraced. . . .
>
> 'In your trust, my companions, is the past, the present and the
> future of Britain. . . .'

British Union did not in fact fight any elections during 1939. Its
principal activity in the eight months that remained before the
outbreak of war was an energetic peace campaign, with propaganda
marches, distribution of leaflets and the posting of chain letters.
There were violent attacks on Poland, which Mosley described as 'a

sink of iniquity'. In the East End appeared gigantic whitewashed slogans: 'Why should you die for Poland's 3,500,000 Jews?' The campaign produced support from one or two unexpected quarters. Hugh Ross Williamson, Labour Parliamentary candidate for West Dorset, appeared as a contributor to *Action*. His case, as presented in a speech at Parkstone in May 1939, was that 'German control of Eastern Europe would be no menace to the people of England – to you and to me – but it might be a menace to the great capitalist profiteers who rule England'. The distinguished novelist of the First World War, Henry Williamson, joined the Movement and contributed anti-war articles to *Action*.

The campaign reached its climax with a mass rally in July 1939 at Earls Court. It was the last of the great British Union demonstrations addressed by Mosley and also the biggest. He could hardly have asked for a better setting for a valedictory appearance. For weeks beforehand the Blackshirts marched through London to advertise the rally and, on the night, coachloads of supporters arrived at Earls Court from the East End. The total attendance was 15,000, the largest number, British Union claimed, which had ever attended an indoor political meeting anywhere in the world.

Half an hour of pageantry with bands and processions opened the rally. For the occasion the Movement had purchased sixty new banners in bright red, each emblazoned with the initial 'M' in gold. Round the walls in huge capital letters ran the British Union slogans: 'Britons fight for Britain only', 'Fight to live not live to fight' and 'Mind Britain's business'. Mosley spoke from a towering, twenty-foot-high rostrum with a Union Jack as big behind him. Looking like a puny doll in the floodlights, dwarfed by the vastness of the hall, for two and a quarter hours he flung his challenge at the political establishment. There was perfect order. The only interruptions were the cheers of the Blackshirts.

His peroration, spoken slowly in cold passion, was in the grand style of oratory:

'We are going, if the power lies within us – and it lies within us because within us is the spirit of the English – to say that our generation and our children shall not die like rats in Polish holes. They shall not die but they shall live to breathe the good English air, to love the fair English countryside, to see above them the English sky, to feel beneath their feet the English soil.

'This heritage of England, by our struggle and our sacrifice, again we shall give to our children. And, with that sacred gift, we tell them that they come from that stock of men who went out from this small island in frail craft across the storm-tossed seas to take in their brave hands the greatest Empire that man has ever seen; in which to-morrow our people shall create the highest civilization that man has ever known. . . .

'So we take by the hand these our children, to whom our struggle shall give back our England; with them we dedicate ourselves again to the memory of those who have gone before. . . . To the dead heroes of Britain, in sacred union, we say: "Like you we give ourselves to England – across the ages that divide us – across the glories that unite us – we gaze into your eyes and we give to you this holy vow – we shall be true today – tomorrow – and for ever – England lives!" '

The outbreak of war in September 1939 faced British Fascists and ex-Fascists with an agonizing crisis of conscience. At one extreme were the patriots, of whom A. K. Chesterton was typical. Chesterton, in his fortieth year, immediately joined the Army and, by an ironical twist of fate, ultimately found himself fighting to free Abyssinia from the Italians. At the other extreme was William Joyce who, with his wife, slipped quietly over to Germany on a British passport a few days before the war to offer his services to Hitler. Joyce's intention had been to fight in the German Army and his job as a broadcaster in the Propaganda Ministry came as a surprise. The original Lord Haw-Haw was an army officer, Captain Baillie-Stewart, who had sided with the Germans. Somehow the nickname became attached to Joyce, for whose harsh voice it was peculiarly unsuitable. His 'Gairmany calling, Gairmany calling' on thousands of British radio sets brought him the fame that he had never found in politics. Arnold Leese and the Imperial Fascists had no doubts about their correct course of action. As early as 1934 Leese had declared in *The Fascist*: 'There is one thing that no member of the Imperial Fascist League will do; he will not join the British forces to fight the battle of the Jew against men of his own Nordic race.' Leese and his followers lived up to their word.

Mosley and British Union trod very cautiously. On the outbreak of war *Action* missed one week's publication through delay at the censors, to whom the printers had insisted that copy should be submitted. When it finally appeared it carried the following instructions from Mosley:

To our members my message is plain and clear. Our country is involved in war. Therefore I ask you to do nothing to injure our country, or to help any other power.

Our members should do what the law requires of them, and if they are members of any of the forces or services of the Crown, they should obey their orders, and, in particular, obey the rules of their service. . . .

The censors had cut out a phrase in the message which said: 'This war is no quarrel of the British people; this war is a quarrel of Jewish finance.'

Mosley's frequently declared principle was to oppose the war, seek constitutionally to overthrow the Government and work for a negotiated peace. He insisted that neither he nor British Union would sabotage the war effort. As precedents for his attitude he cited the examples of Ramsay MacDonald in the First World War, Lloyd George in the Boer War, Charles James Fox in the Napoleonic Wars and Pitt the Elder in the American War of Independence. His argument that the war was a ramp by international finance was very close to that of the Communist Party, who, now that Stalin was friends with Hitler, denounced it as 'imperialist aggression'. Thus the Fascists and Communists, coldly ignoring each other's existence, found themselves bedfellows in the same anti-war campaign.

The apathy of the 'phoney war' period offered Mosley a shred of hope that he might win at last. Might not the British people, disgusted with the war, turn at last to British Union and a negotiated peace? Might there not come the awakening of the people that Mosley had long expected? Early in 1940 British Union decided for the first time to contest Parliamentary by-elections. Through the electoral truce between the main parties, Mosley declared, the Government 'refuses the right of the people to vote; this is the only chance the people have of expressing their will. British Union owes to the people the duty of giving them that chance.'

The first fight was in Silvertown, once the seat of Keir Hardie, 'the first National Socialist'. It was a sensational affair with Harry Pollitt standing for the Communists and Thomas Moran for British Union. The result, declared on 23rd February 1940, was proof that British Union had derisory support even in a constituency adjoining its East London strongholds. Moran polled less than one-sixth of Pollitt's vote:

J. H. Hollins (Labour)   14,343
H. Pollitt (Communist)   966
T. P. Moran (British Union)   151

(Labour 93 per cent, Communist 6 per cent, British Union 1 per cent.)

The next election came three weeks later in North-East Leeds and the result was slightly more encouraging, the absence of a Communist candidate enabling British Union to scoop the whole anti-war vote. The British Union candidate was a Yorkshire poultry breeder.

Craik Henderson (Conservative)   23,882
Sydney Allen (British Union)   722

(Conservative 97 per cent, British Union 3 per cent.)

Action was very pleased. The Leeds result marked 'a substantial advance' and seventy-two per cent of those who had attended British Union meetings had voted for the British Union candidate. The three per cent poll was contrasted with the 2·7 per cent won by the German National Socialists in 1928.

The following month the 'phoney war' ended. Hitler invaded Norway and Quisling was elevated to the rank of Prime Minister in a puppet government. Mosley continued to call for peace amid circumstances of increasing difficulty. His speakers, including Raven Thomson and Anne Brock Griggs, were being arrested on charges of using insulting words. Opposition everywhere was so vocal as to make it difficult for British Union to secure any hearing at all.

The final electoral battle was to be fought at Middleton, Lancashire, in May 1940. It took place under the shadow of Hitler's conquest of the Low Countries and at a time when invasion of Britain appeared imminent.

In *Action* Mosley wrote:

The question has been put to me why I do not cease all political activity in an hour of danger to our country. The answer is that I intend to do my best to provide the people with an alternative to the present Government, if, and when, they desire to make peace with 'British Empire intact and our people safe'. . . . I can conceive no greater tragedy than the British people desiring to make such a British peace and having no means to express their will.

Mosley was, in any case, sceptical about the possibilities of invasion which, he said, 'any Government with even a shred of efficiency could repel with consummate ease'. In the event of German troops actually landing in Britain, British Union would throw itself 'into the effort of a united nation until the foreigner was driven from our soil'.

Mosley was very nearly lynched at Middleton when he attempted to speak from the roof of a van. It was his last public appearance as Leader of British Union and it ended with his being escorted back to the local headquarters under strong police guard. Outside the headquarters gathered a crowd of several thousand, hurling stones until every window was smashed. The election result was:

> E. E. Gates (Conservative)   32,036
> F. Haslam (British Union)   418
> (Conservative 99 per cent, British Union 1 per cent.)

Polling was on 22nd May and on the same day Parliament was rushing through amendments to the Defence Regulations which, among many other things, extended the scope of *Defence Regulation 18b* to empower the Home Secretary, John Anderson, to imprison without trial anybody he believed likely to endanger the safety of the realm. It was much wider than the original *Defence Regulation 18b*, under which five comparatively minor members of British Union were held at the outbreak of the war, and its new form required no proof of enemy associations or of acts prejudicial to the safety of the realm. Under the new regulation, which remained in force until May 1945, the Home Secretary's powers of imprisonment were virtually unlimited. There was a tribunal, headed by Norman Birkett, to review the cases of the detainees, but the Home Secretary was not obliged to take its advice and in a number of cases did not do so.

Anderson acted within hours of the new regulation becoming law, his task eased by the regular reports which had reached the Home Office from a spy planted in British Union headquarters. Early on 23rd May Mosley was arrested in his flat at Dolphin Square and lodged at Brixton Prison. Later the same day eight other leading members of British Union were arrested, including Francis-Hawkins, Raven Thomson, Hick and Norah Elam. The police occupied the headquarters at Sanctuary Buildings, and began a three-day search of the files; outside the Fascists marched angrily up and down on the pavement, periodically saluting each other. Two other arrests on 23rd May were of John Beckett, who had just become Secretary of the Duke of Bedford's People's Party – a non-Fascist group with a policy that was part syndicalist and part social credit, the whole flavoured with pacifism – and A. H. M. Ramsay, Conservative MP for Peebles, President of the Right Club and an open supporter of Hitler. There were wholesale arrests of British Union speakers on charges of using insulting words.

The police, having found no evidence on which to base a prosecution, withdrew from British Union headquarters on 27th May. By then between seventy and eighty leading members had been detained, but the Movement made a last, desperate bid for survival. Moran took over the leadership and published a message: 'It may be that more of us will see the inside of a prison, but where Mosley goes we gladly follow. . . . Go ahead, every one of you, and prepare the minds of the people for the greatness that will be theirs when Mosley leads as Mosley most surely will.' A truncated *Action* appeared on 30th May with a screaming headline 'FREE MOSLEY – SAVE BRITAIN' and an attack on the appointment of Stafford Cripps as Ambassador to Moscow. The same day the police returned to the headquarters. Acting under the Defence Regulations, Anderson dissolved British Union and banned its publications.

Did Mosley in his cell ponder on his far-off words of 1932: 'We shall win; or at least we shall return upon our shields'?

CHAPTER 14

Aftermath

B RITISH FASCISM ended in May 1940 and, apart from one short-lived group, has not since been revived under that name. The subsequent activities of the ex-Fascists and their organizations are, therefore, outside the main scope of this book. To round off the story, this chapter outlines what happened during the war and afterwards; it in no sense claims to be a full history.

After May 1940 the arrests under *Defence Regulation 18b* accelerated until in August there was a peak number of just over 1,600 British subjects in prison without trial. Of these about three-quarters had belonged to British Union and represented almost the entire active membership. A few managed to escape by volunteering for the forces – in at least one case a London Blackshirt was warned by the police of his impending arrest and reached the recruiting office just in time.

By any normal standards the Home Office action was harsh and arbitrary. It appears that during the summer of 1940 mere membership of British Union was sufficient cause for arrest. Some Blackshirts were arrested while serving in the Local Defence Volunteers and in Civil Defence. One member, an amateur yachtsman, was arrested immediately after a hazardous voyage to Dunkirk in which he had helped to evacuate British troops. It may be considered, however, that the summer of 1940 was not a time when normal standards could have been expected to prevail. The impetus for the arrests came from War Office Intelligence, which feared that a German invasion of Britain might produce the same kind of Quisling and 'fifth column' activities as had aided the success of Nazi arms elsewhere. The only safeguard was to take into custody anybody who by any stretch of the imagination could be regarded as a potential danger to security. Throughout it was emphasized that the detentions were preventive and were not a punishment for any act which had actually been committed.

The last prominent Fascist to be caught was Arnold Leese, who in May 1940 had gone into hiding. He eluded arrest until November 1940, when he paid a visit to his home, The White House, Pewley Hill, Guildford, and found that it was being searched by detectives. One officer was bending over a chest of drawers and the burly Leese could not resist the temptation to creep up behind him and kick his buttocks. Removed to Guildford Police Station, Leese smashed up his cell and started his detention with a three-month sentence for assault and wilful damage.

The leading detainees, including Mosley, were held in 'F' wing of Brixton Prison. Their cell doors were unlocked during the daytime and they were allowed freedom of association and the right to purchase their own food from outside. During the hot summer of the Battle of Britain they played cricket in the courtyard under the tuition of Gordon-Canning and Ramsay. Sometimes the ball went over the high prison wall and they had to wait patiently inside for some passer-by to throw it back. The women, including Diana Mosley who had been arrested a week after Mosley, were kept at Holloway. From 1941 the husbands were driven across London once a fortnight to see their wives, first for half an hour and later for an hour at a time.

Ramsay's arrest was considered by the House of Commons Privileges Committee, which ruled that as an MP he had no greater rights under *Defence Regulation 18b* than any other British subject. He was allowed to continue his Parliamentary activities to the extent of tabling questions to ministers for written answer, which he did regularly on constituency matters, the activities of the Jews and the detainees' grievances. Apart from Ramsay, the arrest which attracted most public attention was that of Admiral Sir Barry Domvile who, with his wife, was arrested on 7th July 1940. Sir Barry had been chairman of the Anglo-German friendship group 'The Link' and a friend of Himmler and other Nazi leaders. He had held high naval appointments until his retirement in 1935, including that of Chief of Naval Intelligence. He had a somewhat naïve approach to politics and international affairs which, more than anything else, appears to have been the cause of his downfall. He saw the war as 'an attempt at national suicide' and, during his stay at Brixton, decided that the Jews and Freemasons were to blame. He coined the expression 'Judmas' to describe the 'mysterious power at work behind the scenes controlling the actions of the figures visibly taking part in the government of the country'.

From September 1940 the number in detention fell rapidly. Most of the rank-and-file British Union members were released, those of military age on condition that they join the forces. By the middle of 1941 only 400 remained in detention, the majority of them people of non-British descent who only by a technicality had escaped imprisonment as enemy aliens. Herbert Morrison, who had succeeded Anderson as Home Secretary, made arrangements in 1942 to enable detained husbands and wives to live together. The Mosleys had a four-roomed flat at Holloway Prison with facilities to cook their own meals and permission to pay other detainees to perform domestic services. All but the most prominent detainees had by this time been removed to a camp at Peel in the Isle of Man.

Parliament took a close interest in the detainees' affairs. It was difficult for MPs to ignore their fate, for the detainees bombarded them with letters, but even apart from that there was concern lest people were being unnecessarily held. As the danger of invasion receded, MPs on both sides of the Commons – notably Irvine Albery among the Conservatives and R. R. Stokes in the Labour Party – questioned Morrison and on two occasions forced critical motions to divisions. Their main plea was that there should be some right of appeal to a tribunal over the Home Secretary's head. Morrison, who personally supervised each detention order, said that he found his powers distasteful to exercise but that he believed the best way to run the system was through a minister answerable to the House of Commons.

There was plenty of pressure the other way – in favour of keeping the Fascists in gaol. It reached a peak in November 1943, when Morrison released the Mosleys on doctors' evidence that Oswald Mosley was suffering from thrombo-phlebitis and that continued imprisonment might permantly endanger his health or even cause his death. The release was on condition that Mosley reported monthly to the police, undertook no political activities and made no attempt to contact his former followers. Without police permission he was to travel no more than seven miles from his home which was, at first, at The Shaven Crown, Shipton-under-Wychwood, Oxford-shire. There was a storm of protest in Parliament, mainly from Labour MPs. In Downing Street an angry crowd of 5,000 war workers gathered demanding that the decision should be revoked. Morrison's attitude was that if it had not been for the health con-siderations, Mosley 'as the leader and most influential person in the Movement . . . would have been the last to be released'.

Soon afterwards, Beckett and Leese were freed on similar grounds of illness but with less publicity. Domvile was released in July 1943 and Ramsay a year later, both on the general grounds that their detention was no longer justified. Ramsay remained an MP until the 1945 general election. The final group of twenty-two detainees – including Francis-Hawkins – remained in detention until *Defence Regulation 18b* was revoked by Parliament on VE Day.

Very few made the attempt to return to political activity and some of them seemed to have lost heart. Ramsay, Domvile and Raven Thomson had lost sons in the war. Francis-Hawkins tried to return to his job in surgical instruments but was driven out within a week by a protest strike of his fellow employees. He died a few years later, still a comparatively young man.

William Joyce made his last broadcast from Germany on 30th April 1945, and was arrested by British troops a month later and brought to London for trial on a charge of treason. His counsel had little difficulty in proving that he had been born at Brooklyn, New York, and that his father had been a naturalized American citizen. Soon after arriving in Germany in 1939 he had taken out naturaliza-tion papers as a German, which were valid since the United States and Germany were not then at war. It was, therefore, as a German citizen that he stood in the dock of the Old Bailey. The prosecution case rested on the fact that he had travelled to Germany on a British passport. By accepting the protection of the British Crown he had accepted the obligations of a subject. On this very narrow point he was convicted and sentenced to death. The Attorney General, Sir Hartley Shawcross, granted his fiat for an appeal to the House of Lords, which upheld the conviction by four votes to one.

Apart from the German leaders themselves, Joyce was at that time probably the man most hated by the British public. It was felt that he had mocked his fellow countrymen in their deepest agony. There was anger, too, that in some cases his broadcasts had been genuinely effective. Yet, despite the hatred he attracted, there was favourable comment on the courageous way in which he bore himself in court. He had a nihilistic attitude, believing, perhaps, that with the death of Hitler he had little to live for. He had been brought up a Catholic and, while he was awaiting execution, his brother suggested that he should see a priest and be reconciled to the Church. Replied Joyce in his sardonic way: 'Don't you think I've had enough trouble with passports to which I was not entitled without trying to get into heaven with one?' He was hanged at Wandsworth Prison in January 1946. On his way to the gallows, it is said, he stopped and with a cynical smile looked down at his trembling knees.

The first of the Fascists to return to politics was Arnold Leese, who celebrated VE Day by publishing a book called *The Jewish War of Survival*, in which he argued that with the defeat of Hitler the Jews and Freemasons had won a battle but that they could still be routed by a determined policy of anti-Semitism. He followed this with a monthly newsletter called *Gothic Ripples* which he continued until his death in 1956. *Gothic Ripples* was devoted almost entirely to attacks on Jews, a somewhat surprising exception being the amount of space he devoted to attacks on the fluodorization of water supplies. He was worried about the ancestry of the Duke of Edinburgh, in which he detected traces of Judaism, and was much exercised in weighing the rival merits of a republic and a new dynasty headed by the Duke of Gloucester.

Leese made no attempt after the war to run a political party but movements came into being which acknowledged him as their mentor. Colin Jordan, born in 1923, a Coventry schoolmaster and a friend of Leese, founded the Birmingham Nationalist Club in the early 1950's. At a time of racial tension involving West Indian immigrants in the Notting Hill area of London, Jordan moved his activities to London and founded a group called the White Defence League. Another group with similar ideas formed at about the same time was the National Labour Party led by a technical journalist, John Bean, who was born in 1927. In 1960 the White Defence League and the National Labour Party united to form the British National Party under the presidency of a Norfolk landowner and former Conservative parliamentary candidate, Andrew Fountaine. Jordan was National Organizer of the new party and Bean the Deputy Organizer. The headquarters were at Arnold Leese House, Princedale Road, Notting Hill, which is the property of Leese's widow, Mrs. Winifred Leese.

Jordan and Bean quarrelled in the spring of 1962 and Jordan broke away to form a new organization, the National Socialist Movement. Jordan retained the support of Mrs. Leese and the use of Arnold Leese House. Although the National Socialist Movement has been very small in numbers – well under fifty – it secured during 1962 a great deal of publicity for its imitation and adulation of the pre-war German Nazis, its members wearing in private grey uniforms and knee breeches and practising unarmed combat. In August 1962 Jordan organized a country camp for his followers in Gloucestershire with the American Nazi leader George Lincoln Rockwell as one of the visitors. Jordan and Rockwell formed a World Union of National Socialists under Jordan's leadership. 'I place myself under the orders of Colin Jordan. He is the leader now of all world Nazis and I will obey him implicitly,' said Rockwell. Later, when Jordan was in prison, Rockwell proclaimed himself 'international commander' of world Nazism. In October 1962 Jordan was prosecuted for running an illegal, paramilitary organization and sentenced to nine months' imprisonment.

Jordan is bitterly anti-Semitic and the violence of his opinions led during the summer of 1962 to a revival of disorder in the London streets on something approaching the pre-war scale. When he attempted to speak in Trafalgar Square he was shouted down and pelted with missiles.

The British National Party, under Bean and Fountaine, is also anti-Semitic but has pursued more moderate tactics than those of Jordan. It has pledged itself to run parliamentary candidates and to try to win power by constitutional means. Its main centre of strength appears to be in the Deptford area of East London. At different times it has claimed membership figures varying between 700 and 5,000; its true active strength is probably between 100 and 200.

Another stream of post-Fascist development has been the League of Empire Loyalists founded by A. K. Chesterton in 1953 and largely financed, until his death in 1961, by R. K. Jeffrey, a rich British businessman living in Chile. The Empire Loyalists represent the super-patriotism which formed one strand in the pre-war British Union. It stands on a platform of preserving the British Empire and accuses 'international Jewish interests' of conspiring against Britain. Chambers-Hunter, the former Aberdeen British Union leader, is a member of the executive, which also includes members of non-Fascist background. During the late 1950's the League showed considerable talent in attracting publicity by interrupting speeches by Harold

Macmillan and other Conservative personalities. John Bean of the British National Party started his political career as an Empire Loyalist.

Mosley's followers after the war were for a while fragmented into a series of 'book clubs' and 'discussion groups' scattered around Britain and united by the 'Mosley Newsletter'. A more vigorous development was the British League of Ex-Servicemen, founded by Jeffrey Hamm in 1946. Hamm had been a relatively minor member of British Union in Harrow before the war and, on release from detention, had joined the Royal Tank Corps. The League of Ex-Servicemen ran open-air meetings in the East End of London and attracted a good deal of opposition, especially at its Ridley Road pitch. Hamm proved himself a forceful speaker and used publicly to call for Mosley to return to politics.

Mosley himself returned in 1948 with the conception of a united 'modern movement' for the whole of Europe. The time had passed, he declared, for the narrow nationalism, as Fascism and Europe could survive as a force in world affairs if united as a single nation under vigorous leadership. European colonies in Africa should be pooled to provide a common living space and source of raw materials. There was also, at first, a vague idea of bringing in South America. He rejected any idea of renewing the campaign against the Jews but his African policies led him to another form of racialism. Africa, he declares, should be partitioned between black and white, the black territories being allowed complete independence. In the white territories – principally South Africa, the Rhodesias and Kenya – the Africans should be allowed no political rights. He campaigns actively in favour of racial segregation and South African Apartheid.

The pre-war scheme for a corporate state was replaced by a creed of 'European Socialism', an attempt to combine the virtues of private enterprise with those of syndicalism. Small industrial enterprises would be allowed complete freedom under private ownership but, once they passed a certain size and when the founder no longer exercised active control, they would pass to the ownership of the people who worked in them. He dropped, too, the idea of the one-party state, saying that opposition parties should have the right to contest elections. He proposed a 'fool-proof' Habeas Corpus law which would make it impossible for the executive to imprison any-one without trial.

The new organization, Union Movement, was formed in London on 7th February 1948. 'It is the task of a new movement to build where the old parties have destroyed.... We will create a third empire after they have lost two empires,' said Mosley at the in-augural meeting. The leading officials of Union Movement have included Hamm, Raven Thomson (who died in 1955), Robert Row who became Editor of the revived *Action*, and H. G. McKechnie, pre-war National Meetings Organizer who succeeded Sutton as Mosley's private secretary. Mosley is the unquestioned leader. The rank and file of the Movement are very young, the great majority of them aged in their teens and twenties. Very few of the pre-war British Union members are still active. Official statistics of member-ship remain, as always, a secret but at the beginning of 1962 the Movement probably had a little over 1,000 paid-up members.

There is a good deal of latent anti-Semitism in Union Movement but it is rarely expressed publicly. Instructions issued to speakers in February 1961 included the following passage:

> Our speakers may not mention Jews because we do not want attention diverted from the main issues which are the economic crisis and the responsibility of the old parties. If questioned on the subject, speakers are to reply: 'We do not attack any man on account of his race or religion, only on account of what he does. Our policy brings to an end both the power of international finance and international financial corruption. These laws will be applied impartially to Jew and Gentile.'

At a conference in Venice in April 1962 Union Movement linked up with the Deutsche Reichspartie of West Germany and the Movimento Sociale Italiano of Italy and the Jeune Europe and Mouvement d'Action Civique of Belgium to form the 'National Party of Europe', a shadowy organization which has neither perma-nent headquarters nor a staff of its own. All four parties 'declare with pride our European communion of blood and of spirit'.

As anti-Semitism became the most prominent feature of the pre-war British Union, so has the 'colour problem' become very promi-nent in Union Movement and the one on which it attracts most of its supporters. During the 1950's the main centre of activity changed from the East End of London to the Notting Hill and Brixton areas, the main centres of West Indian immigrants. Mosley adopted a policy of expelling from Britain all coloured people, except students, and on this basis tried to build up a mass following. His followers were involved in sporadic scuffles with opponents in the streets but violence came nowhere near its pre-war level until Colin Jordan's National Socialist Movement received much publicity in the summer of 1962. A month after Jordan's Trafalgar Square meeting dissolved in disorder Mosley attempted to speak in the same place. An angry crowd of several hundred smashed the speaker's stand and the police banned the meeting before Mosley even started his speech. A few days later Mosley was knocked down in the street when he attempted to speak in the East End. Union Movement has been at some pains to prevent any revival of the pre-war reputation of the Blackshirts for violence and the disorders of 1962 sprang primarily from Mosley's opponents.

In the 1959 general election Mosley stood as parliamentary candidate for North Kensington. He polled 2,821 votes, eight per cent of the total, and for the first time in his career forfeited his deposit. In the same election William Webster, a public-house licensee, stood as National Labour Party candidate for St. Pancras North, winning 1,685 votes, four per cent of the total. During 1961 and 1962 Union Movement fought two by-elections, winning five per cent of the votes at Manchester Moss Side and under two per cent at Middlesbrough East.

Prolific in speech and writing, Mosley has continued to dream of victory. He no longer, he says, wishes to become Prime Minister of Britain but he would like to be the British representative on the ruling council of 'Europe a Nation'. His speeches are more closely argued than before the war, but seem to have lost some of the emotional fervour which once made his oratory so compelling. The standard of his writing has risen and, had he avoided the temptation to return to active politics, might have earned him a considerable reputation as a political analyst. But he retains the apocalyptic vision that one day there will be a great crisis in which the people will at last turn to him.

'What matters,' he wrote in 1955, 'is to have a new idea in a new epoch, and to find the real men in each generation who are prepared to face the steel test of standing for a new truth. More than ever are they needed in this greatest of all ages of decision.'

Note on Sources

Mention of British Fascism occurs in almost every work of history, biography and autobiography covering the relevant period. The list of such works is long and need not be given here; where a particular book is relied on for a particular fact it is acknowledged in the text.

The other basic sources have been contemporary newspapers, periodicals and pamphlets and, especially, the publications of the Fascist organizations themselves.

The Fascist publications were:

British Fascisti Bulletin (1924–25).
British Fascist Bulletin (1925–26).
British Lion (1926–29).
The Fascist (1929–39).
Blackshirt (1933–39).
Fascist Week (1933–34).
Fascist Quarterly (1935–36).
British Union Quarterly (1936–37).
Action (1936–40).

The New Party published a weekly paper, *Action*, from October to December 1931.

The following books deal substantially with British Fascism or with the career of Sir Oswald Mosley:

Louis T. Bondy: *Racketeers of Hatred* (1948).
A. K. Chesterton: *Oswald Mosley, Portrait of a Leader* (1936).
Barry Domvile: *From Admiral to Cabin Boy* (1946).
'James Drennan' (W. E. D. Allen): *Oswald Mosley, B.U.F. and British Fascism* (1934).
R. Palme Dutt: *Fascism and Social Revolution* (1934).

William Joyce: *National Socialism Now* (1937).
Arnold S. Leese: *Jewish Ritual Murder* (1938).
Arnold S. Leese: *The Jewish War of Survival* (1945).
Arnold S. Leese: *Out of Step* (1947).
Oswald Mosley: *The Greater Britain* (First edition 1932, revised edition 1934).
Oswald Mosley: *One Hundred Questions Answered* (1936).
Oswald Mosley: *Tomorrow We Live* (1938).
Oswald Mosley: *My Answer* (1946).
Oswald Mosley: *The Alternative* (1948).
Anonymous: *Mosley, the Facts* (1957).
Frederic Mullally: *Fascism Inside Britain* (1946).
E. Mandeville Roe: *The Corporate State* (1934).
W. A. Rudlin: *The Growth of Fascism Inside Great Britain* (1935).
John Strachey: *Revolution by Reason* (1925).
John Strachey: *The Menace of Fascism* (1933).
A. Raven Thomson: *The Coming Corporate State* (1935).
Rebecca West: *The Meaning of Treason* (1949).
Ellen Wilkinson and Edward Conze: *Why Fascism?* (1934).

Index

ABERDEEN, 75
Acland, Sir Richard, 124
Action: New Party organ, 50, 52, 53;
    BUF organ, 141, 155–7, 164, 166,
    170, 172–4, 178, 180–1, 185–7, 189–
    92, 194; post-war, 202
Albert Hall, rallies at: 1926 (Conser-
    vative), 62; Apr. 1934, 98–100, 109;
    Oct. 1934, 126–8; Mch. 1936, 157–8
Albery, Sir Irvine, 197
Allen, Clifford (later Lord Allen of
    Hurtwood), 103
Allen, Rev. M. Yate, 141
Allen, Sydney, 192
Allen, Warner, 90
Allen, W. E. D., 42, 46, 48, 52, 86, 119,
    183, 187
Amalgamated Engineering Union, 144
Amery, L. S., 44
Anderson, Sir John (later Lord
    Waverley), 61, 193–4
Anstruther-Gray, W. J., 112, 115
Armstrong, Rear-Admiral A. E., 60, 61
Ashton-under-Lyme by-election, 47, 49
Astor, Lady, 14, 85
Attlee, Clement (later Earl Attlee), 33,
    37, 54, 94, 103, 160, 176

BAILEY, J. A., 166–7, 174
Baillie-Stewart, Capt., 190
Baldwin, Oliver (later 2nd Earl
    Baldwin), 31, 43, 46
Baldwin, Stanley (later 1st Earl
    Baldwin), 12, 16–17, 27, 58, 77, 101,
    113, 117, 129, 147–8

Barker, Dudley, 138, 154
Barrington, Mercédes, 180
Batey, J., 43
Baxter, Angus, 108
Beamish, Henry Hamilton, 120
Bean, John, 199, 200, 201
Beaumont, M. W., 115
Beaverbrook, W. M. Aitken, 1st
    Baron, 25, 40, 56, 100, 117, 124, 127
Beckett, John: ILP whip, 42, 104; in
    BUF, 103–6, 131, 134, 138, 139, 144,
    156–7; dismissed from office, 169–
    71; forms National Socialist League,
    171–2; in prison, 194, 198
Bedford, 12th Duke of: People's Party,
    194
Bell, Dr. G. K. A., Bishop of
    Chichester, 141
Bellairs, Carlyon, 98
Bentinck-Budd, Charles, 142, 179
Bergner, Elizabeth, 166
Bevan, Aneurin, 12, 23, 42–5, 131, 181
Bevin, Ernest, 25, 30, 36, 51, 89, 129
'Biff boys', 49–50, 69
Birkett, Norman, KC (later Lord
    Birkett), 143, 193
Birmingham, 22–3, 28, 31, 49, 78, 97,
    108, 132, 142, 146, 199
Black and Tans, 14
Black House (Chelsea), 86–8, 92, 96,
    98, 107, 137; closed down, 138
Blackshirt, 70, 78, 83, 90, 108, 116, 119,
    123–5, 128, 132, 138–41, 148, 164,
    166, 171, 178
Blakeney, Brig.-Gen. R. G. D., 59–62,
    64, 82

Blue Lies and Red Violence, 114 n.
Blueshirts, 95
Boothby, Robert (later Lord Boothby), 14, 23–5, 38, 40, 85
Box, F. M., 48, 87, 100, 138
Bracken, Brendan (later Lord Bracken), 48
Bristol, 78, 106, 108
British Fascisti: aims and work of, 57–62; *Bulletin* of, 58, 60, 61; officials of, 60
British Lion, The, 59, 62
British National Party, 199, 200
British Union of Fascists (BUF): formation of, 62, 64–72; Defence Force of, 68–70, 97, 139; policy and aims, 72–5, 117, 128; inner life and symbols, 75–7, 139; youth movements and clubs, 76, 137, 155; personalities and categories, 78–81, 87, 133–4; anti-Semitism, 78, 98, 101–2, 116–28, 151–61, 166; clashes with anti-Fascists, 81–4, 106, 110–11, 125; headquarters, *see* Black House; finances, 88–93, 138, 169–70, 184; branches and membership, 105–8, 130–3, 137–9; Westminster office, 138; title changed (1936), 139; new rules and constitution, 140; in general election (1935), 147; success in East End of London, *see* East End movement; in LCC and municipal elections, 165–8, 180–1; decline of, 169 *et seq.*; participation in Parliamentary elections, 179–81, 188, 191–3; peace campaign (1939), 188–91; dissolved under Defence Regulations, 194. (*See also* Mosley, Sir Oswald Ernald)
British United Fascists, 82
Britons, The, 120, 122
Brockway, Fenner, 29, 41, 103, 104, 160
Brown, W. J., 26, 31, 42, 43, 45, 46, 104
Bruce, Sir Michael, 60
Burges, Col. Dan, 60
Burke, Owen, 151
Burn, Col. Sir Charles, 59

CABLE Street, battle of, 159–61
Calder, Ritchie, 114
Call Back Yesterday (Dalton), 29
Cambridge, 61

Campbell, J. R., 131
Camrose, Lord, 156–7
Carruthers, General, 60
Carson, Edward Henry, Baron, 144
Chamberlain, Joseph, 23
Chamberlain, Neville, 22, 52, 187
Chamberlayne, A. R., 12
Chambers-Hunter, W. E. A., 75, 108, 180, 187, 200
Chesterton, Arthur Kenneth: member of BUF, 79–80, 102, 105, 108, 131, 134–5, 137–8, 164, 172; offered post by Germans, 184; edits *Action*, 185; resigns from BUF, 186; joins Army, 190; founds Empire Loyalists, 200
Chesterton, Doris, 186
Chesterton, G. K., 86
Cheyney, Peter, 53
Churchill, Randolph, 97
Churchill, Winston, 10, 12–15, 28, 40, 53, 54, 85, 94, 100, 104, 165
Citrine, Walter (later Lord Citrine), 30, 51, 129
Civilization as Divine Superman (Thomson), 79
Clarke, E. G. ('Mick'), 151, 154, 166, 179
Clynes, J. R., 18, 37
Cole, G. D. H., 23, 34, 36
Coming Struggle for Power, The (Strachey), 48
Communism, Communists, of Britain, 48, 49, 52, 61, 68, 70, 75, 83, 88, 90, 91, 95, 108, 131, 143, 146, 148, 154, 160, 161, 176, 183, 191–2
Conservative Party, 11, 15–17, 21, 22, 26–8, 39–42, 47–8, 51, 54, 58, 59, 62, 63, 82, 88, 90, 96, 100, 102, 113, 117, 148
Conze, Edward, 131
Cook, A. J., 21, 23, 26, 41, 43
Cooper, Alfred Duff (later Lord Norwich), 179
'Corporate State', Mosley's, 16, 24–5, 40, 53, 73, 96, 117, 133, 150
Cove, W. G., 43
Cripps, Sir Stafford, 54, 94, 96, 142, 194
Crowley, Aleister, 140
Cumings, Leslie, 48, 68
Cummings, A. J., 181
Curzon, George Nathaniel, Marquis of Kedleston, 14, 16, 29
Czechoslovakia, 187

DALLAS, George, 35, 41
Dalton, Hugh (later Lord Dalton), 13, 25, 29, 33, 35, 41
Davison, J. E., 26
Decline and Fall of the Labour Party (Scanlon), 155
Disraeli, Benjamin, 16
Dolan, Charles McEwan, 145
Dollan, Patrick, 19
Dollfuss, Engelbert, 95
Domvile, Admiral Sir Barry, 196, 198
Donovan, B. D. E., 134, 152
Dorman, Geoffrey, 173, 185, 187
Dorman, Pamela, 79, 173
Downe, Dorothy, Viscountess, 179
Drennan, James, *see* Allen, W. E. D.
Dudgeon, Major Randolph, 52
Dukes, Charles (later Lord Duke-stone), 118
Dundas, Ian Hope, 79, 87, 110, 173
Durham: Mosley at, 26
Dymock, Rev. Geoffrey, 141

EARLS Court rally (1939), 189
East End movement, 149–53, 169, 173–9, 186, 189, 201–2
Ede, Chuter, 91–2
Eden, Anthony (later Earl of Avon), 12, 54
Edinburgh, 108, 132, 146, 168
Edinburgh, Prince Philip, Duke of, 199
Edward VIII, abdication of, 164–5
Elam, Norah (Mrs. Dacre-Fox), 180, 193
Elliot, Walter, 40, 44
Emery, John, *see* Scanlon
Empire Loyalists, League of, 200
Erroll, Earl of, 98
Ex-Servicemen: Leagues of, 103, 154, 201; Mosley's interest in, 12

FASCISM, Fascists: in the 1920's, 57–62; different groups in Britain, 57–64, 81–2; Lord Rothermere's campaigns for, 95–7; organizations on the Continent, 95, 183; post-Fascist leagues, 199–203. (*See also under* British *and* Scotland)
Fascist, The (Imperial Fascist League's organ), 64–5, 153–4, 190
Fascist Quarterly, The, 144–5, 171, 173, 183

Fascist Week, The, 102–3
Fascists at Olympia (pamphlet), 114 n.
Findlay, A. G., 184
Firuski, Maurice, 15
Flowers, John, KC, 142
Fontaine, Andrew, 199, 200
Forgan, Robert, 43, 46, 48, 52, 65, 67, 87, 88, 90–1, 100–1, 112, 131, 145; resignation of, 123–4
Frampton, Walter, 145
Francis-Hawkins, Neil: joins Mosley, 65; works for BUF, 69, 87, 102, 111, 123, 133–4, 138, 152, 160, 169–70, 172, 184; arrested, 193; death of, 198
Franco, General Francisco, 140, 159, 182–3
Freitas, Geoffrey de, 101
Fuller, Maj.-Gen. J. F. C., 140, 179

GAME, Sir Philip, 155, 159–61, 175, 177
Gardiner, Gerald, 143, 145, 157
Garvin, James, 16, 44
General Strike (1926), 25, 61, 62
Geoghegan, General, 60
Germany, *see* Hitler
Gibson, Jack, Mayor of Lambeth, 178
Gilmour, Sir John, 84 106
Gilmour, William Weir, 108
Glasgow, 19, 46, 49, 108, 132
Glasgow, Captain the Earl of, 60
Goebbels, Josef, 80, 97, 162
Goering, Hermann, 84, 119
Gold Standard, 21, 25, 34, 45
Gordon-Canning, Robert, 172, 196
Gothic Ripples, 199
Goulding, J. ('Mick'), 154
Grandi, Dino, 91, 92
Grattan-Doyle, Sir Nicholas, 115
Greater Britain, The (Mosley), 65–7, 72–3, 90, 96, 107, 117, 119
Griggs, Anne Brock, 166–7, 179, 192
Gueroult, Leonard, 105
Guinness, Mrs. Bryan, *see* Mosley, Diana

HAILE Selassie, Emperor of Abyssinia, 140, 165
Hamm, Jeffrey, 201–2
Hardie, Keir, 20, 155, 191
Harold Laski (Martin), 32
Harrow: Conservative Party of, 11, 15–16, 22

Hastings, Sir Patrick, 18, 107, 143, 145, 155
Hawke, Mr. Justice, 107
Haworth, Sir Lionel, 179
Hayes, J. H., 26
Henderson, Arthur, 18, 19, 21, 30, 32–4, 38, 47
Hick, U. A., 134, 193
History of the Labour Party, A (Cole), 23, 36
Hitler, Adolf, 9, 45, 55–6, 70–3, 77–8, 83, 89, 95–8, 101, 110, 116, 119, 122–3, 141, 155, 162, 164, 167, 171–3, 182–3, 185–7, 190, 192, 194
Holmes, Valentine, 143, 157
Hons and Rebels (Jessica Mitford), 162, 163
Horrabin, J. F., 31, 43
Houston, Lucy, Lady, 57, 90
Hughes, T. W. Mainwaring, 98
Hull, 146
Hutchinson, St. John, 142, 143
Hyde Park rally (1934), 124

I Fight To Live (Boothby), 23–4
Iddesleigh, 3rd Earl of, 101
Imperial Fascist League, 64–5, 79, 81–2, 102, 122, 140, 152–3, 171, 190
Independent Labour Party (ILP), 17–23, 25, 38, 42–3, 86, 88, 103–4, 108, 155, 160; 'living wage' policy of, 20, 21; delegation to Soviet Union, 29; leaves Labour Party, 68. (*See also* Labour Movement *and* Parliamentary Labour Party)
India, 29, 33, 53, 94, 100, 104, 117, 132, 171–2
Industry and the State, 40

JACKSON, Major Ward, 16
Jameson, Storm, 114
January Club, 101
Jebb, Ralph Gladwyn, 179
Jeffrey, R. K., 200
Jenks, Jorian, 179
Jewish Defence Committee, 123, 154
Jewish Ex-Servicemen's Assoc., 154
Jewish War of Survival, The (Leese), 199
Jews: Beamish's campaign against, 120–2; BUF's campaigns against, 118–28, 151–61, 173–4, 177, 187–8,

197, 200; other Fascist attacks, 63–5, 78, 80–2, 93, 171. (*See also* East End movement)
Joad, C. E. M., 50, 97
Johnston, Tom, 33
Jones, Morgan, 35
Jordan, Colin, 199, 200, 203
Jowett, Fred, 17
Joyce, William, 59, 80–1, 87–8, 97, 100–2, 104–5, 123–4, 134, 140–1, 151, 155, 164–7, 175; dismissal from BUF, 170–3; admiration for Hitler, 171–2; in Second World War, 190, 198–9
Joynson-Hicks, Sir William (later Viscount Brentford), 61

KEMPTHORNE, Rev. J. L., 60
Keynes, Maynard (later Lord Keynes), 21, 24, 25, 36
Kirkwood, David, 26
Kitchen, Gordon, 98
Knebworth, Antony, Viscount, 95

Labour and the Nation, 30
Labour Movement: attracts Mosley, 13, 15, 17–19; first Labour Government (Jan. 1924), 17, 21, 58; in 1920's, 19–35, 39–40, 103; Party Conference (1930), 40–1; Beatrice Webb comments on, 45; attacks Mosley's New Party, 47; opportunities for Mosley in, 54–5; weakness in 1930's, 54, 77, 94–5; opposes BUF, 118. (*See also* Independent Labour Party *and* Parliamentary Labour Party)
Lansbury, George, 26, 29, 31, 33, 35–7, 41, 46, 54, 85, 182
Laski, Harold, 15, 18, 32, 119
Law, Bonar, 15
League of Nations, 13, 14, 65, 140, 182
Leaper, W. J., 87, 102
Lee, Jennie, 42–3, 131
Leese, Arnold Spencer, 62–5, 79, 81–2, 122–3, 140–1, 152–4, 171; imprisoned for anti-Jewish activities, 156; during and after the war, 190, 196, 198, 199
Leiter, Levi, 82, 119
Lenin, 122

Lewis, Cecil Courtney, 78
Lewis, T. 'Kid', 49, 52, 102, 119
Lewisham 'Parliament', 62
Liberal Party, 15, 17, 18, 22, 30, 39, 41, 51, 88; *Yellow Book* proposals, 30, 36
'Link', The, 183, 196
Lintorn-Orman, Rotha, 57–9, 62, 65
Liverpool, 107–8, 132, 185–6
Llandudno: Mosley at Labour Party Conference (1930), 40, 41
Lloyd, Geoffrey, 113, 115
Lloyd, George Ambrose, 1st Baron, 101
Lloyd George, David (later Earl Lloyd-George), 11, 12, 14, 16, 40, 85, 86, 94, 156, 191
London County Council elections, 103, 159, 165–8
Lovat-Fraser, J., 43
Lowther, James William, 15
Luttman-Johnson, Capt. H. W., 101
Lutyens, Edwin, 85
Lynskey, G. J., KC, 145

MACDONALD, James Ramsay, 17, 18, 19, 21, 26, 29, 30, 32–3, 37–8, 51, 53, 54, 58, 77, 85, 94, 103, 129, 191
McGovern, John, 43
McKechnie, H. G., 202
Macmillan, Harold, 12, 21, 40, 48, 54
Macmillan & Co. Ltd., 45
MacNab, John Angus, 171–2, 179
McShane, J. J., 43
Madagascar, 153
Manchester, 9, 47, 49–50, 52, 69, 70, 78, 107–8, 125, 132, 170, 181, 187; Fascist rally at Belle Vue (1934), 125
Mann, Tom, 143
Marchbanks, John, 145–6
Markham, Frank, 43
Marsden, Victor E., 122
Martin, Kingsley, 32, 124
Massingham, Henry William, 16
Matteotti, Giacomo, 56
Maxton, James, 42, 85, 104
Mein Kampf (Hitler), 72, 98
Melville, Cecil, 50
Menace of Fascism, The (Strachey), 38
Metcalfe, E. D. ('Fruity'), 164
Mile End Road pogrom, 161
Mitford sisters, 162–4, 177

Moir, E. ('Panther'), 154
Moore, Thomas, 99–100, 114
Moore-Brabazon, John T. C. (later Lord Brabazon), 44
Moran, Thomas P., 105, 191–2, 194
Morris, Hugh, 17
Morris, Sir William (later Lord Nuffield), 44, 48
Morrison, Herbert, 19, 26, 29, 33, 35, 41, 160, 197–8
Mortimer, Raymond, 50
Mosley, Lady Cynthia (*née* Curzon), 14, 16, 19, 20, 26, 27, 29, 42, 43, 46, 52, 82, 84, 89, 164; visits Soviet Union, 29; MP for Stoke, 30, 47; death of, 84–5
Mosley, Diana (*née* Freeman-Mitford, formerly Mrs. Bryan Guinness), 162, 196
Mosley, Maud (*née* Edwards-Heathcote), 9–10, 76
Mosley, Sir Oswald (4th baronet), 10
Mosley, Sir Oswald (5th baronet), 9–10, 27, 29
Mosley, Sir Oswald Ernald (6th baronet), family background and schooldays, 9–10; First World War, 10–11; first seat in Parliament, 11–15; supports League of Nations and disarmament, 14; elected as Independent (1922), 16–17; joins ILP, 18–22; association with Young and Strachey, 23–5, 35; champions the miners, 25–6; on National Executive of Labour Party, 26, 28–30, 32, 35, 41, 47; MP for Smethwick, 26–8; visits India and U.S.A., 29; Chancellor of Duchy of Lancaster (1929–30), 33, 37; breach with Labour Party, 38; outstanding speech on unemployment, 38–9; speech at Llandudno, 40; forms New Party, *q.v.*; last Parliamentary speech, 52; tours Italy and Germany to study modern movements, 56–7; forms British Union of Fascists, *q.v.*; visits Fascist Exhibition in Rome, 84; leads Fascist marches, 86, 124, 146, 177–8; speech at Albert Hall (1934), 99, 126; campaign against tithes, 107; speaks at Olympia, 110–11; campaign against British Jews, 118–28; relations with his followers, 134–5; reorganizes

Mosley, Sir Oswald Ernald—*contd.*
BUF, 137–40; peace campaigns, 140–1; attitude to religion, 141–2; lawsuits, 142–6; fencing as relaxation, 147; at general election (1935), 147–8; in East End, 149–61; address at Albert Hall (1936), 158; visits Hitler in Berlin, 162; second marriage, 162; cuts BUF staff, 169–70; in 1938, 181; knocked unconscious at Liverpool, 185; valedictory appearance at Earls Court, 189–90; attitude to the war, 190–2; imprisonment, 193, 196–7; post-war policy, 201–3
Mosley 'Conversations', 40
Mosley Group, 42–4
Mosley Manifesto (Dec. 1930), 43–6
Mosley Memorandum, 36–7, 43–4, 51
Mosley Newsletter, 201
Muggeridge, H. T., 43
Mullens, Bernard, 142
Munich, 56, 187
Mussolini, Benito, 9, 24, 38, 56–8, 60, 64, 68, 71, 73, 76, 84, 89–93, 96, 97, 101, 104, 119, 141, 182; invades Abyssinia, 140, 182
My Answer (Mosley), 89, 93

NATHAN, H. L. (later Lord Nathan), 101
National Confederation of Employers, 50
National Council of Labour, 118
National Fascisti, 61
National Government (1931–5), 51–4, 77, 94
National Labour Party (1931), 43
National Labour Party (1958), 199, 203
National Policy, A (pamphlet), 44–5
National Socialism: adopted as title of BUF, 139; East End interest in, 159, 169; Mosley on, 136
National Socialism Now (Joyce), 171
National Socialist League (Beckett and Joyce), 171–2, 183
Nazi Movement, 56, 116, 119–20, 141, 157, 183, 185, 196
Newcastle: Fascist meetings at, 106–8, 132, 145; club at, 137
New Cross Empire rally, 19
New Party, Mosley's, 44–52, 65, 67, 68, 108, 119; youth clubs of, 48–9

Nicolson, Harold, 14, 50, 52, 53; leaves New Party, 56
Nilus, Sergei, 121
Northumberland, 8th Duke of, 57

OBERON, Merle, 166
O'Connor, T. J., 112, 114
O'Duffy, Owen, 95
Oliver, Roland, KC, 156–7
Olympia: mass meeting at (1934), 109–16; press comments, 112–15
One Hundred Questions Answered (Mosley), 72, 152
Oswald Mosley, BUF and British Fascism (Drennan), 120
Out of Bounds (Romilly), 111
Oxford: BUF at, 97, 146

PAGE-CROFT, Sir Henry, 62
Pakenham, Frank (later Earl of Longford), 146
Parliamentary Labour Party, 17, 38, 42, 88, 118, 133, 148, 174, 182
Parry, Vice-Admiral R. St. P., 179
Partridge, Eric, 50
Pearson, Lady, 179
Petrie, Sir Charles, 101–2
Piercy, Eric Hamilton, 69, 83, 106
Pilcher, Maj.-Gen. T. D., 60
Piper, Capt. R., 147
Plathen, Richard, 83, 107, 108, 145
Plymouth: Mosley at, 125
Poland, 188–9
Pollitt, Harry, 26, 191–2
Portrait of a Leader (Chesterton), 134, 184
Portrait of the Labour Party (Wertheimer), 19
Portsmouth, 60, 75, 132, 179
Powell, Vice-Admiral G. B., 75, 179
Pratt, Sir John, 52
Price, G. Ward, 97, 99, 114
Price, Phillips, 43
Pritt, D. N., KC, 145
Protocols of the Learned Elders of Zion, 121–2
Public Faces (Nicolson), 53 n.
Public Order Act (1936), 106, 161, 174, 177

QUENNELL, Peter, 50

RAMSAY, A. H. M., 183, 194, 196, 198
Randall, E. D., 71, 176
Ravensdale, Baroness, 89, 123
Reavell, Kenneth, 62
Revolution by Reason (Mosley and Strachey), 23–5, 36
Richardson, Mary, 98
Right Club, 194
'Rignano Principle', 74
Risdon, Bill, 22–3, 47–8, 68, 80, 98, 131, 133, 138, 157, 187
Roberts, Rev. Ellis G., 141
Robertson, E. Arnot, 50
Rockwell, George Lincoln, 200
Roe, E. G. Mandeville, 60, 62, 65, 179
Roehm, Ernst, 116
Rolleston Hall, 9–10, 29
Rome: Mosley in, 56
Romilly, Esmond, 111, 164
Romilly, Giles, 111–12, 116
Roosevelt, Franklin D., 29, 37, 95
Rothermere, H. S. Harmsworth, Viscount, 40, 90, 100–2; campaigns for BUF, 95–8; withdraws support from Mosley, 116–18
Row, Robert, 202
Ruhr, The, 15
Russia, 20, 29, 48

SACKVILLE-WEST, Victoria, 50
Samuel, Herbert, Viscount, 176
Sankey, John, Viscount, 32
Sassoon, Sir Philip, 58
Scanlon, John, 155
Scotland: Fascism in, 78, 108, 132, 180
Scrymgeour-Wedderburn, J. (later Earl of Dundee), 112
Seaton, John, 157
Sharp, Lt.-Col., 91–2
Shaw, George Bernard, 86
Shaw, Tom, 18
Shawcross, Sir Hartley (later Lord Shawcross), 198
Sherrard, Leslie H., 64
Shinwell, Emanuel, 155
Simmons, James, 31, 43
Simon, Sir John (later Lord Simon), 91, 156, 160, 161
Simpson, Henry, 63
Simpson, Mrs. Wallis, 164–5
Sitwell, Osbert, 50, 176
Skeels, Serocold, 61
Slessor, Sir Henry, 59

Smethwick: Mosley as Labour MP for, 13, 26–8, 30, 54
Smith, Ellis, 118
Snowden, Philip (later Viscount Snowdon), 21, 25, 28, 30, 33–4, 37, 45, 51, 104
Social Credit Party, 161, 168
Socialist League, 94
South Africa, 200
Spanish Civil War, 159, 182, 187
Spengler, Oswald, 79
Squire, Sir John C., 101
Stalin, Joseph, 116, 191
Stamford, 63
Stanley, Oliver, 21, 40, 180
Star libel action, 143–5
Stockton-on-Tees, 83
Stoke, 30, 47, 49, 52, 107, 118, 138
Stokes, R. R., 197
Strachey, E. John St. L., 23–4, 30–1, 35, 38, 42–9, 79, 133
Streicher, Julius, 65, 153
Strong, L. A. G., 50
Sunderland, 146
Sutton, George, 23
Swaffer, Geoffrey, 96
Swaffer, Hannen, 54

TAWNEY, R. H., 30
Taylor, Admiral, 100
Thomas, J. H., 18, 32–5, 37, 41
Thomson, Alexander Raven, 72, 79, 102, 105, 151, 166, 172–3, 179, 192, 193, 198, 202
Thurtle, Ernest, 176
Tomorrow We Live (Mosley), 72, 135–6, 152
Trade Union Congress (TUC), 26, 30, 51, 61, 118
Trade Unions, 74, 118, 129, 131, 175
Transport and General Workers Union, 35, 89
Tremlett, Rex, 87
Trevelyan, Sir Charles, 26, 29, 30
Tupper, Admiral, 60
Turvey, Arnold, 175
Tyndell-Biscoe, General, 60

UNEMPLOYMENT, 16, 20–1, 25, 28, 33–41, 45, 48, 50, 51, 60, 74, 77, 129. (See also *Mosley Memorandum*)

Union Movement, 201–3
United Empire Fascists, 61
United Empire Party, 40, 100, 117
Unity Band, 62
Upton, Hon. H. M., 98

VENICE: the Mosleys in, 23–4, 27
Verdon-Roe, Sir Alliot, 98
Vickers, Vincent, 25
Victoria Park ralley (1936), 159

WEBB, Beatrice, 17–18, 25, 34, 45
Webb, Sidney (later Lord Passfield),
17, 18
Webster, William, 203
Wegg-Prosser, Charles F., 166, 167,
173
Wertheimer, Egon, 19–20, 22

Whinfield, Edward, 179
Whinfield, Muriel, 179
White Defence League, 199
Why Fascism?, 131
Wigs on the Green (Nancy Mitford),
162–3, 177
Wilkinson, Ellen, 131
Williams, Prof. Rushbrook, 101
Williamson, Henry, 189
Williamson, Hugh Ross, 189
Winter, Gen. Sir Ormonde, 60
Wood, Edward (later Earl of Halifax),
15
World Union of National Socialists,
200
Worthing: 'riot' at, 142
YOUNG, Allen, 22–3, 35, 45, 46–9

ZINOVIEV, Grigori, 22